D1557672

OUTRAM IN INDIA:
THE MORALITY OF EMPIRE

By Roy Digby Thomas.

Bloomington, IN Milton Keynes, UK

authorHOUSE™

AuthorHouse™
1663 Liberty Drive, Suite 200
Bloomington, IN 47403
www.authorhouse.com
Phone: 1-800-839-8640

AuthorHouse™ UK Ltd.
500 Avebury Boulevard
Central Milton Keynes, MK9 2BE
www.authorhouse.co.uk
Phone: 08001974150

First published by AuthorHouse 06/28/07

ISBN: 978-1-4343-0460-5 (sc)

Library of Congress Control Number: 2007903286

Printed in the United States of America
Bloomington, Indiana

This book is printed on acid-free paper.

*Painting of The Relief of Lucknow on the cover reproduced by kind
permission of the National Portrait Gallery*

OTHER BOOKS BY THE AUTHOR.

DIGBY:
THE GUNPOWDER PLOTTER'S LEGACY.

GEORGE DIGBY: HERO AND VILLAIN.

For my grandchildren, Gavin, Duncan,
Edward and Isabel.

CW00954057

ACKNC

There are many p........ ....   a
foreign culture, and there are few more exotic cultures than
that of India. In researching what happened in that country
in the 19th Century, I have needed to unravel many puzzles
and seek explanations for occurrences which were not within
my knowledge or experience. I was fortunate to have in Dr
Sushama Arur of Bangalore an historian who combined
historical knowledge and expertise with a background of Indian
culture, and I am deeply indebted to her for the guidance and
help I received.

The front cover of this book is from a famous painting by
Thomas Jones Baker in the National Portrait Gallery, London,
depicting the epic meeting of Generals Haverlock and Outram
with their Commander-in-Chief at the final relief of Lucknow
during the Sepoy Rebellion of 1857. It shows graphically all the
colour and drama of that famous moment, and I am grateful
to the Gallery for granting me permission to reproduce it.

It would be difficult to make sense of the terrain and
location of the many places on the Indian sub-continent
which play an important part in this book without clear and
comprehensive maps. I have been very fortunate to have in
my good friend Alan Bridges an artist who could not only
make sense of my scribblings, but who had the talent and great
ability to produce beautiful maps in support of the narrative. I
am greatly indebted to him

My sons, Glyn and Warren, acted as sounding boards
in the early drafting of this book, and helped enormously in
steering me towards what was important and relevant. It is fair
to say that without their input the book would have been very
different, and worse for it. They took time off from very busy
lives to help, for which I am grateful.

Finally my wife, Eileen, spent many evenings reading every word and going through the tedious business of editing. As ever, her support and encouragement was invaluable.

CONTENTS.

List of Maps. xiii

Introduction xv

Chapter 1.   Where It All Started. 1

Chapter 2.   India.. 12

Chapter 3.   The Bhil Corps.. 27

Chapter 4.   Settling Down. 41

Chapter 5.   Sind.. 57

Chapter 6.   British Annexation Of Sind. 79

Chapter 7.   Conflict With Napier. 104

Chapter 8.   Political Repercussions Of Sind. 133

Chapter 9.   Return To Baroda. 146

Chapter 10.   Lucknow... 163

Chapter 11.   Persia.. 182

Chapter 12.   The Indian Mutiny...................................... 197

Chapter 13.   The Relief Of Lucknow. 217

Chapter 14.   The End Of The Mutiny. 230

Chapter 15.   An Office Job. 245

Epilogue. 255

Glossary Of Indian Terms. 259

Bibliography. 265

Notes. 269

Index.. 279

LIST OF MAPS.

India in the 19th Century.   xxii

Bombay Presidency.   26

Sind and Afghanistan.   56

The Indian Mutiny.   196

Lucknow.   216

INTRODUCTION.

In London's Victoria Embankment Gardens stands the statue of a soldier leaning on his curved sword, trophies around his feet, the Star of India on his breast. To the inhabitants of London, and to sightseers, this memorial has little significance: few would recognise the name Sir James Outram, or have any knowledge of why he is celebrated in this fashion. Only the great heroes of Britain's illustrious past are given such a prominent accolade, so who is he? And why do so few people recognise his name or his achievements today?

In the twenty-first century Britain's historical involvement in India is regarded with some embarrassment. As a nation we suffer feelings of guilt over our colonial past. At best the story of Britain's long period of rule in India is considered unfashionable, at worst shameful. This has led to a relative lack of interest in comparison with other periods in British history such as the Tudors and Stuarts. Yet, regardless of our discomfort, the career of James Outram is not only remarkable for his achievements from difficult beginnings, but is also significant in the context of the evolution of British intervention in India during the nineteenth century.

James was two years old when his father, a leading industrialist, died suddenly in 1805, leaving his mother impoverished. As a consequence James was denied the benefits of the social standing and good education which he might have expected. Victorian Britain was dominated by the aristocracy; they filled the positions of power in Parliament and the military, they controlled appointments and patronage. This was particularly true for those who served in India. Promotion was slow and erratic; often what you said was less important than how you said it. James was not equipped with any of the social graces or tact and fluency of expression required, and his career was seriously impeded by these deficiencies.

Yet his achievements, and the plaudits that followed, were exceptional. How was it possible that this humble man could reach such heights?

Much of what Outram achieved, and many of the conflicts in which he became embroiled, have to be seen in the context of the climate of opinion that prevailed in India at the time, and the policies of its rulers. British involvement in India developed primarily through the activities of the English East India Company ("the Company"), which by the beginning of the nineteenth century had seen off French and Dutch competition. It started as a trading venture, seeking to establish warehouses and factories in India in order to exploit the country's huge natural resources and manufactured goods. But once the British were drawn into the tangled politics that prevailed at local and regional level, they found themselves taking an increasingly dominant role in the administration of the territories. They argued that to protect the Company's trade, intervention in local affairs was essential. By 1850, the Company had become primarily a military and administrative power[1] and ruled virtually all of India. It claimed rent from peasant-farmers, revenue from princes. It believed it had a duty to educate and improve Indian society, and to criticise the "barbaric" religious practices it encountered. Such was the imperialistic mood, prevalent in Britain, that it believed it was always right.

The cost of administering and policing the acquired territories was immense. Politicians and the public in England became increasingly uneasy with what was happening in India. The annexation of states caused raised eyebrows in Parliament, and this concern spread to the public. The conquest of Sind in 1843 caused major protests in the streets of England. After the so-called Indian Mutiny in 1857, the British government stepped in and took over the rule of India from the Company. A new, imperialistic style of rule was employed. Evangelical ideals held sway in Britain. Burgeoning self-confidence, brought on by the achievements of the Industrial Revolution and scientific break-throughs led to a sense of national superiority. Throughout this period James Outram was at the centre of affairs in India, often at odds with the accepted British view, and frequently quarrelling with his superiors.

Opinions vary radically on James. He was certainly feted during his lifetime. He enjoyed enormous popularity with his peers and subordinates, and gained the confidence and support of local princes and military leaders wherever he went in India. He was given a hero's funeral in London, and is commemorated in Westminster Abbey. He was showered with awards. Parliament, which in the nineteenth century looked for heroes among the men sent to run India, loved him. In 2005 Richard Holmes wrote: "Perhaps the greatest British general to serve in India never actually became Commander in Chief. Sir James Outram had Havelock's courage without his chilliness, Campbell's skill laced with Nicholson's dash, and the most open of human faces."[2] But he was denied honours and advancement until the accumulation of his achievements and pressure from Parliament forced the issue. Despite his great success and public popularity, when he retired to England, although he had been knighted, he was not a wealthy man, and was not offered any important posts.

There is another perspective on his life. A respected historian writing in 1980, took a different view of him: "More by accident than design Outram came to embody the ideals of integrity and honesty....He was one of the most notable political strategists to emerge from the Afghan war...But in his ruthless determination to seize every opportunity that might advance his own interests...he contrived to leave behind him a wholly deceptive image."[3]

Certainly he clashed with his superiors on numerous occasions. He fell out with two of his commanding officers, and his dispute with Sir Charles Napier became a major public debate.[4] Successive Governors-General of India overlooked him for promotion and saw fit to censure him. One of those who championed Outram and advanced his career wherever and whenever possible, nevertheless recognised his shortcomings. Referring to his tendency to antagonise his superiors, Lord Dalhousie wrote: "I shall...give him to understand that we shall get on very well provided he obeys orders and keeps a civil tongue in his head."[5] Later he wrote that the Court of Directors was critical of Outram and that one of the directors, Hogg had told him: "Col. Outram's proper place is at the head of an Irregular Cavalry Regiment, no higher."[6]

What is the truth about James Outram? That he was exceptionally brave is irrefutable: there are countless tales of his courage. But he was not destined to march to the tune of the Company. His background, education and circumstances caused him to stand aside from the conventional wisdom in India. He was, perhaps, one of the first men in the British administration of India to recognise that it was better to work with the local leaders than to oppose them and remove their power and influence. He quickly found himself adopting a more sympathetic attitude towards local affairs than his masters. He achieved remarkable results by sitting alongside these local leaders and winning their confidence. He often found himself defending the local Indian rulers against insensitive or materialistic British decisions. Undoubtedly his career was adversely affected by these differences of opinion. Yet he managed, eventually, to rise to a position of great prominence and influence. This was in part due to the support of Governors-General who promoted his interests, but it was also due to his persistence and courage in standing up for his own ideals. In doing so he gained the respect of many Indians, the appreciation of the newly emerging rulers in England, and, perhaps most influentially, the accolade of the public. Even most of his harshest critics acknowledged his high-minded honesty and integrity, and this feature will play an important part in this book.

The men who ruled India throughout the nineteenth century were a chosen group. In the main the Governors-General were "high-principled aristocrats from Britain's political elite."[7] They believed they had a civilising mission: technology, public works, education and law would produce a social and economic revolution.[8] Despite their claims to enlightenment, many of them held the Indians in great disdain. They likened them to children, requiring guidance and a firm hand. Marquis Wellesley declared in 1800 that the part of India governed by the British was "..the most opulent, flourishing part of India, in which property, life, civil order and liberty are more secure, and the people enjoy a larger proportion of good government than any other country in this quarter of the globe."[9] There can be no doubt that these men honestly believed that they knew best, that British rule brought greater integrity to those governed, and that what they were doing was in the best interests of India. Christian belief and ethics led them to believe that Indian society was barbarous, in dire need of rescue – and that rescue would be the imposition of western values and ideals.[10] Macaulay's brother-in-law Charles Trevelyan expressed this view clearly: "The natives will not rise against us, ...Trained by us to happiness and independence, and endowed with our learning and political institutions, India will remain the proudest monument of British benevolence."[11] Nevertheless the Company was a commercial concern, bent on profiting from its operations, and this aim was never far from its considerations. The contradictions between commercial ambition and philanthropy kept surfacing.

As the nineteenth century progressed, so did attitudes in Britain. Political change brought men to power that pursued liberal views. Reformers, who believed that tradition should be challenged and not taken for granted, that tests of reason and usefulness should predominate, came to be heard. Adam Smith's laissez-faire (free trade) economic thinking, Utilitarian philosophy (which emphasized the happiness of the majority), and Evangelical Christianity caused them to examine afresh their attitudes to the empire and its people.

In the twentieth century the nation's attention was drawn away from India to other, weighty world events, and nothing more has been written about James Outram. He had been the subject of two previous biographies: one by Major-General Sir F.J.Goldsmid in 1880 and the other by Captain Lionel J. Trotter in 1903. These books therefore stand as testimony to his extraordinary life. Trotter's book is slight and straightforward; Goldsmid's, in two volumes running to nearly nine hundred pages, is substantial. Goldsmid knew James Outram slightly, and had access to his living relatives when writing the book. It is nothing less than a hagiography, extolling Outram's escapades, adventures and achievements in terms which would leave no doubt as to his bravery, intelligence, astute leadership and good moral sense. Time and again he is described as bringing success to everything he did, often selflessly and often at his own personal expense. There is not the slightest hint of criticism or question of whether he made the right choices. He seems too good to be true.

Does Outram's statue on the Embankment deserve its position of prominence in the country's capital? We have seen that there are widely differing opinions about James. Certainly it is puzzling that if he was as heroic as Goldsmid says, he was the subject of such controversy, and was shunned by a succession of high-ranking officials. On the other hand, the earlier biographies do not place his life in the context of the evolving British Empire, and its controversial role in India. This book aims to unravel some of the paradoxes that surrounded James Outram's career. It also reflects the changing face of India through the 19th century, and the influential part James Outram took in those changes. It is as much about the way the British Empire evolved as it is about a famous man who stood up for his beliefs, regardless of the consequences.

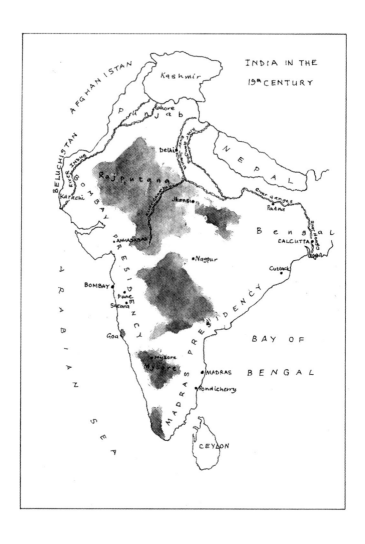

CHAPTER 1.

WHERE IT ALL STARTED.

In 1857 the Indian soldiers serving in the Bengal army mutinied against their British officers and ran amok. The rebels captured many of the key cities in north-east India with no mercy shown to any Europeans living there. Delhi was occupied, and for a few months the future of British rule in India was in severe danger. Had the mutiny spread to other parts of India, or had the rebels managed to retain the key cities, it is difficult to see the British recovering their position But neither of these conditions occurred; Delhi was recaptured, reinforcements poured into the country and the so-called Indian Mutiny was defeated. One of the key cities in the struggle was the capital of the province of Oudh, Lucknow. After Delhi was recovered, it became the focus for the rebel forces, the most important city in the north-east, which had not fallen. A small band of British soldiers and officials, besieged in the Residency there, resisted all attempts on their enclave, and their heroism was to become a legend in the history of the British Raj.

The British garrison sheltering in the Residency at Lucknow came close to exhaustion and despair. For more than three months one thousand and seven men, protecting five hundred and fifty women and children, resisted constant onslaught from a surrounding horde of over eight thousand mutinying Indian soldiers, supported by local officials and police. Reports from other cities told them what to expect if the Residency fell: they would all be killed. The bombardment was incessant: there was little time for rest. Their only hope was that relief would come from the distant British force, battling up from Calcutta and Kanpur. Rations were low, disease was rife, women and children at the end of their tether. All the buildings in the compound had been shattered by round shot and damaged by torrential rain. Constant attempts by mutineers to burrow into the compound and destroy the defences with mines had been resisted. Word came from the advancing relief column that they were still at least twenty-five days away; the message was: "Do not negotiate, but rather perish sword in hand."[12]

Just before midnight on September 22, 1857, a messenger came running through the lines with exciting news: the relief force had crossed the Ganges at Kanpur and would be at Lucknow within a few days. Spirits were raised by the sound of distant gunfire, growing closer: heavy artillery, rifles and muskets. Then, at 6pm on September 25, along the straight road leading up to the gates of the Residency, through the middle of the city, there appeared bearded Highlanders and Sikhs. They advanced steadily through withering fire directed from the houses and palaces crowding closely around the street. They did not hesitate. At their head rode the two heroes of the campaign, Brigadier-General Henry Havelock and Lieutenant-General Sir James Outram. As the gates of the Residency came into view, a new vigour was apparent in the step of these soldiers, and there was a surge forward. At the embrasure guarding the gates Outram's horse balked, and the Highlanders heaved him and his horse bodily across it. The spontaneous cheer which rang out could be heard for miles. The most significant battle of the so-called Indian Mutiny was won, and Havelock and Outram were to be lionised and feted by a Britain desperate for good news.

It was the most triumphant moment in the long and distinguished career of James Outram. He was to have statues erected to him in Calcutta, and on the Victorian Embankment in London, and he was to end his career in India as an important member of the Governor-General's Council in Calcutta. Yet his life had been hard. There had been many setbacks, much disappointment and frustration. He had none of the social or financial advantages of most of his fellow officers. The odds against him achieving high position in India were very great. Somehow, his many attributes shone through in the long run, and projected him to the fore. What was it about this unassuming man that led to such success?

The birth of James Outram at Butterley Hall, Derbyshire on January 29, 1803, was unremarkable. Nothing in his heritage could have presaged the man he was to be. None of his forbears were soldiers, none were leaders of men, and none were particularly wealthy. And if a young man was to make his mark upon the world, wealth and position were essential ingredients in nineteenth century Imperial Britain. James's father, Benjamin, born in 1764, was the eldest of eight children. He was said to have been named after Benjamin Franklin, "a family friend."[13] Franklin certainly visited Derbyshire in 1759, and may have met Benjamin's father, Joseph Outram, although he was not in the country between 1759 and 1770. Joseph described himself as an "advanced agriculturist"[14] and he certainly came from farming and gardening stock. But he was also a leading land agent and commissioner for parliamentary enclosures, and was well respected in Derbyshire. He owned some land, and had an investment in local collieries.

Benjamin joined his father's business after a modest education, and made a reputation as a land surveyor. He was ambitious to improve himself, and left the business to become a civil engineer. The Industrial Revolution was about to burst upon the country, and there were exciting developments taking place in iron works, canal building and steam locomotion. He became interested in canal construction, and was involved in more than one new canal in Derbyshire as the industrialisation of the Midlands gathered momentum. He soon recognised that water transportation had its limitations, and his thoughts turned to alternative forms of transport. He took up residence at Butterley Hall, near Ripon, where with two associates, John Wright and William Jessop, he founded an ironworks known as Benjamin Outram and Co. of Butterley. This was the forerunner to the better-known Butterley Company. Benjamin could see that the developments in railways which were starting to appear offered significant advantages over canal traffic, so he set about developing means of conveying goods by horse-drawn iron railways and tramways, and became an established engineer in this industry. Such was the success of his enterprise that in 1800 he withdrew from the land agent practice and invested his entire wealth in the Butterley Company.

In the same year Benjamin married Margaret Anderson, the only daughter of James Anderson, an impoverished Doctor of Law, Fellow of the Royal Society and distinguished Scottish economist. Anderson's main distinction appears to have been the invention of a small two-horse plough without wheels known as the Scotch plough. He rented a farm of 1300 acres in Aberdeenshire, but when in 1794 the government engaged him to make a survey of the western coast of Scotland with the aim of developing fisheries there, he abandoned farming. He eventually moved to London in 1797. His daughter was only seven years old when her mother died, and he came to depend upon her to run his house. Either through a selfish desire to keep her tied to his domestic needs, or out of a firm conviction that women did not require formal education, Margaret's schooling thereafter was sporadic, and dependent upon her own desire to learn. From her letters, it appears that she possessed plenty of common sense, intelligence and drive however, which helped her develop into a resilient and self-sufficient young woman. Inexperienced in the ways of society, she was sometimes too honest for her own good, and rather forthright in her comments.

Margaret entered marriage with high expectations. She wrote in later years that: "Mr Outram was full of hope and energy, and the picture of health and with promise of long life, our prospects were great and…his sanguine disposition and knowledge of his own successful projects made him flatter me into the belief that fortune would place us on the highest pinnacle."[15] To a young woman whose childhood had been narrow and confined to modest surroundings, Butterley Hall must have appeared very grand. Encouraged by her husband, Margaret set about furnishing and decorating her new home with enthusiasm and some extravagance. Later she reflected upon this time: "By the surrounding country I had been treated as a superior being, looked up to by the ladies as the leader of fashion and manners, and by the gentlemen with admiration, for to my other misfortunes I was considered to have a handsome person, and vivacity that attracted too much attention. Ignorant of the world, naturally saying everything I thought, credulous and believing in the veracity of others, even when gross flattery ought to have made me suspicious, I was a child of nature, with talents, but no regulation of mind."[16]

On May 15, 1805 disaster struck. Having left home in good health for a trip to London, Benjamin collapsed en route and died of a "brain fever". In expectation of the wealth his burgeoning business was to bring him, he had invested all his capital in the ironworks. Moreover lavish improvements at Butterley Hall had been financed by borrowings in excess of £10,000 (some of it in the name of the company without the knowledge of his partners) and at the time of his death he was heavily in debt. His young widow found herself in a difficult position. Benjamin owed the ironworks money, and she had no private funds on which to fall back. The partners in the Butterley Company were unsympathetic. Margaret set out her dilemma lucidly: "His [Benjamin's] affairs were entangled beyond the power of arranging them, and there being no will, no person was responsible to take charge of us. Up to Mr Outram's death, the Iron Works were in full swing, with promise of development into a large and lucrative business, but his sudden decease cast all into confusion. There was no one to take charge of the Foundry, none of the other partners understanding the management, and trade being depressed at that time owing to the fear of French invasion, the value was made out as merely nominal. Indeed, when the statement of affairs was issued, practically only the bricks and mortar were taken into account. Everything was against us. The minerals on the estate that Mr. Outram used to sell to the Works for four or five hundred per annum, were declared to be worked out, and were now got from an adjoining estate, belonging to one of the partners. The house which he had improved for himself, (laying out about £3,000 upon it) no one would take, being so near the Iron Works, and one of the partners therefore got it at the nominal rent of £50, with all the fixtures for nothing, and even of this trifling rent and what was got for the land, half was claimed…..I believe nothing, or very little more was got for us, than five per cent, paid to me on £2,500 that I have mortgaged upon it."[17] Margaret and her family of small children were forced to leave Butterley Hall. A protracted legal wrangle ensued, during which further debts were discovered, leading finally to Margaret ceding her share in the Butterley Company to Wright and Jessop. A further ruling released her of all additional financial obligations on payment of £1290.[18]

Between 1801 and 1805 Margaret had borne five children, of whom James was the third eldest. When she was turned out of Butterley Hall the eldest child was only four years old, and she was near to penury. She took lodgings in Worksop, where she was sustained by an annual sum of £200 from her seven brothers. Perhaps regretting their harsh treatment of her, the Butterley partners also contributed £50 a year until such time as her eldest son, Francis, reached maturity. Margaret did not settle in Worksop, and quickly alienated the small town's inhabitants: "When they came forth from bakers' and butchers' shops, and small farms and malt-houses to call upon me, my pride would not stand it, and I not only returned none of their calls, but with that want of judgment, and foolish openness which marked my character, I treated them with some contempt, and expressed my displeasure at the intrusion."[19] Her outspokenness and stubborn pride was inherited by James, often to his disadvantage.

She stayed at Worksop for three years, and another two nearby at Barnby Moor, but conscious of the need to educate her children, in 1810 she moved back to Aberdeen where the schooling was good and the cost of living reasonable. As the daughter of Dr James Anderson she was able to claim a small annuity from the government for her father's services. She harboured great dreams for her eldest son and favourite, Francis. Her elder brother secured a position for Francis in a well thought-of charity school in London, known as the Blue Coats, and the boy boarded there for seven years from the age of nine. Later she bitterly regretted the move: "I attribute the singularity of his character, his morbid sensibility, and distaste for society, added to his high-toned mind and wonderful talents, to the tears that he ever saw me shed when I beheld him in his charity dress."[20] At sixteen he transferred to Marischal College, Aberdeen, where he made a favourable impression. However he did not like Aberdeen, and when the prospect of a cadetship in India arose he leapt at the opportunity. He distinguished himself at Addiscombe, the East India Company's military college, and was first in his class. This enabled him to enter Chatham as an officer of Engineers with a first-class record.

James, a quiet and thoughtful boy with an enthusiasm for mathematics and the sciences, was admitted to the Udney School at the age of 10 in 1814. The headmaster Dr Bisset described James thus: "Though perfectly healthy, he was somewhat pale, and was neither so tall nor so robust as most boys of the same age. His countenance was singularly prepossessing, full at once of modesty and ingenuousness. He had his mother's black, glossy hair, and dark, hazel, beaming eye, which kept time, as it were, with whatever was going on, and marked his quick appreciation of, and sympathy with every scintillation of wit, drollery or humour. His usual manner was quiet and sedate."[21] James was commended for his draughtsmanship, and showed a talent for carving in wood. But it was out of doors where he really shone. Although very small for his age, he showed an aptitude and enthusiasm for all sports, and by the age of fourteen was "the recognised leader of the school" in cricket, football, shinty (a Scottish game similar to hockey) and bowls.[22] He was an excellent wrestler and swimmer, and often would tread where others feared to go. His sister remarked: "I never remember his evincing the slightest sign of bodily pain."[23] The glory of Waterloo in 1815, with soldiers returning to Aberdeen recounting the epic battle in detail, was the one event which, by his own recollection, was to set him decisively on a military career.[24]

His teachers did not consider him very studious, and he preferred active pursuits to reading. He showed an early interest in military matters, hardly surprising in an age when the army and its exploits were front-page news. He liked to drill his schoolmates, and could often be found around the army barracks or at the docks talking to the sailors. He acquired the sobriquet of "Captain Outram." A fellow student later described him thus: "I always looked upon James Outram as the bravest and most genial boy I ever knew. He was passionately fond of outdoor games. …[He] was the life and organiser of the school sports….Those who had Outram on their side were sure of victory. Was there honour to be won by diving to the bottom of the deepest pond, or was there a rook's nest among the branches of the highest and most inaccessible tree, it was the little Captain who dived the deepest and climbed the highest. …Though many of us were stronger, none would meddle with him."[25] Another wrote: "I was very young when he was the bold and generous Captain of his school, so that I can only record impressions of a very general character. My affection and admiration for him were unbounded. Nothing gave me greater pleasure than to be carried on his back, and his great good nature often gratified my wishes. He was always kind to me, protecting me from the bullying of older boys, and I believe he was equally generous to others. He drilled us regularly."[26] His bravery and fearlessness was illustrated yet further by a third friend, who told of meeting a savage mastiff which suddenly set upon the boys. "Jimmie rushed in with feet and fists, and so surprised the infuriated animal that he turned and fled. He did not know what fear was."[27]

James' sister recollected another incident that illustrated his qualities: "His great enjoyment …..was to associate with the soldiers at the barracks, or the sailors at the docks – we, in the meantime, never knowing where our missing brother had gone….. He was the delight of the regiment, but even still more, if possible, the sailors' pet. There was a mutiny among the latter - I can't remember the date, but I think he must then have been about twelve or thirteen years of age. All Aberdeen was uneasy; my brother, of course, not at home. The sailors were drawn up in a dense body on the pier. The magistrates went down to them, backed by the soldiers, whose muskets were loaded; and they were held in readiness to fire on the mutineers, if necessary. Between the latter and their opponents, Jemmy Outram was to be seen, with his hands in his pockets, stumping about from one side to the other, like a tiger in his den, protecting his sailor friends from the threatening muskets; resolved to receive the fire first, if firing was to be. All ended peacefully, however; much to the general satisfaction, and to our particular thankfulness, when we were told how our brother had exposed himself."[28]

After four years at Udney James moved to a school that had the reputation for being the best in Aberdeen, run by the Reverend Esson. This was a stepping-stone to Marischal College, where he attended mathematics, and natural and experimental philosophy. He did not distinguish himself at these subjects, but had a reputation as a good student, well behaved and co-operative. Outside of school, he was seen in a different light. His naturally aggressive nature led him into a number of scrapes in the town. On one occasion a lady

9

friend paying a considerable fine on his behalf saved him from disgrace. He was to admit later that after leaving college he dared not return to Aberdeen as there was a reward on his head for leading a disturbance in which a number of windows had been broken.

His studies were soon to come to an end, for in 1819, like his brother, he secured an Indian cadetship. It was not easy. His mother, aware of his liking for matters military, had sought the help of a cousin, Colonel Henderson, to get James into the army. This was an age when to make progress in the forces a young man needed sound financial backing, for the pay was pitiful and officers were required to fund much of their own equipment. Commissions and promotion in the regular British army were bought individually. Henderson discouraged the idea, and another cousin responded in similar fashion when he was asked to help James join the navy. Margaret therefore considered the clergy as a career for her young son, but his lack of studiousness counted against him. When he heard the proposal he said to his sister: "You see that window; rather than be a parson, I'm out of it; and I'll 'list for a common soldier!"[29]

At around this time, with Margaret not knowing where she could turn to find a career for James, the Member of Parliament for Aberdeen, Captain Gordon, came to the rescue and secured James a direct Indian cadetship with the English East India Company. Unlike the regular army, the "Company," as it was familiarly known as, did not expect its officers to have private means. He was also offered as an alternative a nomination to the Company's staff training centre, Addiscombe College, to study as an engineer, but chose the direct commission, remarking that if he went to Addiscombe he would, after three years of further study, at best emerge as a cadet for the infantry. In passing up this opportunity he was to place himself in the position of being an outsider, not one of the mainstream graduates, which was to tell against him in career progress, for like so much of British society in the Victorian age, who you knew and what your background was counted for more than how you performed.

It was acknowledged that the East India Company offered young officers the opportunity of rapid advancement and responsibility at an early age. Before an officer reached the rank of captain, he was required to have been in command of troops on distant marches, to have guarded posts and strongholds, attended to the logistics of supplies, and dealt with recalcitrant local rulers.[30] To the impatient youngster, militarily inclined, experience in the field in a position of some responsibility was an enticing prospect. The new cadet was expected to pay for his own, expensive outfit, and it was a measure of the Outram family's penury that his mother was forced to borrow £50 from a friendly banker to pay for it.

At the tender age of sixteen, therefore, James set out for India, where he was to spend virtually the rest of his life, and to forge his reputation. As he had not passed through Addiscombe he in fact arrived there two years before his elder brother, still training as an engineer.

CHAPTER 2.

INDIA.

The East India Company, or to call it by its official name, "The United Company of Merchants of India trading to The East Indies" was formed in 1602 to explore trade with the Far East. The first century of its existence was an extremely uncertain one with many severe setbacks that threatened its very survival. In addition to hostile natives, the Company was competing for trading positions against the Dutch, Portuguese and French, who actually posed greater physical threats than the local inhabitants. Britain's rising dominance of the seas eventually told, however, and by 1800 the other European powers, with the exception of the Portuguese (who still possessed Goa), had been seen off. A practicable monopoly was established in India and the surrounding territories. Initially the British were solely interested in trading with the Indians, buying silk, cottons, spices, sugar, indigo dye and saltpetre in return for silver bullion, other metals, tapestries and mechanical novelties. Later, an acquired taste for tea led to a burgeoning trade in that commodity which eventually overtook the other goods and became by far the largest import. Taxes were extracted by the Company from the local people. As an indication of how important India had become to Britain, by 1740 Company trade represented over ten per cent of the country's entire public revenue.[31] It had become the foundation stone of the new, burgeoning British Empire.

Although India was nominally an Empire ruled from Delhi by the Mughals, it was far from integrated. There were parts of this vast country where the Mughal's rule was tenuous, to say the least. Such was the disparity of terrain and races that at best local satraps, or Nawabs sustained Mughal rule. In Central India the Deccan region alone had over a thousand fortified towns or villages, each dominated by its own landholder, or zamindar. Although the zamindar did not own the land, he collected the rent and taxes from tenant farmers on behalf of the Emperor. Whilst under the rule of the Emperor, the zamindar considered himself a partner in government.[32] The Mughal Empire had started to crumble in the seventeenth century, when oppressive taxes were resisted and local rulers took the opportunity to challenge a regime which was over-extended, and exhausted physically and financially by constant wars to preserve its domain. By the mid-eighteenth century large, semi-independent states with their own rulers had arisen in Mysore, Hyderabad, Oudh, Bengal and Deccan. Whilst paying lip-service to Delhi, these new princes represented themselves locally as the legitimate successors to the Mughals.[33]

Gradually, as the Company's trade spread inland from the coast of India, clashes with the local rulers led to the Company taking a more aggressive role in the administration of the territory. The proud princes, who had prized their independence so highly, found themselves at a disadvantage. Deprived of support from Delhi, they could only defend themselves with local resources, which by and large proved inadequate to resist the advance of the British, with their modern weapons. Trading agreements were extended, but the Company increasingly preferred to take over the administration of the territories in which it operated. Local resistance was overcome, often peacefully, by offering protection against intruders in turn for control over the territory. But the Company's demands were backed up with military might. The Indian Army, as it came to be called, was an amalgam of European professional officers and trained Indians, employed by the Company. Possessing modern weapons, well drilled and organised, it was easily able to dominate any armed resistance it met from local rulers. It has often been asked why, when this army was such a small force, it was able to establish such ascendancy. The answer lay in the cloak of invincibility that it assumed. It was assiduous in ensuring that no challenge to its authority ever went undefeated.

By the time James Outram first arrived in India, the country was largely under the control of the Company, although nominally many states were still ruled by Nawabs. The head of the Company in India was the Governor-General, whose seat of government was in Calcutta. For historical reasons, following the development of British involvement in India, the cities of Bombay and Madras also had governments that administered surrounding territories. While subordinate to Calcutta they had Presidents who possessed considerable authority and latitude in respect of the territories they governed. They also had separate armies, which over time developed individual and different characteristics. They recruited their Indian troops – the sepoys – from different races. The Bengal army, operating out of Calcutta, was regarded as the elite, because it recruited from races that were physically taller, of higher caste and higher status – mainly from the province of Oudh, in the north-east. But the Bombay army would argue that their men were hardier under privation, more loyal and courageous than those in the Bengal army were. Sir Charles Napier, commanding officer said "I feel fearless of an enemy at the head of Bombay troops."[34] The Bombay Presidency, as it was called, was responsible for the important southwestern part of India.

Back home in England the Company structure was equally complicated. The shareholders were known as the Court of Proprietors, who met quarterly to decide on dividends and major issues involving investment and funding, and to elect directors from time to time. The direct management of the

Company was in the hands of the Court of Directors, operating out of a rather grand building in Leadenhall Street, London. However, once the Company became directly involved in running parts of India, Parliament became interested – and not a little alarmed at what a private enterprise was doing in the name of Britain. On several occasions proposals were made to Parliament to abolish the Company and assume direct rule, without agreement being reached. Finally the India Act of July 1784, presented to Parliament by William Pitt the Younger, provided for a Board of Control to oversee the operations of the Company. This Board monitored the Court of Directors by a system of close scrutiny, consultation and accountability that reduced the Court to little more than civil servants. The Board also insisted upon appointing Governors-General, who henceforth were almost always from outside the Company, and became increasingly influenced by political considerations.

The Puritan movement in Britain, enjoying a resurgence in the mid-nineteenth century, saw the Indians as heathens ripe for conversion, and their customs in urgent need of reform. The influential English philosopher Jeremy Bentham believed in strong central government, "enlightened despotism"[35] and although liberal in his leanings, did not think the Indian people ready for self-government yet. The Whig government echoed his views. Thus the relationship between the British and the Indians, initially that of trading partners, evolved steadily and inevitably into the political sphere. The British people's attitude towards India and its people, and the way India was governed was to have a crucial influence on the events of the nineteenth century. James Outram, never one of the establishment, was to find himself frequently at odds with official policy and established attitudes. This was to have a profound effect on his life and career.

James sailed from England on the York on May 2, 1819, reaching Bombay on August 15. The cost of a passage to India in those days was around £95. In addition, to sit at the table of one of the ship's officers required a further fee. Impoverished James must have found it difficult to meet these demands. On arriving in Bombay he had the gentlest of introductions, staying with his cousin Dr Ogilvy when not on duty. He looked upon himself as a puny lad, for at the time he was only five feet one inch tall, and although he was to grow to five feet eight he was known as the smallest staff officer in the army. This lack of stature, combined with a lack of personal wealth, placed him at a considerable disadvantage among his peers. He joined his regiment at Sirur and then at Pune, from whence he wrote his first letter home on October 5, 1820. Such were his financial problems that he was forced to borrow money from Ogilvy. He wrote to his mother: "You insist upon my repaying my Cousin Ogilvy. I believe I need not tell you, that it has always been my first wish, and frequently have I endeavoured to make him allow me to do it, but he never would hear of it, and I am afraid, never will, until, perhaps when I have got an appointment. In the meantime, my kind-hearted Cousin will accept of nothing but my grateful thanks, and I am truly grateful." He added a postscript: "I have not had a moment's sickness."[36] The letter took five months to arrive. Throughout his time in India James was assiduous in writing regularly to his mother, and the affection and concern he showed for her indicate a close relationship born out of the hardships the family had experienced.

By July 1820, at the age of 17 James was an acting adjutant and a lieutenant in the 4th Native Infantry, stationed at Pune. He gained valuable experience from this position, being at the heart of the regiment's activities, having to learn how to handle Indian soldiers and his superior officers as well as the political implications of the job. At first he considered it an easy option, but soon found the administrative burden oppressive. Adjutants normally had two writers: one provided by the Government, the other retained at their own expense to cope with the paperwork, which was considerable. James could not afford the luxury of employing a writer, and in addition was without the Government-appointed assistant for some time, so that the full weight of administration fell on his shoulders. As we have seen, administration and letter writing were not among his strengths. It was six months before the regular adjutant relieved him. He was formally promoted to a full adjutancy on January 15, 1822.

Generally, the life of an officer in the employ of the English East India Company at that time was a life of some ease. The most resistant of the local tribes, the Marathas, who had controlled central India, were finally conquered in 1819, and the way was open for the Company to enjoy a period of untroubled dominance. Although the Company administered vast territories within India, they also employed vast numbers of servants to perform the menial tasks, so there was substantial time for leisure pursuits and plenty of opportunity to indulge them. James' love of the outdoor life, and his natural aggression, soon led him to develop a taste for hunting. Wild hog hunting was the main sport in the part of India where he was stationed, and he frequently joined the Sirur and Pune hunts. But without any wealth or a private income, James found it difficult to make ends meet. A junior officer spent more than half his salary on servants and maintaining his household: a cook, a bearer and a housekeeper – the minimum requirement – would set him back between 32 and 64 rupees per month, the equivalent of between £3 and £7. The financial authorities of the Company decreed that young officers should be paid less than a living wage, as anything more would encourage them to be extravagant.[37] The financial burden of campaigning in India was heavy: an officer was required to equip himself, at his own expense, with a tent and furniture, a good horse, bullocks to carry his baggage, containers for provisions, hog-spears, a hunting knife, a protective hunting cap and plenty of ammunition. It was advisable to keep an additional horse. As a result most officers found themselves heavily in debt, only paying it off when they became majors.[38] Promotion was important, for the difference in pay was noticeable: an ensign received 100 rupees (£10) a month while a lieutenant received three times as much.

Money was to remain a preoccupation throughout James' career, as his letters home show. He was particularly conscious of his mother's impoverished circumstances, and promised to do his best to send back anything that he could save. He wrote to her: "From talking to Frank [his brother] about your circumstances I find you are ten times worse off than I had any idea of, for though I knew you were far from affluent, yet I had no conception that you were so miserably off as you really are….I am astonished how you could have subsisted at all. I, for one, am extremely sorry that I have not been more prudent, for I certainly ought by this time to have been able to send you at least something, for I got the allowance for the acting Adjutancy for eight months out of the ten which I acted, after a reference to Government, and after all found myself but barely even with the world, and since, having been on Garrison pay, have not had an opportunity of saving…... When I rejoin my corps I shall be in receipt of 600 Rupees per mensum (£60), as the corps is at present in the Field, out of which I shall at least be able to save 300 Rupees a month. The Garrison pay is about 400 Rupees a month, so that in the Field I shall save about 350, and in Garrison about 150 Rupees a month, which makes about £180 a year, all of which is of course dedicated to you, and much greater pleasure will spending it in this manner afford me, than if I were amassing riches upon riches on my own account."[39] Throughout his military career James was very quick to volunteer for active service in the field, and it may be that this eagerness had something to do with the increased earnings he would receive. An allowance called batta was paid to all troops on a campaign. Although initially intended to defray expenses, it became a pay increment which officers took for granted. It could be substantial, as James' letter above shows.

Early in 1822 the regiment moved on to Baroda, north of Bombay, but on the way to join it, perhaps worn down by his burden of work, James succumbed to a high fever and was forced to return to Bombay. The cost of his journey back fell to him, as did much of his keep in Bombay. This drained him of his already meagre resources, and he was forced to borrow more money and was unable to pay anything to his mother. Later, in April 1823, he wrote to her from Ahmadabad: "When I left Bombay, I found myself considerably in debt, which I was not in the least aware that I should be when I wrote my last letter…I am very unfortunate in my horses, as the one I brought from Bombay fell lame at Surat…I am afraid I shall be obliged to have him shot. I left a horse at Baroda when I went to Bombay, and when I came back, I found him also perfectly lame. I am trying to sell him for a few Rupees, and have been obliged to buy a hack for about nine guineas, which must do till I can afford to get another, but that time shall not be till I have first sent something to you."[40]

Doctors were of the opinion that he should return to England to rebuild his strength, but this he resisted strongly, and was soon preparing to rejoin his regiment. Embarking upon a boat with horses and kit to cover the first part of the journey by sea, he decided at the last minute to participate in a gala evening which was in full swing, with fireworks being let off at the harbour. It is not clear what happened, but it appears that he discharged some fireworks from the boat, some of which contained gunpowder, and in the process blew up the boat, scattering debris far and wide. The horses were killed and he was picked up in the harbour, blackened from head to foot. It was only by accident that he was recognised as a European and carried to the house of a local Parsi and thence returned to the care of his colleagues with extensive burns to his face. The skin that replaced the burnt surface was to bear testimony to this incident for the rest of his life. The good news was that any trace of the fever from which he was recovering was eradicated!

By the time James rejoined his regiment it had reached the village of Morassa, north-east of Ahmadabad, where it formed part of a field force assembled to suppress long-standing local disturbances. There he officially assumed the position of Adjutant. Soon thereafter the rebel chief, Konkaji, was captured and the unrest brought to an end. The regiment was despatched to Rajkot, 124 miles southwest of Ahmadabad, and the march provided James and his colleagues with some opportunity for hunting. In fact hog hunting was encouraged by the authorities, as it was felt that hard exercise such as this helped in the training and toughening of a soldier. At Rajkot James bought a house which he shared with a fellow lieutenant, Richard Ord. Hog hunting became their regular exercise, and a keen rivalry developed between the officers. Here James showed early signs of his fearlessness, pursuing hogs into the thickest bush, often dismounting to reach them and showing no signs of wavering when the desperate hog turned on its pursuers. As a result he was easily the most successful hunter in the 1823 season, killing seventy-four hogs while his closest rival despatched a mere ten.

But hog hunting was not the reason for which James had joined the army. During 1823 and 1824 he gained practical experience commanding the 1st battalion of the 12th Native Infantry on service to outlying stations. The regiment was highly complimented by reviewing officers in their Annual Reviews for "smart and soldier-like performance under arms, and the report of their orderly and correct conduct in cantonment."[41] James was twenty-two years old. But action was not intense in the area where he was stationed, so when an expeditionary force was mounted to Burma in March 1824 he volunteered for service. His superiors, who felt that he was better employed in his present position, did not welcome this. James must have betrayed a sense of arrogance in the process, for his general, Sir Charles Colville, replied to his request: "Oh, no, little general, I think we can manage it without you."[42] This so infuriated James that he sought out a second in order to challenge the general to a duel. Predictably, no one would agree to such a madcap move, and he mercifully was forced to accept the admonition. Illness again forced him back to Bombay for treatment.

James' first taste of active combat was not long in coming, however. In September 1824 the Desai, hereditary governor of Kittur, to the south of Pune, died without heirs. The East India Company had a policy that decreed that rulers who died without natural heirs forfeited their territory to the Company. (This policy was extremely unpopular, and in 1834 was modified by the Court of Directors, who decreed that rulers could adopt prospective heirs, but that they would only give permission to the local rulers in cases of failure of lineal successors as a mark of favour and not as a rule). In pursuance of this policy the Company annexed a few petty states - Mandavi, Kolaba and Surat. This was the first step towards the notorious Doctrine of Lapse carried out successfully by Lord Dalhousie who was appointed Governor-General in 1848, under which a number of states were peremptorily taken over by the British.[43]

In order to avoid the cession of their territory Kittur members of the Desai's household first sought to conceal his death, and when this failed, to impose a false successor whom they claimed had been adopted by the Desai. Within the Desai's fort was a considerable hoard of treasure including some valuable jewels, and the British Resident, Thackeray moved to control the fort and secure the treasure. This prompted resistance from the inhabitants of the fort, led by the Desai's wife, who barred entry to the British. On October 23, 1824 the British wheeled up two guns and blew the gates of the fort in, but then encountered such heavy fire from within that they were forced to withdraw. In the struggle, Thackeray was killed and his assistants taken prisoner. This little incident was beginning to take on serious overtones, for the British were so thinly spread across India that they could ill afford the blatant flouting of their authority. Fortunately for them Kittur, 274 miles south-east of Bombay, was readily accessible from the seat of the Presidency, and on November 7 the First European Regiment and a detachment of artillery were despatched from Bombay. It happened that James Outram and his brother Francis were both in Bombay at the time. Francis was required to accompany the expeditionary force in the course of duty, and James volunteered to go as a fighting man.

This force quickly besieged the fort, but was reluctant to force an entry, fearing for the safety of the prisoners. The defenders were persuaded to release their captives, and terms of surrender agreed. The Desai's wife and her followers did not adhere to the terms and preparations were made to storm the fort. James volunteered to lead a storming party, but the enemy quickly saw the hopelessness of their position and emerged without a fight. James returned to Bombay on January 19, 1825, and shortly thereafter rejoined his regiment at Melagoan.

Within a month James was to see action again. An insurrection broke out in Western Khandesh, where a rebel leader with an army of 800 attacked and plundered the town of Antapur, retreating with his spoils to the hill fortress of Malair, between Malegaon and Surat. There he raised the banner of Peshwar and declared his intention of presiding over the state. The nearest troops were stationed at Zai Kaira, twelve miles distant, but were required to remain there protecting the treasury, as this was the chief town of the Malair district. A detachment of 200 men was therefore sent from Malegaon, commanded by James. There were signs that the rebels were attracting local support, with young men flocking to their banner. Speed was thus of the essence. James marched his men 37 miles in seven hours, arriving at Zai Kaira at sunrise on April 6, 1825. An assessment of the position led him to believe that although the number of rebels was considerable; their stronghold would be vulnerable to an attack from the rear. Such a daring move was very risky, and exceeded his written instructions, which required him to protect the village of Malair, two miles from the hill fort, and wait until a brigade of infantry from Surat (150 miles away) and a battering-train reached him. His decision gave his immediate subordinates some concern, but James argued that without prompt action the insurrection was likely to escalate rapidly. Shortly after nightfall he sent two British ensigns, Whitmore and Paul, with 150 men to make a false attack on the front of the hill fort, while he took the remaining 50 sepoys in a circular movement to the rear of the fort. Although the ascent to the fort was a steep one, both parties succeeded in reaching the walls before daybreak. The rebels could not ascertain the strength of the frontal force, and whilst this approach drew their full attention James attacked from the rear. The surprise was total, and the defendants threw down their weapons and fled with virtually no resistance. James pursued them closely, harrying them in such a way that they could not stop to appraise the strength of their assailants. Their leader was killed and the remainder scattered with heavy casualties.

But James did not rest. He first sent out scouts to determine whence the scattered rebels had fled, and whether they were likely to reassemble. Cavalry was despatched to follow them, and many more rebels were found and killed in the sweep. This finally broke their resistance, and the survivors fled individually to their respective villages. The uprising had been decisively crushed, and the unrest that had threatened the area for some time brought to an abrupt end. Both the Division General and the Commander-in Chief commended James for the operation.

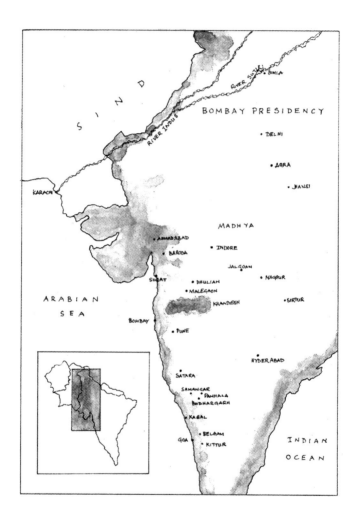

CHAPTER 3.

THE BHIL CORPS.

In 1818 the province of Khandesh was incorporated into British India territory. Situated north-east of Bombay, from which the principal town, Dhulian (now called Dhule), is 181 miles distant, it spanned an area of 175 miles by 128 miles. The terrain can only be described as rugged; thick forest, deep ravines and hazardous mountain passes. Added to this, poor roads and villages scattered sparsely through the countryside made it difficult to move about and to control the territory. Lawlessness abounded, with marauding tribes constantly on the move, terrorising the villagers and looting at will. The most troublesome of these tribes was the Bhils. A contemporary description summed them up thus: "The Kolees or Bheels …were more diminutive than the other inhabitants, and their eyes wore an expression of liveliness and cunning, their turbans, if they used any, were small; their common head-dress was a cloth carelessly wrapped round the temples; their clothes were usually few and coarse; they were seldom seen without a quiver of arrows, and a long bamboo bow, which was instantly bent on any alarm, or even on the sudden approach of a stranger. The natives described them as wonderfully swift, active, and hardy; incredibly patient of hunger, thirst, fatigue, and want of sleep; vigilant, enterprising, secret, fertile in expedients, and admirably calculated for night attacks, surprises, and ambuscades. Their arms and habits rendered them unfit to stand in the open field, and they were timid when attacked, but had, on several occasions, shown extraordinary boldness in assaults, even upon stations occupied by regular British troops. They were independent in spirit, and although professed robbers, were said to be remarkably faithful when trusted, and were certainly never sanguinary. They were averse to regular industry, exceedingly addicted to drunkenness, and very quarrelsome when intoxicated. Their delight was plunder, and nothing was so welcome to them as a general disturbance in the country. The numbers of the Kolees would have rendered them formidable had they been capable of union; but though they had a strong fellow-feeling for each other, they never regarded themselves as a nation, nor ever made cause against an external enemy."[44] The Bhil numbered about 55,000. They imposed a form of tax on anyone travelling through their territory. Although they lived in hill top huts that were easily defended, they were prepared to abandon these homes quite readily and move through the forest if circumstances dictated it.

It is not surprising that, given the description above, the Bhils were strongly opposed to British rule. For seven years the political agent, Colonel Briggs, had tried everything he could think of to bring the Bhils under control. He had threatened them with retribution, he had tried enlisting them in the government service; he had offered some pensions. He had imprisoned the leaders. But little progress was evident. In 1825, in desperation the Bhil agency was established by the Bombay Presidency with express instructions to bring the Bhils to heel, by war if necessary. Three agents were appointed to spearhead the new drive: Captain Rigby in the north-west, Captain Ovans in the south, and Lieutenant James Outram in the north-east, commanding a huge territory, with instructions to raise a Bhil Light Infantry corps under Indian officers. Due to the terrain, and the vastness of the area these three officers were given sweeping powers: to administer and police their territory, to act as judge and magistrate as well as military commander, to arbitrate and conciliate in local disputes – in short to act as God. James was 22 years old.

When James assumed his new post commanding the north-east of the Bhil territory, he unexpectedly started by reducing military operations to a minimum and offering a general amnesty to all Bhils except the worst offenders who had a price on their heads. In doing this he took a huge risk, exposing peaceful citizens to predation, but he saw it as the only way to make progress. He was fortunate in having the support of a far-seeing and humane Governor of Bombay, Mountstuart Elphinstone, who had succeeded Lord Falkland to that post. Born in 1779, Elphinstone had first arrived in India in 1796. Unusually, he attended Fort William College, founded in Calcutta by the brother of the Duke of Wellington, Lord Arthur Wellesley, to educate his fellow countrymen in the ways of India, its languages, religion and culture. He thus possessed a greater awareness of, and a greater sympathy with, the local people. He was the model of a civil servant in India, familiarising himself with the countryside, getting to know the local rulers, learning all the time. He was one of the first administrators to understand that he needed to do these things if he was to earn the respect of the Indian subjects and win their loyalty. He believed passionately that education was the key: by introducing good education the British would improve dramatically the lot of the local people, and equip them for self-rule. There was no reason, he maintained, why Indians should not act as district superintendents, judges and collectors. He believed in greater employment of Indians and was against colonisation. But, inevitably, he had also to act militarily. As Resident at Pune he was required to intervene in a civil war, and rode with Wellesley to part the warring factions. This was followed by a spell in Afghanistan, where he was sent to negotiate an alliance with the ruler, Shah Shuja to prevent a Napoleonic advance upon India. He returned to Pune in 1811 and negotiated a treaty with the Peshwar in 1817 that established British rule over their territory. He was appointed to the post of Governor of Bombay in 1819.

Elphinstone's instinct was to reclaim rather than exterminate.[45] A man of great humanity and vision, he took a rather different line in his governance to that of the normal administrator. In Peshwar he ordered "Officers will be forthwith appointed to collect a regular and moderate revenue on the part of the British Government, to administer justice, and to encourage the cultivation of the soil." He saw his role as preventing "people making laws for this country until they see whether it wants them."[46] Disliking the system of government in place, he returned lands, privileges and judicial rights to local rulers. To the Brahmins he gave back temple lands and provided awards for learning. He pioneered state education. He believed in the authority and usefulness of village headmen and the tribunals through which village elders administered the law locally. He doubted the longevity of British rule in India: "The most desirable death for us to die of should be, the improvement of the natives reaching such a pitch as would render it impossible for a foreign nation to retain the government."[47] It was not surprising therefore that he struck up an immediate friendship with James which was to last to the end of their lives. There can be no doubt that the opinions of this far-sighted man had a profound effect on James.

A free pardon was offered to anyone who surrendered to James' administration. At first this conciliatory gesture provoked a poor response from the suspicious Bhils, long accustomed to a repressive regime, and distrustful of the British. It became evident to James that the Bhils believed his troops could not penetrate their mountain retreats, and were therefore powerless to affect their lives. As they would not come to him, James took the action to them. He made his way to an officer's post at Jatigaon, thirty miles north of his headquarters at Malegaon. Gathering together all the available men stationed there, numbering thirty, with the assistance of a spy he marched on the Bhils stronghold in the mountains. The speed of his move took the bandits by surprise. Reaching their position at daybreak, he caused panic among the Bhils, who fled in all directions deserting their women and children.

James split his party into threes and fours with orders to comb the ravines and forest for fugitives. The bright scarlet coats and sound of musketry gave the impression that the British force was far greater than in reality, and prevented the Bhils from rallying. The ground gained was reinforced with fresh troops from Malegaon, and a more comprehensive sweep of the area resulted in the occupation of many of the Bhil positions, emasculating their local power.

Instead of repressing the Bhils, James set out to recruit them to his Light Infantry. Captives were released on condition that they persuaded relatives to join up. He identified the leading rebels and met them alone in the jungle, gaining "their hearts by copious libations of brandy, and their confidence by living unguarded among them."[48] He finally persuaded five of them to join his infantry. Progress was slow, and his superiors were very dubious about the wisdom of his approach. It was not until July, two months after the first initiative, that James was able to announce that he had enlisted 25 Bhils. Distrust prevailed, particularly when it became clear that the recruits would not be armed. Moreover, the Bhils could foresee the end to plunder, their habitual way of life. By September 92 had joined up, but rumours continued to circulate. James purchased some swords to give his new recruits some sense of security, and this seems to have stabilised the situation. Indeed, when 15 new Bhil recruits fled in fear that they were about to be slaughtered, the remainder went after them and returned with 8 (the rest being out of reach).

Slowly the new infantry corps began to gain momentum. A gang of 13 highway robbers was apprehended, and two rebel leaders, seeing their own kind turn against them, voluntarily surrendered and were treated leniently. James was able to report that the area within 15 miles of his headquarters, which commonly experienced lawlessness and plunder, was now free of crime. Travellers for the first time were able to venture out without protection. The leader of a large body of marauders was apprehended by infiltrating the gang with a loyal recruit, who managed to separate him from his followers and bring him to a village loyal to Outram. By January 1, 1826, the corps had increased to 134 men, and they were developing into a well-disciplined force. James marched them proudly back to Malegaon where the 23rd Native Infantry received them as equals. The Bhils, delighted by this reception, pleaded with James to drill them until they could match their brother soldiers!

James resolved to make his headquarters at Dharangaon, much closer to the Bhil strongholds than Malegaon, and barracks were built there to house his new recruits. The extent of his isolation was referred to in a letter he wrote to his uncle, James Anderson: "These officers are styled Bheel Agents, and I am one of them. The situation is exactly suited to my inclinations, for I care not for the loss of society. I live in a village forty miles distant from any European."[49] Progress with adding to the force was steady: by July 1826, just over a year after he had assumed command, James reported that he had enlisted 308 Bhils. For two months neighbouring villagers had brought not a single complaint against the Bhils. James noted how quiet and orderly they were, and attributed this to the ban on liquor except on public holidays. Lawlessness had not yet been stamped out though. In April 1827 it was reported that two notorious rebel leaders, Mahdeo Singh and Govinda Nayak, were assembling disaffected gangs and attempting to lure away government recruits. When 6 carts and 24 bullocks were seized by this mob, James assembled a detachment of 25 men to pursue them. Again using the strategy of surprise, he marched overnight to Burwari, 20 miles distant, arriving there at 3 in the morning. The jungle around the village was on fire, and James feared that it had fallen to the rebels. When he moved closer the villagers, fearing the rebels were attacking them, opened fire, but on learning whom the visitors were, opened their gates to James.

The rebels had withdrawn to the nearby hills, 6 miles away. They had been kept informed of James' movements, and when he followed them up a rugged ravine, he was ambushed. After the initial shock his troop rallied, but could not attack the rebels who had the advantage of firing from above them, behind rocks and trees. James thus feigned a retreat, drawing the rebels from the heights. The detachment then turned, charged and put them to flight. As there was no prospect of taking the nimble and hardy Bhil on such precipitous ground, with men burdened with arms and accoutrements, and who had marched upwards of thirty-six miles, James again drew them off, and induced the enemy to follow. Another charge totally dispersed them, leaving two killed and several wounded, whom they carried off. James' small party suffered quite heavily too; the Bhil jemadar severely wounded by two arrows, three sepoys with arrows, and about a fifth of the whole bruised by stones.[50]

James was greatly encouraged by the discipline, bravery and commitment of his recruits, almost all of them 18 years old or younger. "The conduct of the Bhil detachment on this occasion is highly satisfactory, being the first opportunity I have had of proving my men when opposed to their own tribe. They have freely risked their blood in our cause, and fought boldly. The quickness with which they rallied, and the boldness with which they charged, together with the fatigue which they had undergone and the eagerness they showed to accompany me on the second night, entitle them to the approbation of Government; especially considering that they were unsupported by regulars."[51]

By 1828, three years after his arrival, there were 600 Bhils in his corps, and the local collector was able to report that for the first time in 20 years his district had enjoyed 6 months of uninterrupted peace. James suggested that a school be opened for the children of his recruits. This was a most unusual step, as previous British administrators had not considered it either their responsibility or in their interests to provide education for the locals. Elphinstone's influence is again seen here. Hitherto the Bhils had resisted any form of education, or indeed regimentation of any sort, but now they were persuaded of its merits and a school was established at the Bhil headquarters for the soldiers themselves as well as their children.

James continued to employ his corps in brief forays against those Bhils who refused to accept law and order. A notable success occurred when the Bhils in the Barwani territory in the Satpura Mountains, north of Khandesh, rose against their Rajahs, sacking several villages and killing a headman. The two rebel leaders were the Nayaks, Hatnia and Esnia. James took 25 of his Bhil corps, 20 horse and 100 auxiliary Bhils, and set out through thick jungle and over mountain passes into uninhabited country in the centre of mountains. The rapidity of his march surprised the locals, and such was his reputation among the Bhils by this time that Esnia was turned over to him immediately, betrayed by his uncle. It was reported that Hatnia had assembled a large force further into the mountains, but James pressed on, marching 24 miles overnight and reaching his camp at daybreak. This was deserted, but the rebels were seen in the surrounding hills. The cavalry, under Lieutenant Hart, succeeded in cutting off Hatnia's retreat and capturing him, causing his followers to flee. Once again James' success surprised his superiors, who had long considered the Nayaks a thorn in their side and did not see how they could be ousted. The capture of Esnia and Hatnia not only neutralised the threat in the Satpura Mountains but also acted as an example to other recalcitrants. James listed three great factors in his success: "1 – placing early trust in them is the only way to make them trustworthy. 2 – show himself their friend and comrade, not an unapproachable Sahib from over the sea. 3 – winning not only the respect but also the devotion of his wild Bhils was his prowess in the chase."[52]

James felt that he had achieved as much as was possible in Bhil territory. He had previously written to his mother asking her to use her influence to obtain for him a position in the political department, where he thought his full talents could be used to better effect, allying his military prowess with civil administration. The political agents of the Company exercised great authority over all aspects of local life, and enjoyed much greater influence than their military counterparts. By this stage in his career James was developing firm ideas about the way in which the Indian territories should be administered, and how their people should be treated. He felt that he could only influence events by becoming part of the civil administration, rather than just a soldier. Sir Charles Metcalfe was about to assume command of the North-West Provinces, and James had his eye on a position under this able ruler. His mother approached Mountstuart Elphinstone, who felt he could not intercede, and wrote back that he was sure Metcalfe was already well acquainted with James' merits. But the Government considered his role among the Bhils to be so valuable that they were not prepared to move him at that time.

Throughout his career, promotion and preferment came slowly to James. His individual views, often strongly expressed, may have given him a reputation as a trouble-maker and iconoclast, but his achievements were such that it is puzzling his worth was not recognised earlier. Perhaps the sympathy he showed towards the local people, and his belief that they should be given more responsibility, told against him in the eyes of his superiors. Nor had he come up through the preferred training path for Company leaders. In 1806 the East India Company had set up a college, Haileybury, to train young men for the political wing of service in India, and after three years graduates from this quasi-university moved naturally into the top positions in India. The Company made the selection of students, and such was the system of civil patronage that almost invariably the students chosen were the sons or relatives of senior Company employees, or from the public school system. Only in 1853, when the Government of India Bill was introduced, was civil patronage abolished and replaced by competitive examination. James had not attended Haileybury, nor had he graduated from Addiscombe Military Training College. Within the regular British Army there existed a system whereby the majority of officers' commissions were purchased, and could be subsequently sold to the next in seniority. This system did not exist within the Indian Army, run by the Company, and the service thus attracted some good men without private means, as well as some misfits.

With peace now the order of the day, and no further immediate challenges to engage him, James turned his considerable energies to hunting. There was an abundance of tigers in the territory, and it was reported that tigers had destroyed 30,000 cattle in one year. The villagers therefore admired and respected anyone willing to hunt them, and James proved himself an expert at the task. Becoming bored with shooting tigers from the relative safety of horseback, he took to stalking them on foot. On one occasion he was attacked by a tiger that felled him, and only the quick use of his revolver saved his life. On another occasion a tiger was cornered in a densely wooded ravine, but it was impossible to see the animal in the undergrowth and difficult to reach it. He ordered the Bhils to climb a tree overhanging the ravine and lower him on a sling down into the ravine, where, dangling in mid-air, he was able to see the tiger and shoot it.

Not content with these feats, James took to hunting with a spear. Having located the tiger, he would ride round it in ever-decreasing circles before striking it before it could spring. At Sirpur when word came of a tiger in the jungle just north of the town he set out with a spear and an assistant armed with a rifle. He followed it for three miles before finally spearing it to death, a feat that became legend in the village. In fact his hunting prowess greatly enhanced his reputation among the wild Bhil, who themselves were expert hunters. Douglas Graham's journal contains several passages of James' daring and prowess, but perhaps the most extraordinary hunt occurred on June 12, 1828. Together with James he followed a tiger into a ravine where the animal took refuge in a porcupine's earth. James dismounted, blocked one of the two entrances to the den and set the brush alight. "At last there was a low angry growl, and a scuffling rustle in the passage. The tiger sprang out, and down descended the long lance into his neck, just behind the dexter ear. With one stroke of his powerful paw he smashed the spear close to the head." James stood "on a little mound, breathing defiance and brandishing his bamboo on high." The tiger gathered: "his huge hindquarters below him for a desperate spring." Douglas Graham shot him twice from the back of an elephant, and recounted: "Had the spear not been directed with the most cool self-possession, so as to arrest the progress of the tiger, and give me the slightest chance of hitting….there would have been an end of one whose like we shall seldom see again."[53]

Another episode showed James' devotion to his men. On one hunt a huge tiger surprised their party and succeeded in killing one of the Bhils before being driven off. A week later Graham was surprised to see James ride into camp with the tiger strapped to his horse. He had followed it for three days through rain and wind over mountains and through the forest before finally getting a shot at it. Nowadays we are conscious of the need to preserve these wonderful animals, and there is no doubt that the predations of these hunters did enormous damage by reducing drastically the number of tigers in India. The villagers saw their extermination as a necessity, for they threatened farmers and village dwellers that had limited means of defence. James saw the hunt as a sport and an exercise in bravery. He noted in his journal that between 1825 and 1834 he and his friends killed 235 tigers, 25 bears, 12 buffaloes and

16 panthers or leopards. He was actually present at the killing of 191 tigers.

In response to his mother's concern at the danger, he reassured her there was none when shooting tigers from elephants. "If I may have been carried away by enthusiasm occasionally to expose myself unnecessarily, believe me I shall bear your advice and admonitions in mind, and abstain in the future. In my situation a little daring was necessary to obtain the requisite influence over the minds of the raw irregular people I command." In another letter "With regard to the subject of tiger hunting, I trust I can set you at ease in a moment. Before I had an elephant I ran some risk, but now I assure you there is none. The tigers also are now nearly extirpated. Pray do not give yourself needless alarms. I keep no tame tiger or any other animal – the tigress I had, I gave away four years ago."[54]

While James was employed in solving the Bhil problem, he and his family suffered a personal tragedy. On September 18, 1829, at the age of 28 his elder brother Francis, an engineer in the Native Infantry, committed suicide in Bombay. Since his arrival in India he had established a reputation for intelligence, zeal and high professional standards. Despite this and his success at military college his position as an engineer paid far less than a field officer and the prospects of advancement were not good. This distressed him. Much like his younger brother he had an independent mind that did not always bend to orders he could not respect. He clashed with a superior and as a consequence was court-martialled and demoted. General opinion at the time was that the sentence was severe, and that he should appeal. Before this could proceed, however, he received another blow. It appears that money had gone missing from an office under his charge, and although he professed to have no knowledge of the defalcation, he felt personally responsible. Many of his friends came forward to testify to his high sense of honour.[55] Added to the court-martial, he felt the disgrace keenly. An attack of cholera two years' previously had undermined his fragile health, and now he fell gravely ill. The surgeon at Ahmadabad who attended him takes up the story: "For six weeks previous he had very bad health and much weakness, but with all this, in spite of my remonstrances he continued to expose himself to the sun. He was however, so ill, that I persuaded him to come to my house, where I nearly made him convalescent. But still it was necessary he should go to the sea-coast, from whence, if not soon better, he was to go to Bombay."[56] A long way from home and depressed by what he saw as the stain on his character, Francis no longer had any will to continue. Goldsmid writes: "…in a fit of delirium, caused by jangal [jungle] fever, he put an end to his life."[57] There is no mention of suicide in any of the many letters which followed this sad death.

James felt his death very keenly, and wrote to the new Governor of Bombay, Sir John Malcolm, in an attempt to clear his brother's name. This was a very unusual step to take; young subalterns just did not address the Governor directly, and the fact that he did so indicated the strength of his feelings. He urged that an inquiry into the cash shortage be held in order that Francis could be cleared of suspicion and the guilty party or parties apprehended. He also offered to repay the missing sum. Far from taking offence Malcolm replied that he fully understood James' concern, that he would attempt to do justice to the memory of Francis and despite some failings he had held him in high esteem. Nevertheless James was profoundly affected by his brother's death, and his suspicion that insensitive government had led Francis to take his life was to inform some of his later brushes with authority.

It seems that James received few letters from his family in England during this time, and the death of his brother reduced familial contact even more. To make matters worse, in 1831 his sister Margaret, who had married a Colonel Farquharson, died in India, and three months later he heard of the death of his uncle, Joseph Outram, in Glasgow. He wrote in his journal:

"All, all are falling; I shall have no relations left to welcome me home, if I ever can return." He threw himself into his work, volunteering for any task that arose.

CHAPTER 4.

SETTLING DOWN.

James must have felt that his achievements in taming the Bhils entitled him to a period of consolidation and relative ease, but it was not to be. To the west of Khandesh lived the Dangehis, a Bhil tribe who had never been suppressed, and who represented a severe problem to the authorities due to their lawlessness and violent nature. The thick jungle to the east of the Sukhain Hills had never been penetrated by troops. James was convinced that through his Bhil troop he could bring about a settlement with the Dang by the age-old tradition of divide and rule. He thus arranged to take a force consisting of 250 Bhil, four companies of native infantry from Surat and Khandesh, 120 auxiliary horse, and 1,100 auxiliary Bhils under their own chiefs, into the heart of Dang territory.

The going was difficult: thick jungle hid isolated villages. Communication between the various elements of the force was virtually impossible. As they progressed, they discovered that word had gone ahead of them, and they encountered one deserted village after another. However the appearance of James and his force had the desired effect upon the population: the Dang leaders became fugitives and the Silput, their chief authority, was deserted by his main followers. On April 18, 1830, four local Rajahs presented themselves with offers of assistance and on May 22 the Silput himself surrendered, his followers having been dispersed. "10,000 bows had vanished into thin air."[58]

Praise and commendations were showered upon James and his Bhil corps, but despite this success he was not promoted, and noted in a letter to his mother that fifty of his contemporaries had superseded him. It was true that promotion in India was very slow, often depending upon the retirement or death of more senior officers. In 1860 fourteen men commissioned before 1830 were still captains.[59] Opportunities were sought by ambitious young men to lobby for promotion through social acquaintances or contacts made in officers' messes. Officers routinely secured testimonials from those under whom they served.[60] James, lacking contacts and to some extent social graces, did not have these advantages, and was not the sort of man to seek them.

Although still very young, James already had a strong sense of social justice. At this time he was writing to newspapers and local magazines pleading for better treatment for sepoys. Their officers regarded them as low life, and he argued that they would perform better if their needs were recognised and they were more sympathetically handled. This would not have endeared him to the disciplinarians among his superiors, who saw the indigenous population as raw savages who needed to be ruled and controlled.

James' success in the campaign against the Dang and other, minor forays with his faithful Bhils in the year which followed finally resulted in his commission as Captain two years later, on October 7, 1832. He was now firmly established in the military hierarchy, but he believed that the political department offered "the only line in the Indian services that allows a military officer to display his talents, both civil and military."[61] His great wish was to be appointed Assistant to the British Resident in Indore, but his requests for a move were still in vain.

Thus James remained in post, revered by his Bhils for his bravery and skill, loved for his sympathy for and understanding of their way of life, until he was required elsewhere. That move was slow to come, but finally in September 1835 James was sent on a tour of Gujarat, the province to the north of Khandesh which had for some time been in an unsettled state and showed signs of adopting a threatening attitude to its neighbours. "It is a change," he wrote, "from an agreeable duty to a very arduous and unpleasant one, from a climate and country to which I am accustomed, to Guzerat, which I never liked, and from old friends and the Bheels to whom I had become sincerely attached, to new faces and turbulent and unruly tribes."[62] The province covered an area of 3400 square miles, being 100 miles from south to north and 60 miles wide. The nature of the people James encountered there would have been familiar to him: isolated villages and fragmented communities where plunder was rife, and individual groups paid allegiance to the head man of the village and no one else. This in itself would not have been of much concern to the British, but these were rebellious and warlike people who were not afraid to attack British camps, and refused to pay their dues. Fairly harsh measures had been taken by the British to suppress any signs of rebellion, and more than once they had intervened in quarrels between rival chiefs. However they had not succeeded in bringing the territory under their control, partly because of the terrain – rugged mountains and heavily wooded ravines – which made troop movements difficult.

The Government in Bombay considered that a possible solution to their problem might be the formation of a military corps from local tribesmen based upon the Bhil model, and James was requested to study the proposal. On September 11 he left Khandesh for Indore, 125 miles north of Dharangoan. From there, after consultation with the British resident, Mr Bax, he set out to tour the province. By November 1832 he was back in Indore, his report complete, although travel through the countryside had been arduous, and the people he had encountered less than hospitable. He came to the conclusion that the area could not be pacified, nor a system of reform introduced, until the unruly bands of marauders had been subjugated and their leaders brought under British control.

The response of his commander-in-chief, Sir John Keane, was to assemble a task force to march against the insurgents. James was invited to command this force, but surprisingly deferred in favour of a friend much his senior. In so doing he pointed out that the appointment of a junior officer (he was a Captain) might give offence where it was important that everyone was agreed as to the action to be taken. Nevertheless he volunteered to serve under the commanding officer. Keane replied that James had the full confidence of the Governor, and having carried out the survey was in the best position to implement his findings. He was to have wide powers of discretion to act against the rebels, and would be invested with civil and political powers that would set him aside from his rank in the army. Keane concluded: "…the military, of whatever rank, must take their directions from you. This is according to precedent and Indian usage; and why should it not be acted on in your case, who possess the confidence of Government, and are looked up to, of all others, as the person best qualified to put their plans into execution?"[63]

Sir Robert Grant, the new Governor at Bombay, was a man of peace and a philanthropist. A founder member of the Clapham Sect, a group including William Wilberforce and Zachary Macaulay who lived near each other in Clapham, London, Grant was a leader of Evangelical and Methodist opinion on political issues. He was an enthusiast for opening India to missionary enterprise. Macaulay had worked in Jamaica and Sierra Leone, and witnessed at first hand the slave trade and the brutal treatment slaves received. He and Wilberforce combined religious fervour with hard-nosed political intelligence to mobilise public opinion, which we know led to the abolition of slavery, not only by the British but also by other nations. There was a sense among the Clapham Sect that the British were an elect people, chosen to spread the creed. A plaque on Holy Trinity Church's wall in Clapham commemorates the Sect for labouring "so abundantly for national righteousness and conversion of the heathen."[64] When the East India Charter came up for renewal in 1813, the Evangelicals successfully campaigned for free access to India by missionaries. Over the next twenty years missionary work in India expanded rapidly. The House of Lords library contains petitions which state: "The inhabitants of the populous regions in India....being involved in the most deplorable state of moral darkness, and under the influence of the most abominable and degrading superstitions, have a pre-eminent claim to the most compassionate feelings and benevolent services of British Christians."[65]

Lord William Bentinck, who was appointed Governor-General in 1828, gave Macaulay powerful support in his campaign. Bentinck was a zealous moderniser, familiar with the scientific and engineering innovations taking place in Britain. He believed steam navigation would bring great benefits to India, and that he could drain the Bengal marshes. He had brought with him a programme of reform. He had been sent out to set the Company's house in order before the East India Charter, due for renewal in 1833, came before Parliament. His immediate tasks were to eliminate the substantial annual deficit and improve the efficiency of the administration. Influenced by the ideals of liberalism, he sought to rule India by bringing improvements to every aspect of Indian life. The aim was to exercise firm but kindly control over the indigenous population, nevertheless imposing western values and practices upon them. He believed in educating Asiatics in the sciences of the west and maintained that Britain could contribute to "the moral and intellectual regeneration of the people of India" by establishing "our language, our learning, and ultimately our religion in India."[66] Ironically, the English East India Company, whilst imposing itself commercially upon India, had exercised scrupulous regard for Indian religions, laws, institutions and customs. Now, under the guise of liberal thinking, came Evangelists intent on imposing their own principles and opinions as well as laws, institutions and morals on the country.

It was not surprising therefore that Grant was somewhat alarmed at the bellicose nature of James report, and could not believe that the troubles in Gujarat had not arisen without just cause. He recommended a full and patient enquiry, with no attempt to disarm until this was completed. His belief that this enquiry alone would resolve the situation led him to reduce the strength of James' force, rather than increase it as he had requested. From being a military commander James was now to adopt the role of a political agent.

James was not a skilled correspondent, and his school record indicates that he did not express himself well. From Ahmadabad on February 2, 1836, he wrote to the Governor expressing his doubts over the suitability of the instructions he had received. Bearing in mind his belief in local rule, he must have felt strongly about the need for military action. He pointed out the unrest that prevailed at that time, and the level of violence between gangs. He continued: "I will pay every attention to your remarks on the subjects you notice, but while Government thus generously pardons the transgressions of these chiefs against us, no provision appears in my instructions for the satisfaction of the claims of others who have suffered at their hands."[67] The tone of this letter caused some offence in Bombay, and he was advised in fairly plain terms as to how he should couch official communications – presumably meaning they should not be critical of government! With his reduced force limiting his capacity to deal with recalcitrant tribes, he could merely issue repeated warnings to them, which went unheeded.

A main cause of conflict between the British and local rulers was the exaction of a tribute called the Ghas Dana, a contribution towards grass and grain fodder for horses. This was acknowledged by precedent and the custom of the country, and was money due to the local ruler. It therefore could not be altered or reduced without the ruler's consent, but the Bombay Government reserved the right to alter the tax rate when it considered such a move expedient. Any reduction would mean that the local chiefs received less from their subjects, and they thus objected strongly when such change was made. James, in an attempt to reach a rapprochement, called a conference of the rulers and offered an amnesty for past offences. This did not suit some of the chiefs, for whom lawlessness was their source of wealth, and it took considerable patience and persistence to persuade them to agree. Over a year later the most recalcitrant, Fath Singh, the Thakur of Rupal, finally agreed, and James was able to report that his mission had been peacefully concluded. In the interests of securing agreement with the Thakur, James had adopted a fairly conciliatory attitude, allowing the Thakur to reach agreement without providing tangible guarantees, which he said would be forthcoming later. James agreed to this although he did not trust the Thakur, and the agreement led to suspicions of mismanagement – and worse – in Bombay. James' response was to state his apprehension that he had lost the confidence of Government. Bombay quickly assured him of their confidence in his actions: "…assure Captain Outram that the confidence of the Government, as it was not lightly given, will not be lightly withdrawn. The ..Governor.. trusts that he will go on cheerfully, under the conviction that though Government may dissent from his judgment on some points, it entertains the firmest general reliance on his zeal, enterprise, and sagacity."[68] The Thakur was to continue to prove troublesome, and whilst James was able to hold him to his commitments during his visit, once he left the Thakur reneged on his promises.

Another chief, Suraj Mall, proved a more serious problem. He had also been reluctant to provide guarantees. A charge was then brought against him, accusing him of holding a merchant hostage and demanding from him 2000 rupees. Mall had been pardoned for his previous misdemeanours, but if true this charge was in direct conflict with the agreement reached. James, already incensed at the lenient treatment allowed these gangsters, informed Mall that unless he released the man within three days and agreed to the terms already settled, he would be declared an outlaw and punished accordingly. James wrote to Bombay hoping for approval, but could not resist adding that he was apprehensive they would be too lenient with Mall. Bombay did not approve of his action, but communications being slow, could not inform him of their attitude rapidly.

Mall refused to tow the line and was declared an outlaw. A small force was assembled to follow Mall up into the mountains where he held his base, and he was persuaded to surrender without force. On April 9, 1836, the Bombay Government wrote to James expressing concern over what had happened and demanding that "without a moment's delay" James explained to them why he had taken action which was not in accord with his instructions and might precipitate the crisis they were at pains to avoid.[69] They considered the treatment of Mall to have been harsh, and that his pursuit of Mall was "the consequence of an unnecessary proclamation of outlawry." But they added: "Under the circumstances…it was an expedient and excellent measure."[70] When Mall came before James together with the released merchant, he was freed without a fine or any further punishment. In the year that followed Mall proved himself a loyal subject to the British, offering active assistance with erring tribes. Bombay wrote with satisfaction at the outcome, commending James on re-establishing peace and good order in the area.[71] Although critical of Grant's approach at the time, his conciliatory attitude towards the local inhabitants and recognition of their rights was to influence James deeply in his future dealings.

At the end of 1835 James travelled to Bombay to consult with the authorities, but more importantly, to get married. When he left England at the age of sixteen he carried with him "a vision…of a beautiful young girl, with gentle manners and star-like eyes, whom he had at that early age decided was to be the wife for him."[72] She was six at the time. He had broken the news gently to his mother several years earlier: "You will see that I begin to think seriously of the married state. I will now confess to you that I have always thought of it, and all my dreams of happiness were connected with my cousin, Margaret Anderson. She would I choose in preference to any. I most sincerely love her, and my greatest ambition is to obtain a return of such sentiments from her." His mother was not pleased – she "had doubtless counted on her son making a brilliant marriage."[73] But James went on to explain that he had been attracted to Margaret since childhood, although there was a ten years age difference: "It was the freedom from selfishness and apathy which distinguished some other members of her family, which engaged my youthful admiration for little Maggy, and I am confident her nature cannot have changed, whatever her education may have been. If she is the same warm-hearted, disinterested girl she then promised to be, I shall be happy."[74] Whilst thus expressing his faith and confidence in his future wife, he was uncertain enough to appeal to his mother: "Should you acquiesce in my wished-for alliance with Margaret Anderson, I am sure you will kindly interest yourself in her education, which will otherwise, I fear, be totally neglected, as her attendance on her younger sisters must be a bar to her own advancement in accomplishments. As far as I am concerned, a very humble share of showy accomplishments would satisfy me, but it would tend much to sweeten the solitary life she might have to pass with me, if she could play and sing prettily (not fashionably) and dance genteelly."[75] Margaret Clementina Anderson came from a large family – six sons and five daughters – in rather impoverished circumstances. There was neither money nor leisure for the children to acquire a good, rounded education. The older sisters were expected to help with their smaller siblings.

Any concerns James' mother might have had about her son, having not seen him for nine years, were put to rest by James' sister, Margaret, who had recently arrived in Bombay, herself to marry: "In every respect I am much pleased with him. His manners are very gentlemanlike and pleasing. I think him remarkably so in appearance also. Though he has seen no female society since he went to Candeish, he is perfectly easy and polite in their company, not a shadow of gaucherie. In fact I think I never saw a young man I admired so much."[76] James himself was nervous. He wrote to his mother: "I fear she must think me a very cold lover, for I cannot write to her so often or so freely as I ought to do. You may recollect that I was always bashful in intercourse with ladies, and a jungle life has not refined me, so that I am not at all at ease in corresponding with them. I fear poor Maggy will be much disappointed in one whose merits have been magnified by prejudiced friends. Such merits as I may possess, are, I fear, of a very rough and uncouth nature, more befitting the Field than society; I trust I should never be deficient in kindness and affection towards her, and she may probably polish me a little."[77]

Ever the considerate gentleman, James broached his intentions first with Margaret's father, requesting that he be permitted to correspond with the girl, now aged seventeen. He planned that she should come out to India in two years' time, ostensibly to join her married sister Charlotte, living in Bombay. This would leave her free of any bond to him, and give the couple the opportunity to become reacquainted after such a long separation. But Margaret returned his affection, and they became engaged. Conscious of his financial problems, James was reluctant to get married until promotion had provided him with the means to keep his wife. As we have seen this was slow to come and delay followed delay. He had hoped and expected her the previous year, but securing a passage on one of the ships coming to Bombay had proved difficult. Margaret's health was delicate, and James worried constantly about the effect the heat would have on her. Presciently, he also foresaw the political problems ahead. In a letter to his brother-in-law, Colonel Farquharson, he remarked: "I foresee nothing but very gloomy prospects for us hereafter - the revenue must continue to fall off - restrictions must continue to be made - thus weakening our own hands whilst the discontent and distress of the country continues to increase, which must break out into constant commotions, gradually becoming more and more formidable, and involving us in ruinous expenses. I suspect that my future years here will not be so quiet as they have been, and almost repent of having involved a sweet girl with one whose future life is likely to be more stormy than pleasant."[78]

Finally Margaret arrived on November 29 and the couple were married on December 18, 1835. Their time together was to be short, however, for within two weeks James was off again on his mission to Gujarat, leaving his new bride staying with her sister and brother-in-law in Bombay. Margaret does not appear to have been too dismayed at their early separation. The British serving in India had established a strong masculine society, based upon games and hunting. Much of this stemmed from the public school background of the leaders. They enjoyed each other's company, and were not quick to marry and settle down. The attitude was one of service: they were in India to do a job, and domestic stability came a poor second. For this reason it was normal for soldiers to spend prolonged periods away from their wives and families, and neither husband nor wife saw this as unusual, or unreasonable.

Margaret was able to join James in Ahmadabad in May 1836, and they established their home at Sadra. James reported to his mother: "My very arduous duties of late have left me little leisure or the freedom from anxiety necessary to private correspondence. I understand that the climate of this country [Guzerat] is more favourable to Europeans than that of Candeish, which is satisfactory to me on Margaret's account.

She, poor thing, I was obliged to leave a fortnight after our marriage, the nature of the task before me not permitting of a lady accompanying me, and I have been so constantly employed ever since, that I have been unable to go to Bombay to fetch her…I am rejoiced to hear from her that you are likely to add to your grandchildren…I have a huge castle of a house at Sadra which is situated on the banks of the Saburmuttee River, about twenty miles north of Ahmadabad. Our only society here is one officer, my assistant, who fortunately is an old friend of mine, and a person I like much. The house is, however, in such a state of disrepair that it will not be habitable for three or four months. Consequently I have been obliged to hire a house for the monsoon at Hursole, a station of troops in my district, about eighteen miles east of Sadra. I hope to be comfortably situated there with Margaret in the course of the next month."[79]

A son was born on September 23 1836, at the cost of Margaret's health. Announcing the news to his mother, James wrote: "The child is to be named after Frank, at Margaret's suggestion, as she said she was sure you would prefer it to any other. My dearest Margaret's most anxious wish is to consult your desires at all times. As soon as she is perfectly strong we shall move to our residence at Sadra, which is much healthier and more commodious."[80]

James remained extremely busy, working seven days a week from dawn to dusk on administrative matters. He was frequently absent on official tours of the region. During the monsoon rains of 1837 he rejoined his wife at Pune, but it was for a very short time. As he told his mother, he did not take to fatherhood easily: "Your grandson is thriving remarkably, but I cannot say that I take much interest in him, for I cannot get over my dislike to infants. I shall be very fond of him no doubt when he begins to speak, but at present we have little to say to each other. Margaret continues very weak, and does not appear at all to gain strength."[81] Margaret remained in poor health, and the doctors considered her return to England imperative. Unable to relinquish his duties and accompany her, James waved goodbye to his wife and new son from the quayside in Bombay.

There remained one rebel chief to be dealt with in the region. Partab Singh, the Rajah of Aglur was one of the most dangerous leaders opposing the British, and was threatening the territory around Ahmadabad in open revolt against his landlord, the Gaikawar of Baroda. The Gaikawar was a member of an important Maratha family who had been feudal lords for centuries. He had solicited help from the British in suppressing Partab Singh, suggesting that the British soldiers available should be placed at his disposal. James was not going to agree to that, but requested a troop of cavalry and a company of infantry to protect the territory under his command, and travelled with this force to Parantej. Four local chiefs were arrested in the hope that this would quell any rebellion, but 500 men took up a position in the strongly defended village of Ransipur on the Sabarmati River and used this as a base to carry out raids on the surrounding district in open defiance of the authorities. A proclamation was issued in the name of the Gaikawar allowing the rebels eight days' grace. If they did not come in and state their grievances they were to be regarded as outlaws. It appeared that Partab Singh had real grievances, which the Bombay Government were disposed to entertain. James however judged that the rebel presence and their marauding was not only a nuisance in itself, but a dangerous precedent if left to fester.

When the eight days' grace expired without response, James proceeded as he had previously agreed with the local commander-in-chief. Hardly consulting with Bombay, impatient that communications took so long, he resolved to attack, and together with 400 local horse and the same number of infantry, approached Ransipur. An ultimatum to lay down their arms was ignored by the rebels, and the attack commenced with artillery setting fire to the town. The rebels attempt to escape was met with withering fire and their losses were considerable. The Thakur of Ransipur was killed by the Gaikawar's troops, and the Thakur of Paria was wounded and taken prisoner.

Although James saw this as a very successful mission, carried out with virtually no casualties on his side (only one infantryman of the British force killed) the authorities were less enthusiastic. Once again they saw reason to censure James for precipitate action, pointing out that they had not sanctioned his attack. They regretted his attitude: "…his fault is that, though perfectly fitted for the performance of civil duties, he is essentially warlike"[82] and continued to hold the belief that much could be attained without force. They also commented that his action at Ransipur was in contrast to the sensitive way he had persuaded the Bhils to conform to law and order. James was quick to respond in his rather straightforward manner, defending his action and pointing out that his success with the Bhils had only been achieved by a mixture of persuasion and the threat of force, which had been recognised and respected. By now the affair had reached the Court of Directors in England, who upheld the Governor's view: "In bestowing the commendation upon Captain Outram we are not forgetful of the fact that on several occasions that officer has shown a disposition to act in a more peremptory manner towards refractory chiefs, and to resort sooner to measures of military coercion than your Government has approved. In all such cases which have been reported to us we agree in the main, or altogether, in the opinion of your Government."[83]

Once again James rashly leapt to his own defence with a lengthy letter defending his position, which merely reinforced their opinion of him. He was at that time seen as an excellent soldier but a poor political risk. Once all the facts were known in London the Directors somewhat modified their views, praising James for his energy and decisive action, and implying that the Bombay President, Sir Robert Grant, had shown excessive leniency towards the rebels. They now accepted that the pacification of the region would never have been possible without "some exhibition and occasional employment of force."[84] They remarked upon the transformation wrought by James' action.

If James felt that after his exertions he was about to enjoy a quiet period of settled, domestic bliss he was to be disillusioned. A new challenge to the British occupation of India was about to arise, and to place James in a spotlight which would be noticed in London, and transform his career.

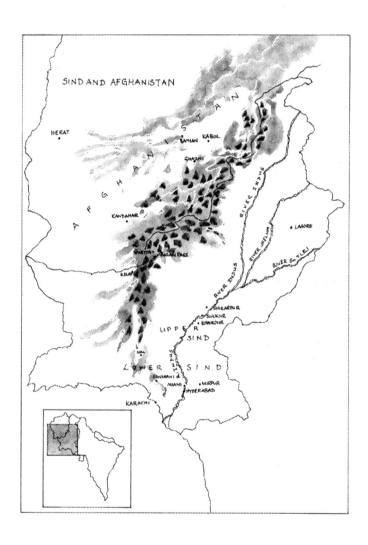

CHAPTER 5.

SIND.

In the latter half of the 18th Century three major powers, Britain, France and Russia were competing to expand their interests in Asia. Britain foresaw a time when all of India would be theirs. France, under Napoleon, had ambitions in Persia and through that country the whole of Southern Asia, possibly regaining a position in India. Russia was alarmed that these two maritime powers would threaten it through Persia, and strove to form alliances with the Muslim rulers of Persia. Russia had for some time been eyeing the immense riches which India offered, and as early as 1791 the British had recorded its alarm at the possibility of Russia moving against them there.

Afghanistan, which at that time was largely unexplored, stood as a buffer between India and both Russia and Persia. A country of 250,000 square miles, it was inhabited by a homogenous people who identified themselves as Afghans, but many of whom were Pathans of Aryan stock. The tribes varied considerably in appearance, but most were poor farmers or adventurers, open for hire by warlords. All were averse to any form of rule other than their own law – Pahtunwali – whose principle teachings related to revenge and hospitality.[85] The western territory was bordered to the north by a 600 mile long range of ice-covered mountains, the Hindu Kutch, while to the south was desert and desolate, hilly country bordered by Baluchistan. The British assessment was that should the Russians wish to invade Afghanistan it would not be practical to enter from the plains of Turkestan, north of the Hindu Kutch, because of the formidable barrier presented by the mountains. It was more likely that they would aim for Kashmir, north-east of Afghanistan, and the Khyber Pass, which offered a narrow, hazardous but accessible way into the country. The only other alternative (and an easier one) was to move east via Persia and south Afghanistan into what is now Pakistan, and at that time was part of India, known as the Sind.

The British relationship with the rulers in the Sind had been chequered. The Sind was a fairly remote region of 50,000 square miles– roughly the southern part of modern Pakistan. The backbone of the country was the Indus River, 2,000 miles long, flowing down from the north to the sea, bordered by rich alluvial soil in a wide valley. To the east were the unforgiving Rajputanja desert and the Rann of Cutch, sparsely inhabited mudflats extending over 9,000 square miles. To the west were the rugged Baluchi hills. The spring and summer rains provided fertile ground on the banks of the Indus for the growing of rice, and the local inhabitants were able to control trade with northern India and central Asia by controlling traffic on the river. The rulers of the Sind enjoyed more independence than most states, and had amicable relations with the British. Due to its inaccessibility foreigners had not troubled it much.

The one million inhabitants of Sind were mainly Muslim, ruled by Amirs of the Baluchi Talpur clan. The country was divided into three and ruled from Khaipur in the north, Mirpur in the east and Hyderabad in Lower Sind. The Baluchis were traditionally nomad farmers who inhabited a wide area, embracing the Upper Sind, Afghanistan and the eastern part of Persia. Formidable and fierce warriors, like the Bhils, many of them made their living by raiding rural villages, and preying on the trade routes. It was therefore not surprising that they jealously guarded their independence and way of life. The British had made several attempts to establish factories in the Sind, but found the Amirs intransigent and fearful that the British wished to control the territory. A treaty signed on August 22, 1809 provided for the residence of an Indian agent in the capital of Lower Sind, Hyderabad, and an agreement to exclude the French. The British were later to play upon the respective rulers' independent-mindedness to agree separate treaties with them in an attempt to "divide and rule."

When the Baluchi leader and head of the clan controlling the Lower Sind, Mir Murad Ali, died in 1833 his power was divided between his two sons, Nur Mohamed and Nasir Khan. The latter's son, Mir Sobdar Khan, received sovereign territory from him, as did Mir Mir Mohamed, son of another Amir. These four Hyderabad princes were to be the central figures in the affairs of the Sind over the next decade. Nur Mohamed was a strict, unpopular ruler who was by nature suspicious and calculating, but Nasir Khan presented a more westernised, urbane impression, and was known to mix freely with British officers.

There is some evidence that the Company was much more interested in the commercial possibilities of the Sind than its defensive importance. The navigability of the Indus offered great potential for trading with the north of India, and the Governor-General's instructions were to seek trading arrangements.[86] A Secret Committee memo to him in Council dated January 12, 1830, reads: "…if the produce of England and India could be sent at once up the Indus to such points as might be convenient for their transport to Cabul we cannot but entertain the hope that we might succeed in underselling the Russians and in obtaining for ourselves a large portion at least of the internal Trade of Central Asia."[87] The Amirs of the Sind did not always act in concert, and their individual interests were not always in the common good. It must also be said that the British strategy was to expand influence in the region, and secure the western flank of India. Their ambitions led them to criticise the Amirs as despots addicted to bhang (a local drug) and opium. They used this criticism to propose replacing bad government with good. They looked to persuade liberals in England to support this approach by pointing out the Amirs toleration of domestic slavery and the practice of killing baby girls at birth. The Amirs found it desirable to maintain friendly relations with the British because they feared the territorial ambitions of their nominal overlord, the Amir of Afghanistan.

The political situation in Afghanistan was unstable. Then, as now, feuding warlords who controlled their own territory ran the country, although it had been ruled until 1809 by a king, Shah Shuja, sitting in Kabul. When he was routed by a local warlord, Mahmud, and forced to flee, he placed himself under the protection of the British. The Sind was nominally in thrall to Afghanistan, and therefore theoretically a possession of Shah Shuja, and the possibility of Britain buying the Sind from Shah Shuja for £200,000 a year was discussed. This would have enabled the Shah to build a strong friendly power in Afghanistan, but this suggestion got nowhere. There followed a period of instability until in 1826, after a long period of internecine strife, another local warlord, Dost Muhammad, emerged as the most powerful man in Afghanistan. Dost Muhammad proved a considerably more able ruler than the Shah, and was recognised by the British as a powerful leader, but despite talks in which they attempted to persuade him not to deal with the Russians, he received the Russian envoy in Kabul. This led London and Calcutta to regard him as an enemy, and although many knowledgeable advisers saw him as the best bet for a peaceful Afghanistan, the Governor-General, Lord Auckland, refused to have anything to do with him.

George Eden, first Earl of Auckland had become Governor-General in 1835, following a successful Whig political career. He was described by the Edinburgh Review as the best that Britain had ever sent to India. One of the youngest Governors-General, he was a brilliant administrator, honest and well liked. It only emerged later that he reacted badly to pressure when he became indecisive and passive, mainly as a result of being able to see several sides of a question. This defect was to cost him, and Britain, dear. But at this point of time he was to be swayed by the advice of the secretary to the Indian government's secret department, William Macnaghten, an orientalist with a high reputation.[88] There was no alternative, in Auckland's mind: Dost Muhammad represented a threat to British interests in India. If he was to be removed British troops would have to be used, and the Amirs would have to be persuaded to support the venture.

The Amirs in turn felt threatened by the Afghans, who regarded the Sind as their possession. Ranjit Singh, the ruler of the Punjab in the north also had expansionary ambitions, and could be seen as a threat. They were therefore prepared to agree to the British plan in return for protection from these forces. This cleared the way for the reinstatement of Shah Shuja to the Afghan throne. To allay fears of a permanent occupation of the country, Auckland stipulated that the British force would be withdrawn as soon as the Shah's position was secure and the independence and integrity of Afghanistan assured.[89] William Macnaghten, fluent in Persian, Arabic and Hindustani who, as we have seen, carried great influence with Auckland, was appointed as envoy to the proposed new royal court at Kabul.

Back in Gujarat, James's house in Sadra, in which he had invested quite a bit of money in renovation, was not suitable for a bachelor, and deteriorated rapidly in the extreme weather. His administrative duties left him little time for hunting or other exercises, and he became quite stout. His letters home showed that he planned to return to England on leave in 1840, but Macnaghten's proposal, and concern that Russia might yet again attempt to occupy Afghanistan, led to plans being drawn up to occupy Afghanistan as a first line of defence. James' regiment was ordered into service there, and James naturally volunteered to join the mission. Although he was now to all intents and purposes a political agent, his reputation as a soldier was such that it was recommended that he be attached to the army in some capacity. One proposal was that he should command the contingent that would occupy

Kandahar and install Shah Shuja as a puppet ruler, but, as in the past, he deferred in favour of more senior officers. The officer commanding the Bombay army, Sir John Keane, appointed him as Extra Aide-de-Camp on his staff. A combined force of the Bombay column and a contingent from Bengal, led by Sir Willoughby Cotton, was to be assembled, and would be known as the Army of the Indus. Ranjit Singh refused to allow the army to march through his territories to the north, so it faced a 1200-mile march through Baluchistan via Kandahar. The logistics were remarkable: 10,000 British and Indian troops, 6,000 irregulars of the Shah's army augmented by camp followers and helpers amounting to four times the number of fighting men. 30,000 camels carried the baggage. In their thick red tunics, white cross belts, gleaming brass helmets and high jackboots the British must have presented a most imposing spectacle.

Far from seeing his new posting as a sinecure, James threw himself into the task with great energy. Suggestions poured from his pen. He proposed that he raise a small body of select horse in Gujarat to be placed under the command of a local Indian nobleman who had already given good and reliable service to the British in previous campaigns. (This was a most unusual suggestion as it was unheard of for Indians to be allowed positions of command). He also suggested the enrolment of a thousand Gujarat infantry under English officers, who could reach the Indus in a month. He criticised the weakness of the cavalry destined for Afghanistan, and proposed that volunteers be called for to augment the force. None of his suggestions were acted upon, and his criticisms were to be borne out when the fighting started.

On November 21, 1838, along with Sir John Keane, James embarked upon the steamer "Semiramis" at Bombay, and sailed west, reaching the mouth of the Indus 6 days later. Further progress was impeded by a lack of camels and boats to move up the Indus, the rulers of the lower Sind in Hyderabad having secretly ordered that they should be unavailable. James was despatched to the Kutch in southern Sind to procure the necessary transport. In the evening he went ashore in a native boat, without servants or baggage of any kind hoping to encourage confidence by displaying that he was totally unattended. His object was ostensibly to look for camels, but in reality also to gauge the feelings of the locals.[90] When James reached Karachi, then a small fishing village, he learnt that the Amirs had not issued orders for camels to be made available. He pointed out that "their backwardness in affording aid must turn to their own disadvantage, by detaining the force so much longer in their own country, or by compelling us to help ourselves."[91] The Amirs had told their local representative that they had received information that forty thousand troops were to follow the present British force in order to occupy the Sind forcibly. James repeated his assurances, and after a meeting he was allowed to commence procuring camels and on his return was able to report success. On December 19 500 camels arrived from the Kutch, having been delayed by the Amir of Mirpur's refusal to allow them to pass, necessitating a detour. In all, one thousand camels had been procured. The adventurer and explorer Henry Pottinger provided an amusing aspect of James' arrival in Karachi. On observing the British vessels approach the inhabitants of the fort fired a signal gun in welcome, but the British took this to be a hostile act and promptly flattened the fort with a broadside, storming the unresisting port.[92]

Whilst in Karachi James saw evidence of the Amirs' hostility towards the British. Although professing friendship towards the expeditionary force, they commenced marshalling all available fighting men between the ages of seventeen and sixty, and concentrated their artillery resources around their capital, Hyderabad. James made the point that even if the army passed through the Sind without trouble it was imperative that the communications of the army should be maintained by a strong force stationed there.[93] Accordingly he was assigned to negotiate a new treaty to enable the establishment of a military cantonment at Thatta in return for a cash payment while troops were stationed in the town. An assembly point at Shikarpur also needed to be secured in readiness for the journey through the Bolan Pass into Afghanistan. He pledged the protection of Sind from foreign aggression and the unconditional aid of the British force if found necessary by the British Government. In case the full implications of these proposals were overlooked, the treaty emphasised that the intention was that the two governments should "really become one."[94] For this privilege the Amirs were asked for a contribution of £200,000 later increased in return for a release from all claims to their territory by Shah Shuja. This money would be used to finance the Afghan expedition. It was expected that wealth would flow into the Amirs' coffers through the British force stationed in the Sind, giving employment to thousands of people. Later writings suggest that James did not fully believe in his brief, and there were suspicions that the British expected the Amirs to reject the terms, allowing them to take control of the Sind. Indeed, there were signs that the Amirs did not trust the British, and were very concerned about Keane's intentions to move through their territory to Afghanistan. They raised objections to the march, and sought to block it. Intelligence was then received by Auckland that the Amirs had written a submissive letter to the Shah of Persia (which was not uncommon at this stage in Sindian foreign relations), and he used this as an excuse to occupy Shikarpur.

From Thatta James, accompanied by Lieutenant Herbert Eastwick, took a steamer up-river towards Hyderabad. The ship ran aground frequently, making progress slow. This suited James quite well, as he used the time to survey the surrounding countryside from a military point of view, in case it became necessary to fight later on. After four days, on January 20, the ship anchored 3 miles from Hyderabad, and the Amirs sent a deputation to welcome the British. On the following afternoon three of the four joint rulers received James, the fourth, Mir Sobdar Khan being on bad terms with the others. In the day since anchoring James had ridden to the town and surveyed the walls of the fort, identifying the various approaches. He came to the conclusion that "artillery would soon breach the fort, which is in itself by no means strong," and formed a low opinion of Hyderabad itself; "…a collection of wretched low mud hovels…and even the boasted stronghold of the Ameers, which surmounts their capital, is but a paltry erection of ill-burnt bricks, crumbling gradually to decay."[95]

The talks started well. The chiefs were polite and welcoming, and prepared to discuss terms. The populace showed every sign of being hostile, however, and soldiers from the Baluchi tribe shouted abuse and threats at the British party. When James asked the chiefs to explain this attitude, the answer was vague and unsatisfactory, so he withdrew. During the night vigilant sentries thwarted an attack on his small detachment of sixty-nine men. A warning was received that five hundred armed men had crossed the river, about two miles below the camp. The warning stated that the Ameers intended marching out at the head of their army during the night, and that their emissaries have been sent down the Indus to direct the boatmen to scuttle all the boats.[96] Measures were taken to protect the boats, and camp was struck in preparation for a swift departure. Finally James received a message from the Amirs to the effect that their answer to the treaty would be given in due course. There was nothing to be gained by lingering, so he joined the boats and sailed back to the main force, which by now had moved forward from Thatta to Jerak.

The build-up of Baluchi fighters in Hyderabad continued. Further requests from the Amirs for clarification over details of the new treaty fuelled suspicions that they were adopting delaying tactics until the strength of their army was adequate to confront the British. The general animosity James had encountered led Sir John Keane to believe a show of military force may be necessary. He sent a message to the Bengal division north of Hyderabad requesting aid, and a section of that force was detached to march towards Hyderabad. They had only covered a third of the distance when a communication came from the Amirs agreeing to the treaty and pledging friendship. On February 1, 1839, the treaty was signed. The Bengal task force returned to the main division and Keane's force moved up-river towards Hyderabad. By February 3 the Bombay division was camped on the right-hand bank of the Indus, opposite Hyderabad. Officers were permitted to visit the town, and James took the opportunity to check his notes of the layout and fortifications. He was commended by his commander-in-chief for having judged the weak points exactly, and identified the best routes of approach.

The mortality rate among pack animals was alarming, and James was deputed to advance to Shikarpur, where Shah Shuja was camped and where William Macnaghten, the Shah's envoy, was based, to obtain more camels. As it was now late February the temperature was beginning to rise and the open, shadeless plains were becoming hardly bearable. The thermometer during the day stood at between 130 and 140 degrees Fahrenheit, and the nights no lower than 90 degrees. On one march of a few hours 116 horses died of sunstroke. Nevertheless James covered the distance to Shikarpur, 70 miles, in a day and a half. Leaving Larkhana, where he had stopped overnight, at 9 a.m. he rode the last fifty-two miles to Shikarpur by camel, arriving there at 10 p.m. without a stop. He was able to secure a thousand camels despite the envoy's disenchantment with the behaviour of Sir John Keane's force and his concern that it was offending the Amirs. Macnaghten was so impressed with James that he immediately sent a request to Keane for James to join his staff, but James politely declined, saying that while there was the chance of military action he preferred to stay with the army.[97]

On James' return to the Bombay contingent he was required to deal with a strike by camel drivers. Numbering over two thousand, they were refusing to advance any further. James' response was to single out twenty of the most influential and confine them. This had no effect: they still refused to budge. One of the prisoners was then given two dozen lashes in front of the assembled throng, and then another prisoner brought forward, each receiving more lashes than the previous one. After the third camel driver received four dozen lashes the remainder yielded, and promised obedience in future.

The intended route into Afghanistan was via the Bolan Pass, a rugged and dangerous path fifty-nine miles in length through the arid mountains. The first twenty-seven miles from Shirkarpur was across desert. The start of the pass was a narrow valley between hills of clay and gravel five hundred feet high with a strong-flowing stream at the bottom that required crossing twenty times in thirteen miles. The middle stretch involved a climb of 1,950 feet in nine and a half miles. William Macnaghten was deputed to travel ahead with the Shah Shuja. James was sent on by Keane to make contact with the royal party. He rode alone all night on a camel through hostile and dangerous country, where the local Baluchi tribe were known to plunder and murder strangers, travelling 41 miles to Gandava, which he reached in late morning. The following day accompanied by two armed guards, he moved on by pony to Bagh, a further 45 miles, where he met Macnaghten on March 18. Macnaghten was concerned at the amount of plundering by the Shah's troops, alienating the locals, who were not well disposed towards the deposed monarch in any event. His train was being harried by hostile Baluchi and opportunistic thieves, and making slow progress. On returning to Keane with news on the progress of Macnaghten and the Shah, James was again despatched to Gandava with instructions to send a messenger on to Macnaghten saying that the army would join up with the Shah at Dadar and accompany him into Afghanistan. By now British soldiers held the Bolan Pass and no resistance was anticipated on the march into Kandahar. A major local ruler, Rustam Khan, was persuaded to grant the loan of a fortress at Bhakkar to the British in order to safeguard their progress.[98]

James suffered an unfortunate accident near Gandava when his horse, turning at speed, slipped and fell on top of him, fracturing his pelvis. This prevented him from riding forward with his chief, but rather than miss out in the adventure he arranged to be carried in a palankeen with the main body of troops. The going was very rough, with many animals falling by the wayside and raids from marauders harrying the force. Baluchi scouts were seen frequently on the ridges, and at one stage it was said that three thousand Baluchi were assembling for an attack. Preparations were made to resist them, and the attack melted away.

On April 16 the combined army reached Quetta. This town, on the main road from Sind to Kandahar, was perceived as the gateway to India, and therefore of immense political and military importance. The officer who had charted the Indus, Sir Alexander Burnes, had also signed a treaty of friendship with the Amir of Kelat, under whose auspices Quetta fell. Ominously this Amir did not appear to meet the Shah despite his vows of allegiance. The Sirdars of Kandahar had assembled a resistance force and marched out to Dil-I-Hadjee to face the Shah and the British, but dissension among them led to withdrawal, and they fled from Kandahar with less than 200 followers.[99] Kandahar was finally reached on April 25, 1839 without serious conflict, and the army set up its headquarters there. The Bengal division soon joined the contingent from Bombay and the Shah made a state entry to the city. A military ceremony was organised, the entire army presenting arms and a salute of 101 guns being discharged. A march past of seven thousand men followed, presenting a most imposing spectacle.[100] To all intents and purposes the Shah was installed as King of Afghanistan. The inhabitants of Kandahar were not impressed; the Shah was not popular, and his arrival was not welcome. Barely a hundred turned out to witness the ceremony. The local chiefs intended to remain aloof until they could gauge whether the Shah could establish himself, and the people saw the Shah as a puppet dependent upon British bayonets. Nevertheless Keane now controlled Kandahar, and the Shah was placed on his throne there on May 8.

James was becoming increasingly uneasy about the expedition, and vented his feelings in letters to friends. He believed that the objective of defending India could be achieved by drawing a line at the Indus and fortifying it. He was concerned that the advance into Afghanistan would be disastrous. He had noted that the Shah was not popular, and that the passage of the British army had provoked hostile reactions. He was concerned that they might be drawn into warfare. He argued that the British army's reputation for invincibility could only be preserved if it was not engaged in a difficult skirmish on Afghan territory, which was notoriously hostile. He felt that a better strategy now would be to set the Shah on the throne and withdraw to the Indus. He was of the opinion that if Afghanistan was threatened from the west, British soldiers could if necessary be moved up to Kabul in good time. Privately he had much sympathy with the position of the local rebel chief, Dost Muhammad, who was popular and maintained good control over his troops. To Major Felix he wrote: "If – as I suspect will be the case - Dost Muhammad prefers temporary exile to submission, seeing that the Shah is only upheld by the presence of a British army which must soon be withdrawn, he will return with tenfold popularity to raise the standard against a King forced upon bigoted Afghanistan by infidel bayonets. Then will Shah Shooja be in his turn deserted by those who are now seduced to his side by British gold, but who can only be held there so long as the golden stream flows undiminishedly. The fact is not to be concealed that Dost Muhammad, at the outset of this struggle, had the

preponderance of personal weight in this country....For our
own sakes I think it better we should pass peaceably through
Afghanistan, and fulfil our mission without hostilities, because
once involved in warfare, we should have to continue it under
lamentable disadvantages in this country. A blow once struck
by us at the Afghans will oblige us to become principals on
every occasion hereafter, much to our cost and little to our
credit."[101] Unfortunately James' views were not confined just
to his friends, but were also communicated to the Governor-
General, Lord Auckland, and William Macnaghten. This
did not enhance his reputation for diplomacy, although
both acknowledged his value as a soldier. Sir Charles Wood,
Chancellor of the Exchequer in a Whig Government, was
equally alarmed at the campaign, primarily from a financial
point of view. He described it as "the greatest disaster which
ever befell us in India."[102]

The advance column left Kandahar on June 27, and James
went with them. Their immediate destination was Ghazni,
a formidable fortress where they expected to encounter
stiff resistance. Dost Muhammad focused his resources on
protecting this stronghold, and cleared the approaches by
destroying orchards and vineyards, much to the dismay of
the inhabitants. Progress by the British was slow with such a
cumbersome force – they only moved an average of 11 miles
a day. This stage was undertaken with very little trouble apart
from occasional marauding, during which two of James' horses
were stolen, one a magnificent Arab worth £200, which must
have been a serious financial blow to him.

By July 18 the combined force was within two days' march
of Ghazni. The column had become strung out, and Keane was
forced to wait until it closed up. Ghazni was reached on July
20. It was one of the strongest fortresses in Central Asia with
walls rising seventy feet, surrounded by a wide moat. It was
defended by elite Afghan soldiers led by Dost Muhammad's
son, Hyder Khan. Mining or scaling the walls would be

impossible. There was no sign of the enemy until they were within one mile of the fort, where they observed scouts who withdrew quickly. On reaching the fort they came under heavy fire. Having left their four heavy guns behind at Kandahar with General William Nott, the chances of taking the fortress looked remote. Fortunately a disenchanted nephew of Dost Muhammad, Abdul Rashid, predisposed to the cause of Shah Shuja, had been forced to flee from the fort and was able to inform Keane that although most of the gates were bricked up, the Kabul Gate was only lightly barred to allow the passage of troops. It could be approached across an unbroken masonry bridge from a good road, and the surrounding terrain offered good positions for the artillery to mount a bombardment. As the army's provisions were down to two or three days' supply, Keane could not afford to mount a long siege. Avoiding head-on confrontation, the army circumnavigated the fort, taking control of the road to Kabul on July 21. During the night, blue lights from the fortress were answered by blue lights along the mountain ridges, and at noon on July 22 five or six thousand men appeared on the heights above the British and commenced descending. In order to prevent them reaching the plain the guns were quickly wheeled into position. A few rounds checked the advance, and a regiment of Bengal cavalry charged to dispel them.

James recorded in his journal that he had galloped out to discern what was occurring. Reaching the scene as the Bengal cavalry advanced, he mustered a body of the Shah's horse and took them round the hills to the rear of the enemy in order to cut off their retreat. Seeing this manoeuvre, the enemy fragmented and fled into the hills. James took over a detachment of 150 of the Shah's infantry and followed them. The infantry fought bravely under a withering fire from the hills, using rocks to shield their progress, and finally reached the top where a green and white standard flew. This was a holy banner set up by a Muslim priest who had convinced the defenders that they were safe under its influence. Once the banner was seized, all further resistance crumbled and the enemy retreated in confusion deeper into the hills. James' men were exhausted and thirsty, so further pursuit was abandoned. James had lost 20 men, while enemy losses were between 30 and 40 with 50 prisoners taken.

With the threat to the Shah dissipated the British were in a position to attack the fort. Early in the morning of July 23, with a howling sandstorm in full spate, a party of engineers managed to place twelve twenty-five-pound sacks of gunpowder against the Kabul gate and bring down the gatehouse and scatter the timbers of the gate. Once through the breach, the attackers were able to sweep the enclosure. James was directed to place guns commanding the western face of the fortress to prevent the garrison escaping, and when this was achieved he used his initiative to ride round to the eastern wall where fugitives were attempting to escape across the gardens. After the fall of the fort Mahommed Hyder Khan, son of Dost Muhammad, was discovered concealed in a tower with about twenty of his followers, He surrendered when his life was spared. Over fifteen hundred prisoners and eight hundred horses were taken at Ghazni, at the cost of seventeen men killed and 165 injured. In spite of the prominent and courageous part James played in the siege, yet again he was omitted from despatches, and was not accorded any of the usual honours or promotion that followed a successful campaign. It is difficult to know why this is. Was he unpopular with his superiors? Had his rather blunt way of expressing himself counted against his advancement?

The loss of Ghazni was a massive blow to Dost Muhammad, who had considered it invulnerable. In the hills above Ghazni Dost Muhammad's eldest son was waiting to fall upon the defeated British. Now Afzul Khan stared in disbelief at the Union Jack fluttering above the fort. Dost Muhammad, on the road to Ghazni west of Kabul with his army of 13,000, implored his followers not to desert. Despite generous bribes to the chiefs, his support began to melt away. He sent an envoy, Jubbul Khan Nawab, to negotiate with Shah Shuja, but when told that an essential condition of any agreement between the two parties was the banishment of Dost Muhammad to India, the envoy declared without hesitation that this was unacceptable, and returned to Kabul. As the British army resumed its march towards Kabul, information was received that Dost Muhammad had fled towards Bamian, north of Kabul. On July 1, 1839, Shah Shuja rode into Kabul on a magnificent white charger, accompanied by Macnaghten and Keane. Despite his glorious clothes Shah Shuja was not popular in the capital either, and the inhabitants showed no sign of welcoming him.

The reaction to the news of the successful march through Afghanistan was not what Auckland expected. Ministers in London, who had paid little attention to what was happening, now became thoroughly alarmed at the far-reaching control being assumed. Those that disapproved foresaw that Afghanistan would become a British dependency.[103] The Board of Control despatched a private letter to Auckland stating that it would never sanction any arrangement having for its objective territorial acquisitions in Central Asia.[104]

Dost Muhammad's popularity was still such that he posed a considerable threat to the success of the mission, and James was deputed to pursue him. A force of two thousand of the Shah's Afghans was assembled, augmented by 100 British cavalry and a body of British officers. Hadji Khan Kakar, or Nasir-ud-daulah (meaning Defender of the State) was appointed to head the Shah's force. He had previously been in the service of Dost Muhammad but had switched his allegiance to the Shah. The terrain was rough, and it quickly became apparent that the Shah's men were not enthusiastic about their assignment. Of the two thousand drafted less than half turned up at the rallying point, and of these only half were effectively equipped, "the residue of those present consisting of

Affghan rabble, mounted upon yaboos and starved ponies."[105] James decided that speed was of the essence, and proposed a short-cut across the hills to intercept their quarry. Hadji demurred, favouring the main road, but James would not agree. They marched during the first night about thirty-two miles, crossing several ranges of hills, and winding along the channels of several rivers. At 7 a.m. they reached Goda, a small village situated in a confined but fertile valley. Although several halts had been made, in order to admit of the stragglers closing up, not more than one hundred Afghans had joined the expedition.[106]

There followed a series of delaying tactics by Hadji which kept James' pursuers behind Dost Muhammad as he moved north. The going was arduous, with high mountain passes and tortuous river channels to be negotiated, and the Afghan force dwindled steadily as the force moved north. Each time James received intelligence that Dost Muhammad was within one march of his position, Hadji would find a reason for a halt, citing the hardships encountered by his men, and the strength of Dost Muhammad's force. Nevertheless, three days into the pursuit, on August 7, James was close behind his quarry. At Hurzar they found traces of Dost Muhammad's encampment from the previous day, and on the road met deserters from his camp who informed James that they had left Dost Muhammad earlier that day at Kalu, and that he showed no signs of departing from there. Hadji immediately protested that it would be madness to press forward, for they would surely be defeated, and that the Afghans could not advance, as they were weary and hungry. James announced he would go without the Afghans, but on reaching Kalu with his small group he learnt that Dost Muhammad had left several hours earlier.

On August 8 they reached the foot of the Kalu Pass, the highest in the Hindu Kutch at 22000 feet. Spirits were raised when two British officers, Captains Taylor and Trevor with 30 troopers and 300 Afghans joined them. They pressed on to the pass of Shutur-I-Gardan, or Camel's Neck, the highest they had encountered so far, and so steep that they were forced to lead their horses all the way through the pass. They stopped at a deserted village at the foot of the path. James intended to recommence the march on Bamian at 2 a.m., but once again Hadji, who had caught up with him, demurred, arguing that he was surrounded by traitors and to take on Dost Muhammad in darkness would be suicide, as "not one of the Affghans will draw a sword against him."[107] James was forced to pause until daylight. He sent two officers forward to reconnoitre. Whilst awaiting their return he formed a battle plan. In the event of Dost Muhammad turning to face them "the thirteen British officers…shall charge in the centre of the little band, every one directing his individual efforts against the person of Dost Muhammad Khan, whose fall must thus be rendered next to certain."[108] He recognised that "all the Affghans will turn against us." He was thus preparing to sacrifice his life in order to carry out his mission of destroying Dost Muhammad. On August 9, as the pursuers were preparing to advance, word came that instead of halting at Bamian their quarry had pressed on, and by nightfall would be outside the Shah's territory, thus ending any hope the British might have of capturing him. In his report James identified at least three places where they might have caught up with Dost Muhammad if Hadji had not delayed them. Disappointed, the party returned to Kabul. Hadji was arrested on the Shah's order for treason and connivance at Dost Muhammad's escape.

The British had not heard the last of Dost Muhammad. Shah Shuja failed to regain any ground with his subjects, and Kabul was a restless and rebellious capital. Dost Muhammad was said to be recruiting an Uzbek army to recover his throne. Gathering disaffected tribesmen as he marched, he closed on Kabul in early November. British artillery was brought to bear on the advancing army, and the Afghan cavalry had no answer to its devastating effect. Without artillery Dost Muhammad could not hope to reinvade Kabul, and was forced to retreat.

The general Afghani populace showed few signs of warming to their restored king. Unrest erupted intermittently in the country. James was ordered to quell disturbances in the district lying between Kabul and Kandahar, where four Ghilzai chiefs were causing trouble, and had not yet submitted to Shah Shuja. He was directed to apprehend these four if possible. He took with him a Gurkha infantry regiment and cavalry and artillery from the Shah's contingent. A gauge of the trust Macnaghten had in James was that he was given carte blanche to exercise his initiative and authority. Moving south, he was able to sweep the country ahead of him, and was joined by a wing of the Bengal native infantry from Ghazni. He soon caught up with one of the chiefs on his wanted list, Mihtar Musa Khan, who surrendered without a fight. He set his sights on Kala-I-Murgha, the fort of another of the wanted chiefs, Abdul-Rahman Khan. This ruler was the principal Ghilzai chief who had harried the British force most on their march north and had previously opposed the establishment of the Shah as king of Afghanistan. On October 5 James marched 42 miles in 24 hours to reach the fort, surprising the chief by his appearance. Facing a further forced march in pursuit of the remaining two chiefs, James paused at the gates of the fort for his force to recover. Unfortunately the garrison were able to ride out during the night and escape by scattering. James had to content himself with the destruction of the stronghold.

Following the ousting of Abdul-Rahman Khan, the countryside appeared acquiescent, and its inhabitants gave James no trouble as he moved on in pursuit of the other chiefs. The forts they came across, some extremely well fortified, were deserted, although in Barukzye he managed to surround two of the local chiefs, Abu Khan and Jubbar Khan. They were prepared to provide information on the whereabouts of others, and the neighbouring villages were cleared of troublemakers.

By the time James reached Quetta on October 31, he could reasonably claim that the Ghilzai were successfully subdued.

It was plain to those who bothered to gauge local reactions that animosity towards Shah Shuja was building steadily. James felt that the entire mission had been misguided, and now took the unusual step of writing to Macnaghten to express his concerns over the actions that had been taken in Afghanistan. His language, as ever, was blunt and to the point: "Having placed Shah Shuha on his throne, we have done our duty by him; but we thus have imposed a further and sacred duty on ourselves, that of seeing that the government we had so mainly contributed to erect is just and beneficial to the people; and we know that oppression and extortion must be the inevitable and immediate consequence of letting loose the Shah's greedy courtiers upon his provinces.....We should best preserve the people from over-exactions, and the Shah from imposition – at the same time performing our duty to both parties and to ourselves....by directly supervising and narrowly scrutinising the first settlement of the Shah's revenues. We should render our interference, as it is an obligation to him, also a benefit to his people, instead of the contrary.....By thus acting the part of mediator between the people and the new government, we should soon convince the former of our superior justice and generosity to anything they had hitherto been accustomed.... So far, our interference would tend to render us popular in this country, instead of the very contrary, which we shall too soon become by continuing only to appear, as at present, in the light alone of supporters to the Shah; and as our future connection with the Afghans must now, of necessity, become most intimate, we cannot too soon secure it on a beneficial footing to all classes – a result, the direct reverse of which the system of non-interference, so far from promoting, must, on the contrary, inevitably insure."[109]

This passage is very illuminating as an insight into James' philosophy towards the local populace. He clearly had severe doubts about the wisdom of the invasion of Afghanistan, and the consequences of the responsibility the British had taken on, and was trying to find the best way of administering the territory in the circumstances. Unlike so many of his peers, and other campaigns, he was making the point that having taken on the task of restoring Shah Shuja to the throne, the British had a responsibility to his subjects to ensure that they were fairly dealt with. This meant avoiding corruption (wherever possible), administering "superior" justice and acting in the best interests of the subjects. In the light of the disaster which was to follow in that country, it is a pity that his words of advice were not better heeded. He was sensitive to the criticism that it was not his place to advise the envoy, for he wrote to his friend, Captain MacGregor: "I fear the Envoy may think me intrusive in thus volunteering my suggestions, but I think not, for he must appreciate my motives – being sent here to do my best for the benefit of all parties.…Time will show whether I am right."[110] However the forthright views of a young officer were not usually welcomed by the hierarchy. And once again James may have offended his superiors.

CHAPTER 6.

BRITISH ANNEXATION OF SIND.

The cost of the Afghan campaign had been exorbitant, and the price of maintaining a large garrison there was likely to be onerous for some time. The Company's debts in India were mounting alarmingly: the net indebtedness had risen to £29 million by 1834, and by 1849 was £48 million. A change of government in England from Whig to Tory had resulted in Sir Robert Peel becoming Prime Minister. The new government considered the Afghan campaign nothing more than an expensive military adventure, and demanded cost reductions. The President of the Court of Directors, Lord Ellenborough, responded by reducing the Kabul garrison and sending the Bombay Division back to Quetta. James marched with the returning army. He had a brief to ensure that the country through which they marched was secure and subject to the Shah's rule. In particular he remained concerned about the position of his old adversary, Hadji Khan, who had sabotaged efforts to capture Dost Muhammad. James therefore gave particular attention to Hadji's strongholds, and deviated from the main march to inspect them. Some he found openly hostile to the British, requiring the forts to be stormed and dismantled; others were inspected and if considered not sufficiently strong to pose a threat, left in peace. The inhabitants of the surrounding villages, who had suffered aggression from these strongholds, often welcomed his actions.

The returning army now faced a more serious problem. At Kelat, the capital of Baluchistan, 100 miles south-west of Quetta, a local ruler, Mihrab Khan, was showing signs of refusing to accept the new regime and the presence of the British. In James' absence Auckland had rejected the treaty of 1838 agreed with the Sind Amirs and replaced it with a more stringent one, which broke up the confederacy of Hyderabad rulers and entered into separate agreements with them individually. The independence of each within his own territory was guaranteed, in return for an undertaking not to correspond with foreign powers without the knowledge of the British political agent. This was aimed at shutting out Russian and French interference. Navigation of the Indus was to be free from tolls for everyone. The Resident in Hyderabad, Henry Pottinger, an arrogant and brash man, delivered a homily to the Amirs pointing out that they had only themselves to blame for the stricter terms in view of their misrule.

Claiming independence in accordance with the new treaty, and thus viewing the approaching army as intruders, Mihrab Khan uttered threats against the British, saying he would expel the filangi (foreigners). It was decided that a punitive expedition was necessary, and an expeditionary force under General Willshire was assembled to march upon Mihrab Khan's headquarters, which had been strengthened in anticipation of conflict. Mihrab Khan sent a letter to the British force directing them to halt immediately or face the consequences. He threatened to move out towards them with his entire army, which was thought to consist of more than two thousand elite Baluchi warriors. James, although not officially part of this expeditionary force, was acting as aide-de-camp to the general, and accompanied the party. As they neared Kelat he was sent forward with an escort of local horse to reconnoitre. He soon saw a small group of mounted scouts who turned and galloped away. As James followed them he encountered fifty horsemen who descended to the road from a ridge. Seeing James' escort drawn up in battle formation they also retreated, stopping only when their pursuers did so. Occasionally they would fire a volley of shot towards James and then turn and gallop away... which James remarked was just as well, for they could not see that the effect of their ineffectual fire was to cause the local horse to turn about rapidly! He wrote: "Had our opponents followed up their advantage, Lieutenant Ramsay and myself would have been left to stand our ground as we best might; but it so turned out that the enemy continued their flight to Kelat, upon perceiving which our party recovered courage, and followed them a short distance."[111]

Kelat proved to be a formidable fortress. As the main British force advanced on the fortress on November 13, they were met by a body of about one hundred horse, who kept aloof, until they observed that there were no cavalry opposed to them, whereupon they became bolder, and, galloping up to the head of the column, discharged their matchlocks. A party of Light Infantry was deployed to keep them at a distance and the advance continued without further molestation for about six miles. Surmounting a small range of hills, the town and fortress of Kelat suddenly came into view. The main gates were open, presumably so that the defenders could retreat into the fortress rapidly if necessary. It was truly an imposing sight. Some small hills in front were crowned with masses of soldiers, and the walls of the towering citadel, which provided a formidable backdrop, were lined with onlookers – "ladies of the harem chiefly, who had assembled to witness the discomfiture of the Feringees."[112]

When the main expeditionary force appeared five guns opened up from the heights, but their aim was poor and they caused no damage. The British force was relatively small in number: 950 infantry, six field guns, 150 irregular horse and a handful of engineers. General Willshire remained cool in face of a significantly larger enemy force, directing an accurate artillery barrage at the walls of the fort under cover of which the infantry advanced. Observing the enemy endeavouring to withdraw their artillery James was despatched with orders to the Queen's Royals, which was the regiment nearest to the gate, to pursue the fugitives, and, if possible, to enter the fort with them – but at any rate to prevent their taking in the ordinance. James, on horseback, led the column to the redoubt and galloped on to it at the very moment that the enemy was vacating it.[113] The Grenadiers followed him down the hill but arrived too late to enter the fort. The defenders hastily abandoned their gun outside and closed the gate after them.[114]

Behind the Grenadiers the heights had been cleared, enabling the artillery to direct their fire at the towers commanding the gate. Two guns were brought down to within fifty yards of the gate, while James brought a band of infantry up to join the Grenadiers, using a mud wall four feet high, about thirty yards from the stronghold, as shelter from the fire still emanating from the fort. The Grenadiers of the Queen's Royals were posted to the opposite side of the gate. These troops were exposed to fierce fire from the walls. James was the only mounted officer present and was lucky to remain unscathed in a uniform that distinguished him clearly from his men.[115]

A few rounds from the field guns were sufficient to blow down half the gate and James led the Grenadiers up to the entrance that they were able to secure. Returning to the general, he was directed to take a regiment of the 31st Bengal native infantry to scale the heights and secure the gate on the opposite side of the fort. As they moved around the western side of the fort they were exposed to heavy fire. Nevertheless they scaled the heights with only minimal resistance and then rushed the gate before the enemy could defend it, thus cutting off any retreat for the fort's inhabitants. Within a short time the innermost keep was stormed and the British standard raised, causing all action to cease. Mihrab Khan and his immediate entourage had been killed in the shooting, but the survivors were spared and 2,000 prisoners removed from the fort unharmed. It was reported that over 400 of the defenders had died at a cost to the British of 32 killed and

107 wounded, a fairly severe toll. James was singled out for mention in despatches.

Danger was never far away in this inhospitable country. General Willshire was anxious to determine whether a more direct route southwards through the mountains to the port of Sonmiani was feasible, saving his troops considerable distance and hardship. If it was, this route could also be developed as a direct communication from the coast to Afghanistan, avoiding the Bolan Pass. Afghanistan was still largely unmapped, and the British had, at best, a hazy idea of what lay before them. Who better than the ever-willing James Outram to find out? The terrain was rugged and the going very difficult. James took with him two escorts who had undertaken to guide him, and two armed guards. The local inhabitants were hostile to the British, and since the move into Afghanistan, in a state of some ferment. His escorts were anxious to precede the news of the fall of Kelat and the death of the chiefs there, so speed and secrecy were essential. They were mounted on four ponies and two camels, and moved fast. On November 16 he was nineteen hours in the saddle, commencing in the dead of night and only resting for short periods. He travelled in an Afghan costume, and they met up with and travelled in the company of a number of assorted itinerants. During this day they passed many groups of fugitive women from Kelat, the men, who ought to have protected them, having either been slain in the conflict, or having preceded the women in flight.[116] When they rested James remained in the background, dressed in poor clothes, while his guides dealt with any questions about them. But he represented himself as a "Pir", a holy man who would have been in much demand in that area. He found himself consequently having to utter a charm over a tuft of hair brought to him by the owner of a sick camel.

The dangers of his journey were great: They were pestered throughout the journey by horsemen galloping up from different directions to enquire of the Kelat disaster, but James' escorts always contrived to place themselves in such a position as to be the first questioned. There was so much of interest to communicate to the enquirers, that James remained altogether unnoticed. "Many were the curses poured out upon the heads of the Feringees, and numerous were the vows of vengeance and retaliation."[117] One night they bivouacked under the walls of a deserted village, but their arrival was noticed, and a crowd soon formed. The escorts were closely questioned. During the discussions that took place James, by pretending to be asleep, avoided the inconvenience of being personally questioned but his companions were compelled to respond to a series of questions. The interrogation lasted until the night was far advanced. The moment the questioners left therefore, instead of resting, as they had intended, until dawn, they resolved to move on.[118]

By the third day, travelling up to seventeen hours per day, they had reached Nal, a large town too dangerous to enter, but where they needed food. They camped in a nearby jungle and sent a guide with two armed attendants to procure grain for the horses. When this party failed to return, the second guide set out to find them. When nobody returned to James' hiding place, he and the remaining members of his party continued at night, as news of the fall of Kelat was the main discussion topic at Nal, and he was concerned that his pale complexion would give him away. Fortunately the second guide spotted them and caught up, having searched all day for the place of concealment. His presence was short-lived, however, for he claimed shortly thereafter that he had only been paid to bring James so far, and decamped. James recruited a local shepherd to help him.

Had James' identity been discovered he would almost certainly have lost his life. Wherever they rested his presence excited curiosity, and they often slept in the jungle away from prying eyes. As they encountered range after range of high mountains, it became apparent that guns could not be hauled over them without considerable effort at creating a passable road. Finally they reached Sonmiani safely, the last leg being a fourteen-hour march without stop. Throughout the entire march James had subsisted on dates and water, in keeping with his assumed status as a holy man. They had averaged forty-seven miles per day over the rough terrain, and he had spent one hundred and eleven hours in the saddle.[119] Desperately hard though it had been, James had proved that the Sonmiani route could be negotiated. But it was doubtful whether heavy guns could be hauled through the rugged terrain. In the meantime, however, it had been decided to retain Willshire's force in Afghanistan, due to unrest following the reinstatement of the Shah, so James' trail blazing had been in vain. Nevertheless his written report proved to be a valuable source of intelligence.

A boat carried James the rest of the way to Karachi. On arrival there he startled his brother-in-law, Brigadier Farquharson, by greeting him in native dress: dirty and threadbare white tunic and trousers, slippers and a small turban. James subsequently learnt that later on the day of his departure from Sonmiani a party led by the son of Wali Mohammed Khan, killed at Kelat, had reached the town in pursuit of him. Only the rapidity of his progress had saved him.

From Karachi James returned to Bombay. For his services at Kelat James was promoted to Major on November 13, 1839. Despite this, the disfavour with which he was viewed is reflected in the absence of his name from Sir John Keane's despatches, and this glaring omission certainly rankled. A man who throughout his life adopted a self-effacing attitude, he was also intensely ambitious, and felt the slight keenly. Had he been mentioned in the initial reports from Ghazni, where it is clear that he performed with distinction and great bravery, he would doubtless have received promotion to Major earlier, and thus a further promotion to Lieutenant-Colonel for his part in the victory at Kelat. A curiosity is that the Governor-General, Lord Auckland, and the Court of Governors in London thought he had been promoted to Lieutenant-Colonel, for a despatch from the Court on February 29, 1840, referred to the brevet rank of Lieutenant-Colonel having been conferred on James on his return. No explanation was ever given as to why this confusion occurred, or why James did not receive this latter promotion. His exploits were recognised however by the new king of Afghanistan, Shah Shuja, who bestowed upon him the second class order of the Durrani Empire for his zeal and gallantry in the dispersing of rebels and the pursuit of Dost Muhammad.

Lord Auckland had, before James' arrival in Bombay, offered him the appointment of political agent in Lower Sind, which James accepted. The title gave him some problems: his predecessor was called Resident and he feared that the change of title would diminish the status of the position. The Governor of Bombay was adamant, however: the Sind was being separated from the Kutch administratively, and the title would draw a clear distinction. Financially James was no better off, for although his remuneration was marginally better the expenses that came with his new post were considerably greater. Although he undertook the posting without demur he did not look forward to it. The climate of the Sind, and Hyderabad in particular, very hot and dry, was not healthy, and he feared that his wife would not be able to live there.

Margaret was still in England, but planned to rejoin him. His letters at the time reflect his feelings. To his wife he wrote that what he had seen of his new territory did not enthuse him, and that the climate at Hyderabad, where his headquarters were to be, was not suitable given his wife's fragile health. He hoped that she would be able to escape from time to time to Karachi, which offered the advantages of sea air.[120] To Macnaghten, shortly before his departure from Bombay, James wrote an altogether different letter. It is illuminating to see what he writes: "I beg to thank you for your two kind letters dated November 4 and 30, in both of which you express the expectation of further warfare in the north-west. My object in now writing is to remind you that in that case my humble services are always at your command, and I trust you will not scruple to command them to the utmost for any temporary military and political service you may think me fit. Most gladly shall I obey the summons, for, in addition to the zeal for the public service and anxiety to distinguish myself, which formerly led me to Afghanistan, I have now the further impulse of personal gratitude to the Governor-General, to you, and to the Shah. Pray remember also that I require no pecuniary advantage, and would accept of none; for the moiety of my salary in Scinde, which I should still receive while absent on duty, is most handsome and far above my deserts. I look upon it not only to more than compensate for any services I may have to perform in that country, but also as the purchase in advance of all that I could ever do hereafter in the public service. My wife will arrive in Bombay about May, but I would not wait on that account. As a soldier's wife, she knows, and will admit, my first duty to be to the public, to which all private and personal considerations should be sacrificed. She has two sisters in Bombay to receive her, with whom she will be more satisfactorily situated."[121]

Commencing his new posting of political agent, James reached Hyderabad on February 24, 1840. His entry into the city was marked with the usual lavish ceremony. On his journey he was met at regular intervals by local rulers and as he neared Hyderabad by members of the family of the four Amirs who ruled there. He was provided with everything he could wish for, and upon entry escorted to his residency with great formality. The Amirs were looked on by the British with considerable distrust, and had a record of hostility and treachery which made for an uneasy relationship. James immediately recognised the magnitude of his task. In a letter to his mother he noted: "We have much to do to set our house in order and I foresee stirring times in which I must take a foremost part."[122]

It appears however that James was quickly on friendly terms with the local rulers. Unlike many of his colleagues and superiors, he believed that the burdens of administration were made easier if the local people were treated with dignity and consideration. He did not fear, as they did, that encouragement in this area would lead to problems. His experience had taught him that given responsibility, they would rise to the occasion. He suggested that the sons of Mir Nur Mohammed be taught English, as this would facilitate communication and understanding. He sought conciliation and put forward the theory that "mutual benevolence" rather than enforced argument, was the path to follow.[123] Negotiations with a troublesome chief, Mir Sher Mohammed of Mirpur resulted in friendly relations being established. The progress he made was manifested by an agreement that all country supplies for the British camp at Karachi would be free of the usual duties. Less successful was an attempt to gain possession of land on the right bank of the Indus in return for giving up a subsidy guaranteed to the British government by treaty. This was resisted by the Amirs, most notably Nasir Khan, who saw the yielding of land as dishonourable.[124] Thus the attempt failed, but was followed later by wholesale confiscation by the British.

James' philosophy was extraordinarily advanced for the time: "As is the case with all semi-barbarous nations, there was occasional oppression practised in Scinde, and appeals were from time to time made to myself and my assistants, against particular acts of individual functionaries. But, beyond friendly intercession, we had no right to interfere with the course of justice, nor with their fiscal arrangements. The systems in force were rooted in, and sprang from, the habits and ideas of the people, and were as much a reflection of the national mind of Scinde, as our own constitution is that of Britain."[125.]

Progressive thinking in England was moving in the same direction: respect the local inhabitants, give them freedom to exercise their own laws and customs, only intervene where it is absolutely necessary. At the same time there lingered a rather patronising attitude, evident in James' use of the term "semi-barbarous." We have seen how Elphinstone had foreseen the day when the British would no longer rule in India.

So well was James regarded by some of the Amirs that when Nur Mohammed fell gravely ill, he summoned James to his bedside. James related: "…seeing me, [he] attempted to rise, which I hastened to prevent ; but his highness, hailing me as his brother, put his arms around me, and held me in his embrace a few minutes, until I laid him quietly down. So feeble and emaciated had the Ameer become, that this exertion quite exhausted him, and it was minutes afterwards before he could speak, when, beckoning his brother Meer Nusseer Khan, and youngest son Meer Hoossein Ali, to the bedside, he then took a hand of each, and placed them in mine, saying, 'You are their father and brother, you will protect them,' to which I replied in general but warm terms of personal friendship."[126] In a report after the death of Nur Mohammed James reflected upon the fruits of his conciliatory style: "…I am satisfied that Meer Noor Mohamed Khan at last perceived that it was wiser to cultivate our friendship than hopelessly to intrigue against our power; and he had sense enough on more than one occasion, when the signs of the times encouraged others to hope for our discomfiture, to prognosticate that temporary reverses, or the machinations of the factions, would but cause the firmer riveting of our power; and I have lately ascertained that, on the occasion of Meer Nusseer Khan's deputing agents to Mecca, Meer Noor Mohamed positively forbade making use of the opportunity to communicate with the Shah of Persia, and strongly expressed his sense of the folly of continuing their former underhand practices, and determination not to countenance them in future."[127]

Although James' wife Margaret had arrived in Bombay at the beginning of June 1840, such was his burden of work and the urgent demands to which he needed to attend, that he was only able to travel to Bombay in January 1841 to fetch her. Comfortable though the Residency at Hyderabad was, by May of that year her health was such that she could no longer stay there, and moved to the cooler air of Karachi, where she stayed with her brother-in-law, Brigadier Farquharson. James and Margaret's time together seemed to be but fleeting moments.

James had so impressed his superiors with the progress he had made in his new appointment that when the political agent in the Upper Sind indicated that he would be forced to leave his post because of ill-health it was proposed that James should assume his duties as well as the Lower Sind. Although unhappy with the increased responsibility in a most inhospitable area, and concerned that there was inadequate accommodation for women there, and that his wife could not endure the harsh climate, James felt honour-bound to accept. It was decided that Margaret should return to England, and that James would follow shortly on much-delayed and well-earned leave.

Having settled this question, James prepared to move north. Then news arrived that the political agent in the Upper Sind, Ross Bell, had died, which made James' assumption of his post urgent. He sailed by steam to Sakhar, a slow journey upstream made tedious by two days marooned on a sandbank. From there he travelled overland to Quetta, two hundred and fifty miles across the desert, arriving on September 2, 1841. The actual time taken travelling from Sakhar to Quetta amounted to 5 days "on the road," a staggering feat in the prevailing climate. With typical zeal he set about reassessing the political situation. He recommended to Lord Auckland the union of the Upper and Lower Sind with Baluchistan under one control, and the strategic positioning of European troops in key spots to respond to challenges of British authority.

The Amirs, who longed to regain their independence, noticed British insecurity in Afghanistan. The first challenge James faced was the scene of his last military action, Kelat. The death of Mihrab Khan had enabled the British to appoint in his place the young, compliant Shah Nawaz, at the same time annexing the region to Afghanistan in a somewhat arbitrary fashion. This had caused considerable unrest among the inhabitants, who rose against the Shah in favour of Mihrab Khan's son, Nasir Khan. Shah Nawaz was forced to abdicate, and the British representative in Kelat was imprisoned and later murdered. The British had little alternative but to back down, as their local military strength was not sufficient to confront a popular uprising. This state of affairs could not be allowed to prevail, however, and in November 1840 a powerful force under Major-General Nott re-occupied Kelat. Nott appointed Colonel Stacey of the Bengal Army to restore relations with the local ruler, Nasir Khan, and this he succeeded in doing.

The aim was to recognise Nasir Khan as the true ruler without losing too much face. This was not an easy task, as he had been alienated by the rather high-handed British attitude, and was wary of striking a rapprochement with them. He could see, however, that any withdrawal by the British may simply lead to another oppressor, the Afghans or perhaps the Sikhs from the Punjab, filling the vacuum. Nasir Khan had ambitions to be acknowledged as head of the Talpur family, the dominant Baluchi hegemony, but recognised that the most compliant of the Amirs, Mir Sobdar, was the British favourite. Colonel Stacey made some progress in persuading the young man that his best interests would be served by agreeing to cooperate with the British, and a meeting was arranged in Quetta

Nasir Khan, accompanied by Colonel Stacey, met James at Quetta. He was accorded a twenty-one gun salute and every courtesy befitting a ruler. In return he pledged himself as an ally of the British and to "live under the shade of their flag."[128] A treaty of friendship was proposed between the Indian Government and the State of Kelat. In return for Khan acknowledging vassalage to Kabul, the districts of Kashi and Mastung (which had been confiscated by the British following the siege of Kelat) would be restored to him. The British or the Shah Shuja would have the right to station troops at Kelat and the local army would assist the British Government if required to do so. British counsels would be paramount, and no negotiations were to be opened with foreign powers without the consent of the British and Shah's governments. Hostile at first, and distrustful of the man who had played a conspicuous part in the assault of his father's fortress at Kelat, Nasir Khan was won over by the quiet sympathy shown by James. Escorted by a body of British troops, James conducted the young Khan back to Kelat, where the treaty of friendship was signed and the prince was installed in the seat of his ancestors. James returned to Dadar where he set up his headquarters.

Despite the successful negotiations, unease was growing in government circles. The Government of India came under severe criticism from the Court of Directors for the cost of the Afghan war, which had not only drained the treasury but also plunged India into heavy debt. The annual deficit was reckoned at £1.25 million, and it was becoming clear that the cost of sustaining the unpopular Shah on his throne would continue to add to the debts for many years to come. The British government would gladly have withdrawn from Afghanistan if they could have found a way of extricating themselves.

News reached James from Kabul that all was not well there. Rebels continued to make life uncomfortable for the British, and desertions swelled their ranks, threatening the occupation of the capital. The snows had arrived, making it impossible for reinforcements to be sent from Kandahar. James foresaw that his support would be needed if the situation in Kabul deteriorated, and he considered that sending troops north via the Bolan Pass was preferable to attempting to reinforce the Kabul garrison with troops of the Bengal army from the Khyber Pass. Although warlike tribes in the vicinity of the Bolan Pass continued to be troublesome, both ends of the pass were considered to be secure. His letters at the time show him preparing to send up "as many troops as the accommodation at Quetta can shelter."[129] This amounted to a company of the 41st infantry regiment (100 men) and a wing of the 25th native infantry. In addition to providing troops in a forward location should they be required, he considered that the sight of British troops moving north through the Bolan Pass at a time when there were rumours that the British may retreat from Afghanistan would provide a morale boost.

But events were about to overtake him. Although news of the calamity would not reach James for four weeks, his worst fears were about to be realised. On December 23 the rebels led by Mohammed Akbar Khan turned against the British in Kabul, who were seeking to negotiate with them, and slaughtered the leaders, including William Macnaghten. The British garrison was penned in under the hills surrounding Kabul, in a camp impossible to defend adequately, and finally all but annihilated. When James heard of the tragedy, he wrote to Colonel Stacey: "This is a lamentable finale to poor Macnaghten's career: but just what he ought to have expected from treating with the rebels at all."[130] Then he turned his mind to ensuring that the disaster at Kabul did not destabilise the British position in the remainder of Afghanistan. He was to write later: "As I have already on more than one occasion said, the cabals of the Amirs were the result of that spirit of intrigue which is inherent in oriental character. Puerile, and easily frustrated by a mixture of discretion and firmness, they originated in a distrust of our intentions, (since, alas, too sadly justified) and were fomented by emissaries from above the passes. At one period, and then only, were they a legitimate source of alarm, when our disasters in Affghanistan placed us in a great measure at the mercy of the Chiefs of Scinde."[131]

His first concern was for the scattered military posts that were not strongly defended, and at such a distance from each other that reinforcement would be difficult. He was forced to turn to local rulers for help: rulers whom the British had treated harshly, and dispossessed of property and rights. The garrisons at Kandahar and Jalalabad came under pressure. The state of Kelat became restive, with Mohomed Sadik, a leader of Afghans hostile to Shah Shuja, seeking to unite the local tribes against the British. Another local warlord, Mohomed Sharif, who had fled British custody at Sakhar, used Sadik's activities to advance his own interests. James responded by seeking to strengthen the alliance with the Brahui, the tribe occupying the plains around Kelat, no friends of the aggressive Baluchis, and turn them against the agitators. This he was able to accomplish.

At this critical time in 1842 Lord Auckland, with gentle persuasion from London, relinquished his post as Governor-General. The Afghan campaign had never been popular in London, and the new government was faced with a rising tide of protest against it. Auckland had pursued a relentless policy of acquiring territory for the British wherever possible, and this had been noticed with some disapproval in London. The previous government had approved the Afghanistan invasion plan, but Peel could disclaim it now. Stringent new economic policies demanded savings, and the cost of the Afghan campaign was exorbitant. Auckland was replaced by Lord Ellenborough, the President of the Court of Directors and a prominent politician, who was despatched with instructions to salvage what he could from the Afghan disaster, and withdraw the army. Ellenborough had originally opposed the expedition on the grounds that it would be too expensive and too dangerous. Instead he had supported a move to uphold Dost Muhammed and to check Sikh expansion.[132] By 1840 he had come round to supporting Auckland's strategy, but on the basis that once Shah Shuja was secure in Kabul the main British force would be withdrawn. It was only on February 21, 1842, when Ellenborough reached Madras en route to Calcutta, that he learnt of the slaughter of the Kabul garrison. He was immediately faced with a crisis, and the possibility that the remaining occupation of that country would be conceded. There were many advisers in Calcutta who thought that in the light of the losses at Kabul the only course was to withdraw the army. This meant abandoning those British who had survived the massacre at Kabul and been made prisoner by the rebels.

James, along with others, argued long and hard against this policy. He believed that not only would it be possible for the British army under General Nott, stationed at Kandahar, and General Pollock, coming from the north, to counter-attack and take Kabul, but that it was essential they did not withdraw. To do so, he wrote, would not only abandon Afghanistan and the British prisoners to the barbarities of the rebels, but would endanger the entire peace of India. It would send the signal that not only were the British not invincible, but that they were prepared to yield without much of a struggle if confronted by an effective force. In a letter to Sir James Carnac on February 10 James vented his feelings: "…who could conceive that 5,000 British troops would deliberately commit suicide, which literally has been the fate of the Kabul garrison? From first to last such a tissue of political and military mismanagement the history of the world has never shown, and such dire disgrace never heretofore blotted the British page."[133] He wrote time and again to the new Governor-General to argue his case. This persistence was to count against him. Good news came shortly thereafter with the capture of Mohomed Sharif by Lieutenant Hammersley, though James reported that he had accompanied the Lieutenant to "afford the weight of his authority."[134]

The Sindhi and Baluchi tribes, fired by the success of the rebels, sought to expel the British from their territories.

The garrison at Ghazni, always the most belligerent of the occupied towns, came under threat and Colonel Palmer, the officer commanding, contemplated abandoning it until James urged him to hold fast. It was necessary to move troops up the Bolan Pass to keep it open, for it was now a vital – and probably the only – feasible line of retreat should that become necessary. Still Calcutta dragged its feet, and would not make a final decision on the deployment of a force to retake Kabul. A further setback occurred when General England, contrary to James' advice and General Nott's orders, moved forward from Quetta towards Kandahar without waiting for reinforcements and was defeated at Haikalzai, a village 30 miles north of Quetta, losing 27 men with a further 70 wounded. This caused great embarrassment and raised again the question of the vulnerability of the British forces in the Sind. Controversy found its way into the Bombay newspapers when it was stated that the military authorities had been misinformed of the strength of the enemy and their fortifications and the blame fell on James' local assistant, Lieutenant Hammersley. Characteristically James defended him vigorously. His name in Calcutta was already in disfavour as a result of his insistent and sometimes strident advocacy of an aggressive stance towards Kabul, and his defence of Hammersley did not help his reputation there. Hammersley was remanded on regimental duty pending an enquiry, but James chose to interpret this order rather liberally by retaining Hammersley in his post at Quetta, pleading urgent requirements. He then petitioned General Nott and Colonel Stacey on Hammersley's behalf, but his voice was alone in support of the young man. The suspension was confirmed; Hammersley died three days before it could be actioned, his mind seriously affected by his treatment.

Frustrated by lack of direction from Calcutta, and concerned that the British position was being undermined by vacillation, Nott moved north out of Kandahar, overwhelming

Ghazni and then establishing communications with General George Pollock advancing from the north through the Khyber Pass. At this stage Ellenborough got cold feet, and on April 19 ordered the two armies to withdraw, leaving the remaining hostages to their fate. He was not to know it, but Shah Shuja had been lured out of his defended position and killed. The two generals, appalled at their new orders, adopted stalling tactics. A fierce debate ensued both in India, where Ellenborough was pressed to change his mind, and in London. The Duke of Wellington, who held a position in the cabinet, weighed in on the side of the generals: "It is impossible to impress upon you too strongly the notion of the importance of the restoration of reputation in the East."[135] Increasingly isolated, Ellenborough relented. He told the two generals they may retreat, if they judged it militarily expedient, by way of Kabul.[136] Fortunately both generals had found good reasons to remain where they were, and a race ensued between the two. Nott was three hundred miles from Kabul while Pollock was only one hundred miles short. Both armies encountered fierce resistance as they closed on the capital. Pollock reached Kabul shortly before Nott, on September 15, to find the enemy had fled the city.

From the start Ellenborough and James did not see eye to eye. Although he had presided over the Court of Directors of the East India Company, Ellenborough had no direct experience of India or Indians. Although he had ruled the Board of Control efficiently, in India he displayed extreme autocratic tendencies. He would not delegate, refused advice from counsellors and regarded any criticism he received as treachery. Auckland reported to the new President of the Board of Control, Sir John Hobhouse, that he thought Ellenborough had no capacity for business, and that he wondered if he were sane.[137] Ellenborough was on record as saying that the spread of education was incompatible with the security of the British Empire.[138] James felt he understood the

Indian mind thoroughly, and was not reticent in voicing his opinions and advice, probably in a rather blunt way. The new Governor-General did not appreciate this. Henry Lawrence wrote in the Calcutta Review of September 1845: "James Outram in one quarter, and George Clerk – a kindred spirit – in another, were the two men who stood in the breach; who forced the authorities to listen to the facts against which they tried to close their ears, that the proposed abandonment of the British prisoners in Afghanistan would be as dangerous to the State, as it was base towards the captives. These counsels were successfully followed: the British nation thanked our Indian rulers, while, of the two men, without whose persevering remonstrances and exertions Nott and Pollock might have led back their armies, without being permitted to make an effort to retrieve our credit – Clerk was slighted, and Outram superseded!"[139]

Retrospectively James' stand in the Sind was to receive glowing recognition in the Cornhill Magazine of January 1861, which in reviewing the war commented: "Outram was supreme in the Sind, and a heavy weight of responsibility fell upon him. But he was equal to the occasion. His was it in that conjuncture not only to maintain the peace and security of the country immediately under his political care, but to aid our imperilled countrymen in the territory beyond the Biluchi passes. He stood on the high road to Kandahar. If that road had been closed, if Sind and Biluchistan had risen against us, it would have gone hard with our beleaguered garrisons in Western Afghanistan. But the country did not rise; and Outram, all his energies roused into intense action, grieving over the dishonour that was falling upon the nation, and vehemently protesting against the recreant counsels of those who would have withdrawn our beaten army within the British frontier without chastising the insolence of our enemies, did mighty service, at a most critical time, by throwing troops, stores, ammunition, and money into Kandahar."

There soon followed a new order, whereby General Nott was given full military control of the territory. This undermined James' position, and although he felt that this move was as a result of his correspondence with the Governor-General, he did acknowledge that in the unusual circumstances it was a reasonable decision. In fact Ellenborough held strong views about the position of political agents. He resented their independence and decision-making capabilities, and was suspicious of their ideas. Wherever possible he sought to superimpose military command, which he could control. James was ordered to move to Quetta and assist Nott. This was almost the last straw to a soldier as loyal and dedicated as James. His position in the Sind, and the way in which his persistent advice had been ignored, was intolerable. He wrote to Mr Willoughby on May 10: "I go up to officiate in the immediate neighbourhood, and as the humble subaltern of General Nott, where so lately I was supreme; I pass through the heat of Kutchee, and the dangers of the Bolan, to the deadly climate, privations and annoyances of Quetta…with undiminished zeal, and determination to fulfil the duty assigned to me…but I must here in justice to myself add, that it is not my intention to remain in this country, in the subordinate capacity so assigned to me, one hour after the withdrawal of the army, and hostilities have ceased; when the necessity for a military dictator in these countries no longer existing, I should degrade myself by continuing in a lower position than that to which the Government had thought proper to raise me, and in which, so far from a single instance incurring displeasure, every act of mine has been highly approved, and every measure successful. Unless, therefore, the Court of Directors are pleased to order that, on the termination of hostilities in Afghanistan, General Nott's political powers over me are withdrawn, I most assuredly must respectfully resign the line in which I have so long endeavoured to serve them, and join my regiment, a poorer man than when I left it, nearly twenty years ago."[140]

Installing Lieutenant Brown in his position at Sukkur, James commenced the tedious journey up to Quetta on June 1. He completed the trip in 10 days, and settled into his subordinate post. A measure of the perils of this journey was reflected in an unusually considerate letter from Calcutta expressing relief that he had reached Quetta safely. Further encouragement came in the form of a despatch dated May 22 which addressed the administrative staffing of the "new" British territories to the north of India. The establishment had become bloated and unwieldy, and it was proposed that a new institution should be established, consisting of an envoy with private secretary, three secretaries of legation but no other European officers. It gave the envoy, who was to be James, power to nominate and remove any and every member of his establishment and afforded him complete control of his staff.

James never was appointed envoy. Why this was so is not clear, but the political decisions taken over Kelat must have played a significant part. James was concerned that the future control of Kelat, a strategically important town, should be secured. In Lord Auckland he had a receptive ear to his ideas, but Ellenborough was a different man altogether. Where Auckland preferred the soft approach and conciliation, Ellenborough was an out-and-out hawk. James felt that the best way of securing Kelat was to ensure the Khan remained a willing ally. He proposed that military aid be replaced by pecuniary aid once the British troops were withdrawn from Kelat. He suggested a grant of one and a half lakhs rupees (£15,000). He was told that his proposals should not be addressed directly to the Governor-General, but as he was now under the orders of the military commander they should go through General Nott. Nott simply acknowledged receipt of the proposals but did nothing: he neither approved nor disapproved of them. He had a reputation as a good general, but a selfish one, "contemptuously indifferent to anything but the welfare and safety of his troops."[141]

James wrote again, this time suggesting that the districts of Shal and Sibi be brought under the rule of the Khan of Kelat. He argued that Nasir Khan, a young man, had been loyal to the British and would respond well to encouragement. Auckland had agreed with this approach, but again Nott merely acknowledged receipt of the letter. Ellenborough, despite his earlier stance, now intervened. He was indifferent as to who possessed Shal, he said, but Britain should not assume responsibility for its fate.[142] He had decided that Kelat should be abandoned, and he instructed James to abrogate the 1841 treaty.

Dangerous intriguers were now active in the state of Kelat. Mohomed Sadik was attempting to unite opposition to the British by forming a coalition of Brahuis, the tribe who had been loyal[143] to the British. He was hostile to Shah Shuja's cause in Afghanistan, and looked to destabilise Baluchistan as part of a broader strategy. James judged that it would be dangerous at this time to terminate the treaty until he could manage to withdraw all British subjects from Baluchistan. This was finally achieved in October 1842. The bringing together of Kelat with Shal and Sibi would have gone a long way to foiling the plans of the intriguers, but James could not obtain a decision. So he took it upon himself to act by signing over the two territories to the Khan, arguing that although he did not have the authority so to do, neither had he been commanded otherwise.

Lord Ellenborough and Nott greeted the news coldly, neither censuring nor approving of James' action. Unfortunately however, in his letter to the Khan, he stated that he had received authority to make over the territory to him – authority that had "just been received."[143] This caused a considerable stir in Calcutta when it became public, and led to a strong rebuke from Ellenborough: "The Governor-General will not now consider to what extent, and under what circumstances, if any, it may be justifiable to resort to fiction in political transactions, but his Lordship must observe that to resort to fiction in communications to a native chief, without the shadow of justifying necessity, if any such there can be, is conduct inconsistent with the character with which he desires the diplomacy of India to maintain, and calculated to shake the confidence of the Government in the fidelity of communications it may receive from its own officers. The Governor-General trusts that he shall never again have occasion to remark upon similar conduct, which he has witnessed with the greater regret on the part of an officer so able and so zealous in the performance of public duty as you have heretofore shown yourself to be."[144] Faced with a fait accompli, Ellenborough was forced to accept the deal, and later took credit for it.

James replied by expressing regret that his measures had caused such severe displeasure, but then his nature could not be suppressed and he sought to justify his actions, concluding: "…here I am, with no instructions or precedents to guide me;…harassed in body and mind by my incessant endeavours to forward the public service; kept in ignorance of the measures intended by the authorities at Kandahar, which I am expected to forward; and surrounded by a fanatical and treacherous people whom I have to preserve in good faith, although naturally opposed to us by religion, and by awe of our enemies their neighbours – besides being goaded by recent recollections of the many hardships they have suffered at our hands, such as spoliation of their territory, sacking of their capital, and slaughter of their Khan and principal chiefs. In successfully working as I have been under these disadvantages to effect almost impossibilities, and at the sacrifice of health and every reasonable comfort, I had hoped to earn the approbation of his Lordship's Government; but although so bitterly disappointed, I shall not relax in the slightest degree my endeavour to forward the public interests."[145]This is a good example of James being unable to resist expressing his true feelings in undiplomatic language.

In October he left Quetta with great relief. Before he went however he poured out his grievances to a close friend and respected adviser, Colonel John Sutherland, in a letter. "....I complain not of military supersession, because where warfare is likely to occur, the responsibility should never be divided, and of course should rest on the military commander; I complain not of being bandied like a racket-ball, up and down this abominable pass, because it is my duty to go wherever it is thought I am most required; but I do complain of the lackey style in which I am treated by the Governor-General; of the bitter reproof he so lavishly bestows on me when he thinks me wrong, and I know I am right; of the withering neglect with which he treats the devoted services of those in my department."[146]

James' immediate duty was to escort General England through the Bolan Pass, but once that was successfully accomplished he pushed on rapidly to Sakhar. A new superior officer of the region had been appointed, and James was required to report to him. The relationship between James and his new superior was to change his life, make headline news in the London papers and lead to endless controversy.

CHAPTER 7.

CONFLICT WITH NAPIER.

The new commander was sixty year-old Major-General Sir Charles Napier, who could not have been less like James. The son of Colonel the Honourable George Napier, he was given a commission in the army at the age of twelve, went to military college and was helped along his career first by General Fox, who appointed him to his staff, and then a cousin who had him promoted to major. He served in the Peninsular Wars, but his temperament proved an impediment to advancement. He was a devout Christian who saw himself as an instrument of God, and constantly sought divine guidance. Hot-headed and demanding, he was not popular with either his regiment or his superiors. Another family friend, Lord Moira, who was Governor-General, offered him a commission in India. He declined, however, feeling repulsed by the stories of corruption and cruelty among the East India Company. After spending two years back in England waiting to be summoned to an attractive posting, he chose the Ionian Isles, where as Inspecting Field Officer he spent several fruitless months negotiating with Ali Pasha, the champion of Greek independence.[147] He was then appointed to the Residency of Cephalonia. All his frustration and pent-up energy was poured out in improving the lot of the islanders; building new roads, establishing schools, hospitals, a market place, a prison and lighthouse. But his headstrong approach was to bring him into conflict with his masters. In 1830, accused of harshness and despotism towards the inhabitants of the island, he was dismissed from the Residency and although offered a similar position on Zante, he refused on principle. Back in England, he champed at the bit. After nine years of enforced idleness, during which he considered those few posts that were offered to him inappropriate, he obtained command of the Northern District in England. Disagreements with the government led to his resignation, which left him with few other options when offered a post in India.

Napier was originally posted to Pune, which he reached in December 1841. There he introduced new drilling methods and battle tactics. He found fault with virtually everything, criticising the Bombay Government's treatment of sepoys, the organisation of the Indian army, the quality of their officers and the lack of officers posted to individual regiments. After submitting to Lord Ellenborough his thoughts on the British involvement in Afghanistan, he was directed in July 1842 to the Sind with orders to assume command of the troops there and in Baluchistan, with complete control over the political agents and civil officers. He complained: "What a Government! What a system. I go to command in Sind with no orders, no instructions! How many men are in Sind? How many soldiers to command? No one knows. I am, if sharp enough, to find that out when I am there."[148] The emergence much later of correspondence between Napier and Ellenborough would tend to indicate that there was a hidden agenda: to seize Sind for the British, whatever the circumstances he found there. As we have seen, the territory was strategically of great importance, situated as it was between troublesome Afghanistan and tranquil India. Furthermore, the Amirs of both Upper and Lower Sind were known to be extremely wealthy.

James arrived in Sakhar on October 12, a week after Napier. Initially he welcomed Napier's appointment, writing in a letter to Captain Durand: "…[his] character seems formed for such a crisis."[149] It had not escaped his notice that the new leader, as a former Radical MP, had once denounced the East India Company for sucking the lifeblood out of Indians. The two men immediately took to each other, discussing the most urgent political questions fully and freely. Both clearly had a high opinion of the other's record. Their first challenge was a breach of the treaty by Nasir Khan of Hyderabad, who had recommenced taxing Sindhi commercial traffic on the Indus. Khan had also banned the transportation of grain from Upper Sind to the British base at Karachi, arguing that it was destroying the market for Lower Sind suppliers. The return of General England and his army led to rumours that the British had been defeated in Afghanistan, and this encouraged Khan and his followers to resist the treaty.

Napier's initial reaction was that those chiefs who had neglected their treaty obligations should forfeit their territories. James enjoyed good relations with the Amirs: he had avoided interference in their internal affairs and he believed the treaty signed with them was working well. He argued that three rulers had committed themselves fully to the British: Mirs Rustam and Nasir Khan of Khairpur, and Mir Nasir Khan of Hyderabad. It should be remembered that Nasir Khan's father had entrusted his son to James on his deathbed. No doubt James felt some responsibility towards the young man, and it is not surprising that he sought to protect him.

Napier's response was to respect James' opinion, writing that "His experience of these countries, his abilities, and the high situation in which he has been placed by the Governor-General, render his opinion very important."[150] But Napier also harboured the view that his political officers were a disaster, and responsible for the problems in Afghanistan. When told of his appointment in Sind, and that all the politicians were to be placed under his orders, he reflected: "Down comes Lord Ellenborough to abolish at one slap the whole of the political agents. This is very hard on Major Outram. I never quarrel with such people if they behave well, and I think them useful in their place: but that place is not as councillors to a general officer: he should have none other but his pillow and his courage."[151]

Napier had never been in overall command of an army, and knew very little of the Sind. Nevertheless he had firm views about the Amirs: "There can be no doubt that most of the Ameers of Upper and Lower Scinde have for some time past been engaged in intrigues against us; in fact they only want the power, not the will, to make an attempt…to expel us from their country."[152] In his later book James reaction to this was caustic: "A quick perception of danger and hostility in Scinde, Sir Charles Napier undoubtedly evinced; a perception so swift, indeed, as to outrun probability, and so keen as to discern sources of alarm which to other eyes were invisible. He arrived in Scinde on the 9th of September 1842, when that province was in a state of complete tranquillity, when all danger of an outbreak had passed away, when British officers of all ranks, and British subjects of all conditions, accompanied by their wives and families, traversed Scinde in every direction, by land and by water, unguarded and unmolested."[153] Lord Ellenborough guided Napier in his attitude. The new Governor-General felt that it was not his position to question the rights and wrongs of his predecessor's policy. He accepted the situation as he found it under the conviction that British interests must be safeguarded come what may.

The situation was not helped by the fact that both Napier and Ellenborough were highly unpopular. Known by his contemporaries as the "Elephant," due to his heavy-handedness, Ellenborough's political ambitions (he aimed to become Foreign Secretary) had been thwarted, while Napier was quoted as "never willingly obeying any of his superiors."[154] They were both romantics: Ellenborough had dreamed of leading an expedition to conquer Egypt while Napier fancied himself as the ruler of Asia, no less.

James was becoming alarmed by Napier's high-handed attitude: "…not only totally unacquainted with the language, feelings, and customs of those whom he undertook to manage, but rude and domineering in his demeanour, prejudiced by anticipation against the Indian character, suspicious and distrustful even where there was no reason to doubt the good faith of the native princes, and probably from this very feeling of his own incompetency to separate truth from falsehood, or discriminate between candour and imposture, naturally, though it may be unconsciously, or even unwillingly, led to precipitate an appeal to that weapon, of which he felt himself to be a greater master – the power of force, and the terror of the British arms."[155] Later, Napier was to criticise James's defence of the Amirs, reiterating that they were not to be trusted, that they were intent on treachery, and that James had allied himself too closely with them. James responded by pointing out that "Our armies were shut up in Affghanistan, and their return, in any state of organisation, the Ameers could, as I have already shown, have easily prevented. Is it not, then, strange – passing strange - that, with so great an object as 'their independence' so steadily in view, they should not have struck the requisite blow, at the time when it could have been dealt with such terrible effect? Strange, that with a deeply laid, and perseveringly entertained determination to attack us, they should not only have delayed hostilities till we had retrieved our disasters in Affghanistan but have supplied to us the resources which enabled us to do so; that they should have waited till, by their assistance, General England's column, with all its munitions of war, was safely in their country, and an army of 25,000 men within a few marches of their country – reinforcements the while pouring in by sea."[156]

James was playing a long game. He hoped to be able to use any evidence of disloyalty by the Amirs to negotiate the abolition of transit duties in exchange for a tribute of £35,000 and the cession to Britain of either Shikarpur and Sakhar or Karachi. But Napier's response to continued infringement of the treaty was direct. He made it clear to the rulers in Hyderabad that he would not hesitate to use army might to enforce the treaty, writing in his journal: "I will strive to teach the Ameers a better use of their power; and if they break their treaties the lesson shall be a rough one." His disaffection was confirmed by the delivery to him of a letter purported to have been written by Nasir Khan from Hyderabad to Bibarak, chief of the Bugti tribe, calling on him to expel the foreigners from his country. This was almost certainly a forgery, as several commentators have since remarked. Earlier a letter purporting to have been written by Mir Rustam to the ruler of the Punjab, Sher Singh (which James thought also inauthentic), pledging himself to subordinate co-operation with the Khalsa Government, had been handed to James by an adherent of Ali Murad, Rustam's brother and would-be usurper. However doubts about the loyalty of these two princes provided Napier with the excuse to tear up existing treaties and impose new, more stringent ones.

Communications between Napier and the Governor-General were difficult and spasmodic: Ellenborough was in Simla, from whence messages to the Sind took nine days. As he moved on to Ferozepur and Delhi the interchange became even less reliable. Ellenborough had never met Napier or James Outram; he prided himself on being able to judge an officer by his correspondence. He had never visited the Sind, and had only a sketchy knowledge of the complications there. Napier expressed the opinion that the Amirs would not fight, because the British force was too strong. He added in his journal: "Major Outram is of my opinion, and I like him much, for that reason probably, for I confess not to like those who differ in opinion with me. I may love and respect them, but do not like them as companions; it is very tiresome to have everything one asserts argued, my temper won't bear it."[157]

A report following Napier's strong reproof to the Amirs showed most of the princes prepared to honour the treaty, with Mir Sobdar particularly loyal to British interests. The only exception remained Nasir Khan of Hyderabad, and James also feared that this rebel had implicated Mir Mir Mohamed, who could no longer be trusted. He wrote in his journal at this time that his impression was that reports of warlike preparations were unfounded, possibly provoked by the Amirs as a negotiating ploy, although Nasir Khan was reported as saying: "we obtained the country by the sword, and if it to pass from us, it shall not be without the sword."[158] Although somewhat disillusioned by Nasir Khan's attitude, James wrote that the Amirs were quite conscious of their inability to oppose the British and had no serious intention of so doing. He added that only extreme provocation and despair would drive them to armed resistance. We shall never know to what extent his pledge to Nasir Khan's dying father coloured his judgement in this respect.

Contrasting instructions were then received from Ellenborough. The first requested Napier to "enter upon operations in the field and to lose no time in moving a force towards Hyderabad, should it be necessary."[159] Two days later the Governor-General wrote: "You may be quite right with respect to the unfriendly intentions of the Ameers in assembling their troops, but I am satisfied that you will weigh the evidence you receive upon the subject of all the chiefs upon the Indus."[160] This was followed rapidly by the decision to impose new treaties upon the Amirs, justified by the lack of co-operation from Khairpur, and the persistent breaches of existing treaties from Hyderabad, Sobdar excepted. The proposed new treaties incorporated the proposals by Napier and James for Sakhar, Bhakar, Rohri, Karachi and Tatta to be ceded to the British in return for the remission of all tribute. There was to be totally free trade on the Indus, and the Amirs were to lose their right to coin money, which would henceforth be supplied by the British Government. This last requirement was in line with a general policy to introduce uniform currency throughout India east of the Indus. These demands went considerably further than James had planned, and in his opinion were unacceptable to the Amirs. This he reported to Napier on November 12, asking him to refer the matter back to Ellenborough, but Napier did not do this until January 30, 1843.

In a letter to his friend Willoughby dated October 22 James expressed fears that he had incurred Ellenborough's displeasure: "My real offences being such as he cannot forget, i.e. my advocating poor Hammersley's cause, and opposition to the disgraceful retreat [from Afghanistan] once determined on; for in the only instance in which he fancied he had room to find fault, he has tacitly admitted that I was in the right - at least so I read the acknowledgment of my letter defending the cession of Shal, without comment or disapproval, which otherwise would have been expressed freely enough I presume.....As my name does not go up with his despatches, announcing the Kabul victories, of course I shall have no share in the honours that will be showered…. But I regret nothing that has passed; indeed you are well aware that I fully laid my account to suffering personally in the cause of Hammersley, months ago; and were it all to do over again, I would not vary my course… I am prepared for the worst, and fully expect it."[161]

The next communication from the Governor-General dated October 25 confirmed James' fears. Not only was there no further mention of his appointment as Envoy, but the Political Department in the Sind was to be totally abolished, and he was to return to his regiment. No explanation for this change, or the humiliating demotion, was offered. No thanks for his remarkable role in the territory over three years was proffered, and the official order was curt and to the point, requesting only that Napier thank Outram "for the zeal and ability…manifested in the collection of the means of carriage and supply, and in …various transactions with the native chiefs and tribes."[162] Letters poured in from friends and colleagues, outraged at the treatment James had received, and recognising his role in the Sind. Napier held a farewell dinner in James' honour, as he felt James had been shabbily treated by Ellenborough. He also wished to express his personal gratitude for James' support and help, and ended his speech with the ringing phrase: "Gentlemen, I give you the Bayard of India, sans peur et sans reproche, Major James Outram of the Bombay Army."[163]

Before James left there was a further twist in the saga. The princes in Hyderabad were alarmed at the news of James' departure. They had come to trust him and rely on him for the settlement of disputes, and they begged for the order to be rescinded. They feared his removal was preparatory to a reimposition of Afghan rule on them. Mir Rustam sent a message to Hyderabad saying he feared British treachery, and urged them to follow his example and assemble men to defend their country. When James was shown the new, draft treaties by Napier he at once pointed out that the demand for cession of territories in the Upper Sind far exceeded the value of tributes, and was therefore impractical. Napier actually held back a further letter from Ellenborough in which he expressed the view that it might be desirable to obtain this territory for a friendly ally, so that the British could rely upon loyal support in this part of the Sind. It is evident that the Governor-General confused Mir Nasir Khan of Khairpur with the Amir of the same name in Hyderabad, for he believed the former was the leading rebel among the Amirs and should be punished by giving up much of the Upper Sind to either the British or neighbouring, friendly rulers whom the British wished to reward. James felt there must be some mistake, for the Khairpur Amir had been an exemplary ally, but Napier either did not notice the mistake or did not care. Napier was empowered to nominate a Commissioner to negotiate the treaties on his behalf, and he naturally asked James to stay. James felt that if he was to be appointed, it should be by Ellenborough himself, and that his political status be reinstated.

His refusal was to cause great problems in the Sind, for Napier was not a patient man, and had a low opinion of the

Amirs. James had warned him that any military move towards Hyderabad might trigger conflict, although the Talpurs were unlikely to fight unless driven to it. Napier wrote in his journal "Outram provokes me: he pities these scoundrels, who are such atrocious tyrants that it is virtuous to roll them over like ninepins. All I want is not to be compelled to slay their poor slaves: however, the soldiers of the Ameers are all Beloochees; i.e. robbers and murderers."[164] It was time for James to return to Bombay, and his reputation was such that Napier could not ignore his achievements. James left on a steamer with Napier's praise ringing in his ears: "I cannot allow you to leave this command without expressing the high sense I entertain of your zeal and abilities in the public service, and the obligations I personally feel towards you for the great assistance which you have so kindly and diligently afforded to me; thereby diminishing in every way the difficulties that I have to encounter as your successor in the political department of Sind."[165]

In contrast to the disappointing end to his stay in the Sind, James' return to Bombay was a triumph. Here, at least, his true worth was recognised. Napier's letter of praise was quoted at length, and the Bombay authorities noted the "eminent zeal and ability with which he had discharged the important duties confided to him during the three past eventful years."[166] He was offered the command of the Pune horse, a prestigious appointment, although the authorities regretted they could not offer him anything approaching the position in responsibility or remuneration he had held in the Sind. Tempting though the offer was, James was torn between seeking active service again and taking his long overdue leave in England. There were rumours of further warfare in the west that attracted his attention, but any thought that he could be involved was firmly squashed by Lord Ellenborough.

He embarked upon a round of dinners in celebration of his achievements. Some of these were official, others given by fellow officers who recognised the scale of what he had done, and wished to give him a good send-off on his return to England. Then, to everyone's surprise, came a change of plan. James recorded it in his journal thus: "Having made every preparation for returning to England after twenty-four years' absence, on the first application for leave from my duty that I had ever made – taken my passage in the steamer which was to sail on January 2, 1843 – written by the previous mail to my wife and mother to meet me in London…by February 10 or 12 – and in the belief that the Government of India had no further occasion for my services after the summary manner in which I had been dismissed, on November 15, from the political control of Sinde and Beloochistan, without thanks or acknowledgement of any sort (and even without the direct communication from Government which courtesy, at least, would dictate towards a person who held one of the most responsible situations in India, and who had committed no error, or, at least, had been accused of none) – I was surprised at receiving, on December 12, the following letter directing me to return to Sind, should Sir Charles Napier require me, but without expressing the slightest consideration for my own wishes or convenience, and without any reference to the Bombay Government, and its Commander-in-Chief, at whose disposal I had been placed."[167] He goes on to quote the letter, from the Secretary to the Government of India, advising him that Napier wished to employ him as a Commissioner for renegotiating the treaty with the Amirs of Sind. James' anger and resentment are all too evident: the seeds were sown for a clash of ideas and wills.

James was advised by his friends to decline the order and return to England, but, as he wrote in his journal: "…the principle which has ever guided me throughout my career of service – implicit obedience to the orders of Government (and when, as in this case, orders were conveyed, and no option was left available to me) – I had no hesitation in following

on this occasion."[168] He left on December 16, 1842 in the
steam-frigate "Semiramis," which arrived at the mouth of
the Indus on December 21. There he transferred to the river
steamer Euphrates. His journey up the river was punctuated
with visits from local Amirs welcoming their old acquaintance
and adviser, and seeking his help in their negotiations with
the British. Wisely he side-stepped these requests by pleading
insufficient time. At Hyderabad he received a request to
entertain the Amirs on board so they could seek his assistance,
but again he hurried on, leaving the message that he would
contact them once he had consulted with General Napier.

A shock awaited him at Sakhar. There he learnt that Napier
had left several days earlier to depose Mir Rustam, prompted
to do so by reports of the hostile intentions and preparations of
the other Amirs. Napier had written to Rustam on December
12: "I laugh at your preparations for war…Eight days have
now passed, and I have not heard that your Highness has
nominated a commission of rank to arrange the details of the
Treaty…Your Highness is collecting troops in all directions, I
must therefore have your acceptance of the Treaty immediately
– yea or nay."[169] Rustam reponded: "God knows, we have no
intention of opposing the British, nor a thought of war or
fighting. We have not the power…If, without any fault on
my part, you choose to seize my territory by force, I shall not
oppose you, but I shall consent to and observe the provisions
of the new Treaty."[170]

Rustam's brother, Ali Murad, was ambitious to "take the
turban" – a reasonable ambition, for either he or Rustam's son
would become Amir on Rustam's death. However Ali Murad
did not propose waiting, and had set out to depose Rustam. He
embarked upon a double game: on the one hand he persuaded
Rustam that Napier was treacherous, and was seeking to seize
all Rustam's territories, while on the other hand he sought
to convince Napier of Rustam's untrustworthiness. This had
the added benefit of casting doubt over the worthiness of

Rustam's son. It was evident to Ali Murad, wrote James, that Napier was "ignorant of Oriental customs, feelings and modes of thinking,"[171] and he traded on this. Ali Murad sought an interview with Napier, purporting to represent Rustam, and managed to persuade him to pledge the turban to him on Rustam's death in preference to the Amir's son. James takes up the story: "While, on the one hand, he endeavoured to excite the Ameers to some open movement, by undervaluing the British forces, and assuring his brother 'that he had seen the whole English force, and that the Ameers need not be under any apprehension to encounter it,' on the other, he contrived then the most exaggerated accounts of the levies made by the Ameers, their preparations for war, their resolution to make a combined attack upon the British force, should almost daily reach the camp of Sir Charles Napier."[172] Napier believed these reports, and prepared to march on Rustam's capital, Khairpur. Before commencing, however, he wrote to Rustam: "My own belief is, that personally you have ever been the friend of the English, but you are helpless amidst your ill-judged family. I send you this by your brother, Meer Ali Murad. Listen to his advice; trust to his care; you are too old for war. If you go with your brother, you may either remain with him, or I will send an escort for you to bring you to my camp, where you will be safe; follow my advice, it is that of a friend, - why should I be your enemy? If I was, why should I take this trouble to save you? I think you will believe me; but do as you please."[173]

On December 20 Rustam abdicated in favour of Ali Murad. Napier, rightly suspicious that somehow Ali Murad had engineered the hand over, sought a meeting with Rustam, but Ali Murad blocked this. At the same time Ali Murad informed Rustam that Napier wished to take him prisoner. The threat caused the eighty-five year old Mir Rustam and his entourage to flee, he himself in one direction, Mir Nasir Khan and Mohammed Hussain in another, while Mir Mohammed Khan withdrew to his fort in the desert at Imamgarh. Each group now rallied their armies, and were able to count on over 10,000 men.

James caught up with Napier at Diji, 30 miles south-east of Sakhar, on January 4. The general was preparing an expedition to attack Imamgarh, one of the most remote of the desert fortresses. He told James he had chosen it because the Amirs believed themselves safe in the desert, and that the fall of Imamgarh would have most effect upon them. James sought to convince Napier that the posturing of the Amirs was all part of the negotiating process, and that Ali Murad was distorting the truth. Napier felt that the time was ripe to appoint a single chief over the territory and disband the oligarchy that prevailed, but James urged him to reconsider, pointing out that diminishing the power and status of the Amirs was the best way to provoke hostility. He reacted in horror to the realisation that Napier intended to appoint Ali Murad as the overall ruler!

On January 6 a messenger approached James with news that Mir Rustam was only a few miles off the line of march from Diji, and that the Amir begged James to represent his good intentions to Napier. James diverted to meet Mir Rustam, taking with him his A.D.C. Captain Brown and two horsemen. They came upon Mir Rustam's camp after ten miles, pitched on an elevated spot in the middle of a jungle. James was embraced by the chiefs as an honoured friend, and taken to the Amir's tent. Mir Rustam was in ill-health and his will appeared weak. James was shocked by his appearance and the conditions in which this once-proud man was living. Rustam immediately launched into a bitter tirade against Ali Murad, accusing him of misrepresenting his intentions. James advised him to return to Khairpur and there await developments. He also suggested that the most senior of his chiefs should accompany him, James, back to Napier to receive his assurances in person, and this was agreed. Ali Akbar (Mir

Rustam's second son) and Dost Muhammad (brother of Mir Nasir Khan) were chosen to go

The meeting with Napier started well. The emissaries signified the willingness of Mir Rustam to sign the new treaty drawn up by Napier and to submit to any conditions that might be posed. They explained that the Amir had fled because he had been misinformed as to the British intentions. Napier adopted the tone of a stern father addressing recalcitrant children, and spoke directly to the emissaries through a translator, ignoring James. This shook the emissaries' confidence: James had always treated them with respect, and led them to believe that they were equals. To make matters worse, on their way back they visited Ali Murad, who persuaded them that his power was now such that they would be better off serving him than Mir Rustam. They reported back to the Amir that General Napier had adopted an angry tone, and that he had ordered them all to proceed with their families to the fort at Diji. Influenced by Ali Murad, they also reported that James had little influence with the general and that therefore no reliance could be placed on his advice.

The relationship between Ali Murad and Mir Rustam was to become a key aspect of the government of the Sind, and the growing differences between Napier and James. It emerged later that in taking to himself Rustam's territories, Ali Murad had also annexed the various estates that had belonged to the Amirs between Rohri and Sabzalkot, although the British had actually possessed these. Throughout these negotiations Napier received a number of letters from the interested parties, many of which were blatant forgeries, while others he suppressed. The treaty which Ali Murad used to take control of the Rohri lands was actually itself a forgery, being the original contract, signed by Napier, amended to include this territory. James consistently and frequently warned Napier against Ali Murad, pointing out the deception that was occurring. (It emerged later that Murad, through his Prime Minister Sheikh Ali

Hasan, had amended the treaty to include three districts, those of Mirpur, Mathela and Meharki, not scheduled in the original agreement). Napier ignored his advice entirely, reacting with anger to what he saw as James' partisan position in defence of the old Mir, Rustam. Later, when Napier and James were to fall out, this dispute was to be at the centre of it.

Napier continued his march on Imamgarh, arriving there on January 11. Mir Mohammed Khan, whom James wrote had no intention of opposing the British, fled, leaving the fort empty except for some old gunpowder, which was used to blow up the fort. A messenger from Mir Rustam arrived with a last appeal to General Napier, but Ali Murad who persuaded the man to come over to his side, intercepted it. The message that was delivered was therefore very different in tone to the original, conciliatory one, and conveyed a sense of belligerence. James heard of this distortion, and warned Napier in advance what to expect. Once again James went to see Mir Rustam, completing a journey of ninety miles in twenty-four hours, but the old chief's confidence in the influence James wielded had been shaken. James was forced to admit that he could not change the details of the new treaty, nor could he undo the elevation of Ali Murad to overall ruler. Mir Rustam indicated that there was nothing more to discuss then.

James remained hopeful that a peaceful solution could be found. On January 12 he wrote to his mother: "....I found, on joining the General, that he had been led into the field by hostile indications on the part of the Amirs.....I had ascertained...and by previous experience of these people, that they were instigated to feeble attempts to arm by mistrust of us, and with a view to defence rather than any idea of acting offensively: and, as my duty is peace-maker, I hope I shall have the happiness to be instrumental towards preserving amity. My present chief, Sir Charles Napier, is fortunately so good and kind-hearted a man that he never would drive the Amirs to extremity so long as he could prevent bloodshed."[174]

Returning to Rustam's camp on January 16, James sought to persuade him to join the other Amirs in a meeting at Khairpur to discuss the new terms of the treaty. He found the old man had augmented his force there, and whilst receiving James civilly, he reiterated that there was nothing more to discuss. Nevertheless he promised to join the meeting in person. Once James had left, however, Ali Murad persuaded Rustam that the meeting was a ploy to capture the old man, and he fled with his followers. Later James wrote: "I had told him honestly that the arrangements with Ali Murad, and the terms of the new treaty, I had no power to rescind or even to modify; that my sole duty was to settle the details of the latter in the most equitable manner. It was not, therefore, wonderful that the old man fell into the snare laid for him by his brother. He proceeded to join his sons and nephews at Koonhera. These, too, had been invited to meet me at Khyrpoor, personally or by proxy, but they came not. Nor is it difficult to assign a reason for their non-appearance."[175]

On January 20 James returned to Khairpur for talks with representatives of the chiefs of the Upper and Lower Sind. Napier had informed the Mirs that James was invested with all the powers delegated to himself by the Governor-General, but it was not clear what these powers were. James was instructed that there were to be no changes whatsoever with the arrangements concerning Ali Murad's reign, which seriously affected the allocation of territory. Napier also let it be known that failure to agree the new treaties would result in possession of territory in the name of the British government. The only representative from the Upper Sind was a minister representing Ali Murad, who remained with Napier. Murad continued to block attempts at a rapprochement between Napier and Mir Rustam who, having fled, was considered to be outlawed. A deadline of January 25 for Rustam to submit came and went without any appearance at the British camp, aggravating the stand-off.

Meanwhile James was becoming increasingly concerned at the worsening political situation. He could foresee a similar conflict arising with the rulers of the Lower Sind, and was particularly worried about the position of the Amirs at Hyderabad, with whom he was still on very good terms. He requested permission to go to Hyderabad, writing to Napier in terms which, for the first time, explicitly disagreed with the policies of his superior: "I am sorry to confess myself unable entirely to coincide in your views, either as respects the policy or justice of, at least so suddenly, overturning the patriarchal government to which alone Sind has become accustomed.... I say patriarchal, for, however we may despise the Amirs as inferior to ourselves, either in morality or expansion of intellect, each chief certainly lives with, and for, his portion of the people; and I question whether any class of the people of Sind, except the Hindoo traders....would prefer a change to the best government we could give them."[176] He particularly criticised the seizure of land as "robbery" and "most tyrannical" and went on: "I consider, therefore, that every life which may hereafter be lost in consequence will be a murder." He defended the rulers in Hyderabad and Khairpur as co-operative and benign: "Although every chief ruled his own people, each brotherhood had one head, or 'Rais,' for the conduct of the foreign relations of the State, and whose power interposed in internal quarrels."[177]

In his journal Napier showed increasing impatience with James: "...in his indignation against Ali Moorad, he every day puts a fresh coat of whitewash on the others that they will soon be apostles...if he will become a partisan for that old animal Roostum there will be no end of our negotiations." [178] He refused to see that Ali Murad was manipulative, and was coming to the conclusion that James had been swayed by some influence other than the facts before him. This he attributed to James' bitterness at being demoted, and feared he would now exceed his brief and attempt to settle everything along his own lines. Napier thus replied to James' letter by reconfirming his view that the Mirs were cunning rascals – in fact "tyrannical, drunken, debauched, cheating, intriguing, contemptible."[179] He asserted Ali Murad's loyalty, and argued that there was no alternative to him. (Lord Dalhousie writing in 1851, said: "I have received orders to pound Meer Ali Morad, the last Ameer of Scinde, and Sir C. Napier's friend. He is a great villain, and played the worst part in that very bad business. I shall therefore flay him with a lively pleasure.").[180]

James responded by arguing that it was neither politic nor just to overturn the traditional, patriarchal form of government. He was by now extremely concerned at where the rise of Ali Murad was leading. The dispossessed Amirs of the Upper Sind were inclined to travel to Hyderabad and seek the hospitality of the Amirs of Lower Sind. James pointed out that Oriental custom would oblige the Hyderabad Amirs to defend their cousins, a move bound to lead to conflict. He was increasingly exasperated at Napier's ignorance of local customs, and attempted to warn him of the consequences. Rather than disturb the status quo, he proposed that the British lease Shikarpur and use it to show the surrounding territories how to govern wisely and fairly. The population of adjoining areas would migrate to the protection of the British flag, encouraging their rulers to improve their regimes. He pointed out that much of what Napier construed as the misrule of the Sind was due directly to British interference. By abolishing the ruling head of the Lower Sind and replacing him with six separate princes, each of whom controlled a separate territory, at the same time undermining the power of the Rais of Khairpur, they had encouraged divisions among the families. The elevation of Ali Murad was the most serious of these blunders, because he would now dispossess many of the feudal lords and introduce foreign mercenaries. Those dispossessed would be troublesome, and Ali Murad would not be able to control them. This in turn would encourage the

Baluchis to recommence raids on the divided territories. The only solution in these circumstances was, in his view, to annex the country and suppress it with numerous garrisons. Even if this was done he questioned whether "we should by that means either pay our expenses, benefit the people, or preserve tranquillity, leaving alone the unwarrantable outrage against justice and good faith we should commit."[181]

In view of these differences of opinion, James offered to resign his position and return to his regiment, but hoped he may still be able to help at Hyderabad. "By going to Hyderabad, I should afford one more chance to the fugitive Ameers, for doubtless, the Ameers of Hyderabad will intercede for them; and, perhaps, should the latter promptly accede to your terms, you might then, without any compromise to your dignity, receive their overtures on behalf of their relations."[182]

An interesting aspect of this exchange was that Napier had written to James advising him that as Commissioner of Sind he would receive a salary of 1,500 Rupees per month. James refused to accept this, pointing out that not only was it 200 Rupees less than the salary he had received in Gujarat many years previously but, more importantly, he felt that he had not, and could not, achieve anything as Commissioner. He chose to rely upon the pay he drew as a Captain in the field.[183] As we know, James' financial position was not strong, and it is surprising that he would pass up what amounted to a pay rise. Perhaps his remuneration as a field officer was, in his eyes, more valuable to him?

Napier agreed to James'proposal to go to Hyderabad, but his letter never reached James as it was intercepted by Ali Murad's minister. Frustrated, James remained at Khairpur. There he recommended a settlement with the Amirs of the Upper Sind whereby two-thirds of the territory remained in the hands of Ali Murad and they agreed not to enter the Lower Sind. Although this deprived the Amirs of most of their territory, it left more in their hands than Napier had envisaged, and he therefore frustrated the deal. James did not believe that Napier intended to provoke hostilities: "He did so, I believe, with no view to precipitate hostilities, by rendering a settlement impossible, but through that fatal ignorance of Oriental feelings and customs, that wilfulness which hurried him from one indiscreet act to another, and that mistaken idea of what constituted a firm and dignified policy, which prompted him to menace and command, instead of conciliating the subjects of his diplomacy. He doubtless imagined, and was taught by Ali Murad to believe, that if he could implicate the Ameers of Lower Scinde in the concerns of their cousins, the presence of his army, and the heavy punishment inflicted on the Khyrpoor Princes, would compel those of Hydrabad, from fear of a like fate, to coax or intimidate the fugitives into a compliance with his demands."[184] From correspondence disclosed later, there must be a suspicion that Napier was under orders from the Governor-General to take possession of the entire Sind.

James finally discovered through a letter written by Napier to Brown that the General assumed he was already on his way to Hyderabad, and he started out on February 4. Having issued a proclamation that subjugated the Amirs of the Upper Sind, Napier also proceeded towards Hyderabad. This James agreed with: "I fully concurred in the propriety of his prolonging his march southward, not only as calculated to expedite the final submission of the Ameers of Lower Scinde, but as tending to dispel any faint hopes the Princes of Khyrpoor might still entertain that by standing aloof they possibly might obtain better terms."[185]

At Hyderabad James urged the Amirs to accept the new treaties, but met with stern resistance from all the chiefs of the Lower Sind, who were assembled there. Rustam had also arrived in Hyderabad on February 4, raising the temperature. The Amirs argued that they had remained true to the old agreements with the British, and that there was therefore no necessity to impose upon them new and objectionable terms as punishment for offences which they had not committed. Despite this disagreement, many of the Amirs agreed to sign the new treaty. However there were strong feelings about the position of Mir Rustam, and the Baluchis in particular demanded his restoration before they would sign. James was powerless to grant this request, and now faced open revolt. He asked that Napier hold back from marching towards Hyderabad, as this would be seen as an aggressive act and the Baluchis would be difficult to restrain.

Napier had halted at Sakarand, sixty miles from Hyderabad, at James' request. The size of Napier's army considerably alarmed the Amirs, who now saw Napier's force as an invasion of their territory. Nevertheless James was confident that he could obtain the consent of all Amirs to the new treaties, and could defer the problem of the reinstatement of Rustam by offering compensation and/or referring the whole issue to the Governor-General. At this crucial juncture Colonel John Jacob, stationed with his Scinde Horse at Kumb Lima to the west, apprehended and disarmed twenty-five well-armed Baluchis who tried to ride through his camp. Letters found on them showed they had been summoned by their chief, Mir Mir Mohamed Khan of Hyderabad, to meet him at Miani on February 9 with every man who could wield a sword. This excited suspicions in Napier's camp, and made him wonder whether he should now move forward.

James finally succeeded on February 12 in obtaining the agreement of all Amirs to the treaties, everyone signing except Nasir Khan of Khairpur, who claimed not to have his seal with him. But at the same time news reached Hyderabad of the arrest of the Baluchis, and this was regarded by the Baluchi chiefs as an overt act of hostility by Napier. A large crowd of Baluchis threatened James and his party as they left the Durbar, and reports came in of huge numbers of Baluchis flocking to Hyderabad. James was escorted back to the Residence by a strong guard of the Amirs' men, but then news reached the

British that the chiefs had sworn not to sheathe their swords until Rustam was restored to his position as ruler. The Amirs were further alarmed by the arrival at the Residency of the light company of the 22nd Regiment. The appearance of European troops convinced many at Hyderabad that the English were preparing to surround them: Napier advancing from the north while the force at the Residency south of the city prevented a retreat. James maintained that the Amirs were most anxious to avoid conflict: "As I afterwards found, the Balooches, inflamed by just indignation at the unmerited wrongs inflicted on Meer Roostum, and despairing of their country's independence, had resolved to exterminate the mission...They were prevented, however, from effecting their purpose by the generous interposition of the Ameers."[186]

Talks to defuse the situation went nowhere. James was unable to agree to the restoration of Rustam, or to redress the allocation of lands taken by Ali Murad. He still hoped Napier would not approach the city unless he heard that hostilities had commenced. When it became evident that no amount of negotiation would assuage the Baluchi's fury, James sent a message to the Commanding Officer of the 41st Regiment, en route to Karachi on the Indus, to stand by. Napier was furious: he saw this as interference by James with his orders, and he instructed the 41st to continue to Karachi. Once he realised the seriousness of the situation facing James he sent a message recalling the regiment, but it was too late. The Amirs sent a message to James advising him to leave immediately, as they could not restrain the Baluchis. A letter from Nasir Khan to the Governor of Karachi, intercepted by Captain Preedy, explained that he was "compelled to agree to take the field, and to proclaim to their subjects the necessity of a war, because the English are determined on seizing the country."[187]

On February 15 the Baluchis attacked the British Residence in Hyderabad with 8,000 men, surrounding the compound on three sides. The fourth side faced the river that the steamer Planet was able to defend from about 500 yards out. For four hours the Baluchis poured fire into the compound, but a band of 100 defenders under the command of Captain Conway resisted all their efforts until the defenders ran out of ammunition. At midday they were forced to withdraw, evacuating the Residence and boarding the steamer Satellite, which had arrived to help, but without reinforcements. From there they sailed upstream under a barrage of artillery fire from the bank, before they were able to make contact with Napier's army advancing towards Hyderabad. There James learnt that Napier, on receiving a copy of his letter requesting the 41st Regiment to stand by, had ordered it on to Bombay, and he was advised he would be censured for interfering with the Governor-General's arrangements. The tally of casualties was two killed and eleven wounded, while more than sixty of the attackers were killed.

James and Napier were reunited at Matari, a town sixteen miles north of Hyderabad. Between Matari and Hyderabad lay the town of Miani, where it was believed the main force of the Amirs was situated. To his horror, James found that Napier was planning to leave his baggage at Matari and advance with "all disposable force, to clear the shikargahs along the road to Miani of the enemy before returning to Muttari."[188] James argued that this would involve hard fighting in conditions favouring the Baluchis, who were skilful forest skirmishers, and that the decision to advance without baggage would delay the main attack on Miani. He proposed that he take a small force on a night raid from the river, where they would be covered by the steamer's guns. The object was to burn the town and surrounding forest in order to prevent the enemy collecting there, where they would be difficult to dislodge.

Napier agreed, and James sailed downstream with 200 sepoys drawn from convalescents unsuited for active duty. They found the shikargahs deserted. The enemy had been informed of his intentions and had moved away the previous night. James set fire to the shikargahs, thus ensuring that the British met the Baluchis on the open plain.

Napier followed up rapidly with the full army, and on February 18 a fierce battle took place on the plain. The scene was vividly recalled by Charles Napier's brother, William: "Thick as standing corn and gorgeous as a field of flowers were the Beloochies in their many coloured garments and turbans. They filled the broad deep bed of the Fullaillee; they were clustered on both banks, and covered the plain beyond. Guarding their heads with large dark shields, they shook their sharp swords, gleaming in the sun, and their shouts rolled like peals of thunder as with frantic might and gestures they dashed against the front of the 22nd. But, with shrieks as wild and fierce, and hearts as big and strong, the British soldiers met them with the queen of weapons, and laid their foremost warriors wallowing in blood."[189] Victory was complete; the Baluchis were routed and the banks of the Indus secured. British losses were 19 officers, 256 men and 95 horses killed and wounded. The enemy suffered 5,000 men killed, including several chiefs. A message was sent by the Amirs tendering their submission, and Napier demanded that they surrender unconditionally or his army would march on Hyderabad. To this they acceded. By February 19, four days after the evacuation of the Residence at Hyderabad, the British were camped on the banks of the Indus, surveying the blackened ruins. In discussion with the chiefs who surrendered, James was able to ascertain that it had indeed been the Baluchis intention to take cover in the forest at Miani, and that his raid had forced them out into the open. James urged that a general amnesty be declared and no further action be taken until the Governor-General's orders were received. Napier, in his dispatch of the battle, reporting on the siege of the Hyderabad Residence referred to "…the residence of Major Outram was attacked by 8000 of the Ameers' troops, headed by one or more of the Ameers."[190] James immediately protested, pointing out that Napier had received no less than five letters stating that the Amirs were seeking to save James from the fury of the Baluchis.

Napier had triumphed, and the "hidden agenda" of taking control of Sind had been achieved. If there was any doubt about his intentions, they can be dispelled by a written note he made: "We have no right to seize Sind, yet we shall do so, and a very advantageous useful, humane piece of rascality it will be." [191] An often-made quote had Napier sending the message to Ellenborough: "Peccavi." (I have sinned). This is almost certainly apochryphal, as it appeared in Punch in 1846. Amusingly, when Oudh was annexed 10 years later, the following couplet was published;
"Peccavi, I've Sind," said Lord Ellen so proud;

Dalhousie, more humble, said "Vovi, I've Oudh.

With misgivings about the future of the Sind, and a heavy heart at seeing the Amirs, with whom he had formed friendly relations, humiliated, James embarked upon a steamer for Bombay. His concern was reflected in a letter to his friend, Lieutenant Brown on February 22: "As you are the custodian of the captured princes, let me entreat of you, as a kindness to myself, to pay every regard to their comfort and dignity. I do assure you my heart bleeds for them…. alas, they have placed it out of my power to do aught, by acting contrary to my advice, and having recourse to the fatal step of appeal to arms against the British Power."[192] James parted on good terms with Napier, who handed him dispatches for the Governor of Bombay and indicated that he was content that James should represent to the Governor his own views of what had occurred.

He was received well in Bombay by the Governor, Sir George Arthur. He submitted his report on the conflict, not thinking for a moment that Napier would not have carried out his express intention of forwarding to the Governor-General his notes on the conferences with the Amirs on February 8 and 12. But Napier had reported nothing to Ellenborough, and this omission was to lead to serious differences at a later stage. Arthur, who recognised the importance of what he was told by James, immediately forwarded James' notes to the President of the Board of Control in London. Napier now realised he may be at a disadvantage, and wrote to Arthur setting out his version of what had occurred. He stated that he had studied the Amirs closely, and his conclusion was: "Such brutes have never been seen! They issued orders to murder all the English, man woman and child."[193] Napier also warned Ellenborough that James held views diametrically opposed to his own, and separately advised James to let Arthur see his private journal. It was evident that a storm was brewing, for public opinion was firmly in favour of the Amirs, and the English merchants were angry that the conflict had disrupted trade. Elphinstone said that the mood prevailing with Ellenborough and Napier was like "a bully who has been kicked in the streets and goes home to beat his wife in revenge."[194]

James had planned to take a ship home to England at the earliest possible moment, but during the passage back to Bombay from the Sind he had had time to reflect upon his position. He came to the conclusion that perhaps his departure from the battlefield had been premature, prompted by a degree of personal pique, and disagreement with the policy being employed. He also felt that perhaps Napier had sent him back to Bombay not out of a sense of disapproval but compassion after his long and arduous tour of duty. He therefore wrote to the Governor offering his services as aide-de-camp to Napier, acknowledging that as such he would have no personal voice in policy matters and promising to apply himself to military matters without raising issues of conscience which had plagued him earlier. This is an interesting letter, in that it speaks of his insecurity, and perhaps regret that he had overstepped the mark and sullied his reputation by disagreeing with the official policy. The Governor replied in encouraging terms, so James then wrote to Napier, saying how much he wished he could be with the General, "as a humble military aide-de-camp (not a political or commissioner) for I cannot but fear you will have a most troublesome time of it."[195] To underline his new approach he ended: "I am sick of policy; I will not say yours is the best, but it is undoubtedly the shortest – that of the sword." But he could not resist a final sally: "Oh, how I wish you had drawn it in a better cause!" The rebuff he received came not from Napier, but from the Secretary to the Government: with reference to his "former position in Sind, and distinguished services," considerations existed which induced "the Hon. The Governor in Council to think it inexpedient that Government should accept the offer." Sir George Arthur had seen both sides of the argument between Napier and James and thought it wise that James was not pitched back into the Sind.

If James had any doubts about the esteem in which his fellow officers held him, this was soon rectified by the reception he enjoyed in Bombay. On March 25 a meeting of his friends resolved to present him with a sword valued at 300 guineas and a valuable piece of plate. This was mainly in recognition of his defence of the Residency at Hyderabad, which had not been officially commented upon although he had played an influential and leading part. It also sought to compensate for the fact that he had not shared in any of the spoils of war in the Sind and Afghanistan. His name had been omitted from the commendations, but he was due a proportion of the prize money as a Major in the army there – a sum amounting to nearly three thousand pounds.

But as he disagreed so vehemently with what had occurred in the Sind, he refused to accept a penny, and insisted that his share be distributed to local charities. One of the most significant donations, to the Indian Missionary Schools, was to be the start of a long and fruitful association between him and the charity.

CHAPTER 8.

POLITICAL REPERCUSSIONS OF SIND.

On April 1, 1843 James returned to England by steamer. He did so with mixed feelings. After an absence of a quarter of a century he was returning to his family, and his letters home show how eagerly he looked forward to that. Having left the shores of England as a young cadet from a very ordinary background, he was returning with a shining reputation, his name ringing in the ears of the highest in the land. He had received news of promotion to Brevet Lieutenant-Colonel and the award of a C.B. (Commander of the Bath), a source of great satisfaction, as recognition for what he had achieved in India. Yet there were friends who argued that these honours should have come to him several years previously, and that had he received his just dues he would by now be an aide-de-camp to the Queen.

Then there was the matter of his feelings towards British policy in the Sind. He felt very keenly the humiliation of the Amirs, particularly that of Mir Rustam, and suffered from a sense of guilt that as their friend and confidant he had been powerless to prevent their downfall. Britain's strategic objective had been to secure the western border by assuming military control in Sind, but Ellenborough was unconcerned about ruffling any local feathers in the process. The Governor-General believed that Sind was "essentially a school in which the people of India would be taught a great moral lesson."[196] James felt that Napier had deliberately provoked a war when the Amirs wanted peace. He argued that Napier, by his actions, had destabilised the Sind, and this had led to the necessity of a 10,000 strong garrison which the Company could ill afford financially and in terms of resources. It now seemed that the Sind would become a severe burden on British finances. Many Baluchis had moved north into Afghanistan, a move that could cause unrest there. Being the man he was, James could not stay silent. Yet he knew that the criticism he would voice might well be political suicide, and precipitate the end of his military career. In his burning desire to have his opinions heard, perhaps he did not foresee the worst consequence of his criticism: the personal falling out which would occur with the man he admired as much as anyone, Sir Charles Napier.

On arriving in London, his onward journey to Edinburgh, to see his mother, became impossible. Parliament was becoming increasingly alarmed at Ellenborough's actions. He appeared out of control: in February 1843 the Prime Minister, Sir Robert Peel, complained that the President of the Board of Control, Lord Edward Fitzgerald, was not effective, and he made no attempt to hide his dislike of Ellenborough. Fitzgerald advised Peel that the charges levelled against the Amirs that led to annexation had not been proven, and accused Ellenborough and Napier of trumping up a case to justify the seizure of the territory. On May 6 of that year the Times published a leading article strongly criticising Ellenborough. It accused the Governor-General of premeditating the seizure of the Sind, replacing James with Napier in order to further his plans, and conducting the campaign rashly and incompetently. It demanded that the Government intervene. James was summoned by the new President of the Board of Control, Lord Ripon, and by the President of the Court of Directors. James expressed his views freely under questioning, and his version of events was taken up increasingly by members of the Government, who considered the possibility of cancelling the treaty with the Amirs and reversing the conquest. Lord Ashley took up James' claims in the Commons, describing the Sind campaign as a stain on the national honour. It seemed that everyone wanted to talk to James: Peel and the Duke of

Wellington became heavily involved. It appeared that many important reports from the Sind had not reached London, particularly James' notes on conferences with the Amirs, and the powers in London were in a state of some ignorance. Peel defended Ellenborough in a rather lukewarm way. The Duke of Wellington pointed out that the affair was extremely embarrassing to the Government, and could put it in danger. Besides, any attempt to roll back the arrangements would weaken the authority of the Government in India and even place Napier in danger. At this point petitions submitted by the three senior Amirs of Hyderabad arrived, fully corroborating James' report and stated position. In spite of these, it was decided that in view of the severe criticism that would attach to the Government if Ellenborough was recalled at this time, there was no alternative for the present but to support the Governor-General, and Ellenborough was given full discretion to take matters forward as he judged.

James stayed at the Burlington Hotel in Cork Street. There he awaited a summons from the Chairman of the India Board, which was several days in coming. Frustrated, James moved to Cheltenham to be with his wife, from whence he could journey to and fro to London. A number of meetings followed, at which he was able to give a first-hand account of the events in the Sind. At the end of summer he and his wife moved back to London and were presented at court. He even found time for a quick visit to Scotland to see his sister and father-in-law. While he was there he received an invitation to a State Ball. This was normally perceived as a command, but, ignorant of the protocol, James excused himself on the grounds of being absent from London. This was a serious breach, but such was the feeling towards him at the time that, not only was the implied slight overlooked, but he was invited to a second State Ball. Unfortunately this invitation only reached him after the due date of the Ball, and his apology was misdirected through a friend, once again breaching protocol.

Conscious of the precariousness of his position, Napier set about defending himself. He argued that the Amirs never had any intention of signing the new treaties, and had been busy assembling an army in order to attack his forces. He referred to James as having been deluded by the Amirs, and in grave danger in Hyderabad. He made no distinction between the Baluchi tribesmen gathering in Hyderabad and the forces of the Amirs, although the Amirs, despite being from the Baluchi Talpur clan, had always distanced themselves from the wilder, lawless Baluchi country dwellers. He believed that they were not negotiating in good faith, but simply biding their time before going on the attack. He rejected James' claim that they sought to protect him, but asserted that they did not have James killed at the conference because they wished to annihilate all the British at the storming of the Residence. James argued that Napier's letters were full of inaccuracies and highly selective "facts," which incensed him. When James went public with these accusations the Bombay press, which hitherto had been reasonably sympathetic towards Napier (who was a regular contributor to the Bombay Times) became very hostile towards the General.

On his return from Scotland James and his wife took some time off to stay at Brighton and to visit Dieppe and Paris. Whilst his wife might have enjoyed the distractions of Paris, James' mind remained full of the problems in the Sind. He was busy arranging papers for possible publication should it be necessary, and his opinion was continually sought. The visit abroad was cut short, and he returned to London. He discovered that the powers in Calcutta had been busy in his absence, providing the Court of Directors, and the British Parliament, with their version of the events in the Sind, which was naturally critical of James' part in them. Attempts by him to have his written report heard by Parliament were blocked on the grounds that it should have been sent through the Government of India. James had indeed thought of that:

before leaving Bombay he had suggested to the Governor, Sir George Arthur, that he write such a report. The Governor felt that the Bombay Presidency should not express an opinion on the Sind, and that should James write an individual report it might lead to him being told to stay in India. Instead James had written to Napier setting out his views.

Whilst in London James received regular reports through a close friend, Major Gordon, who relayed the grievances of the Amirs now in captivity in the hope that their old friend could help them. James used these communications to progress his arguments with Parliament, thus aggravating the conflict with Napier, who felt his old aide was conspiring behind his back. Protagonists fell sharply into two camps, and the debate became sharp and unpleasant. The first Blue Book on the Sind was presented to both houses of Parliament in August. The Court of Directors informed the President of the Board of Control that it had passed a resolution condemning Ellenborough's policy in the Sind. It was pointed out that if this was made public, they would have no alternative but to recall the Governor-General at a particularly sensitive time for India, and no successor had been chosen.

Within three months James was on his way back to India. The ruler of the Punjab, Ranjit Singh had died in 1839 and the state had been in some confusion since then. The Company, concerned by the dangers of the situation, and seeing an opportunity to take a dominant position in the Punjab, had strengthened the military establishment on the border of the territory. The annexation of Sind alarmed the Sikhs and unrest increased. The inhabitants of Lahore rebelled and the Maharajah, Sher Singh, was murdered. War with the Sikhs, appeared inevitable, and James hoped his services would be required. He applied to Lord Ripon to be allowed to volunteer in any capacity they might need him. Fortunately his request was referred to the Duke of Wellington, Commander-in-Chief of the British Army, who knew the value of a good soldier.

Armed with the Duke's letter of support, James wasted no time in boarding a steamer for Bombay. He did not tarry long there, and was soon on his way to join Sir Hugh Gough in Gwalior. But all was not plain sailing. Word reached him that in his absence he was being heavily criticised by his enemies in London, and his friends in Bombay made him aware that his reputation in Calcutta was such that the offer of his services in Gwalior might well be refused. Napier's brother William, Governor of Guernsey, mounted a stinging attack on him, claiming that had his brother followed James' advice not to advance on Miani the army would have been cut to pieces. The temperature was raised by the appearance of a letter from Sir Henry Pottinger, previous Resident in the Sind, which described the treatment of the Amirs as "the most unprincipled and disgraceful that has ever stained the annals of our empire in India."[197]

Coincidentally, on his way up-country James found himself in the same camp as the Governor-General, Lord Ellenborough, at Indore. He offered to attend Ellenborough, as was his duty, and to show him the respect due him despite his criticism in England. Ellenborough declined to meet him "unless I would state my reasons in writing."[198] Thus they did not meet, although Ellenborough made it clear that he objected to James joining Gough, and offered him the position of political charge and revenue manager of Nimar, close to Indore. This post was actually less important and paid less than James had enjoyed ten years previously, and Ellenborough made the offer in the expectation that it would be turned down. James, however, accepted. He hoped that his labours in this job would raise him to a more important position in due course, and did not dislike the conditions of the residence he now found himself occupying: "It is situated on the banks of the Narbudda, on the road between Asirgarh and Mhow, called Mandlesir. There we shall have a good house and garden, a doctor and his wife, and one or two officers."[199]

Now he was settled he was anxious for his wife to join him, but worried that her poor health would prevent it. His life was indeed one of quiet routine, a life that would have been welcomed by many, but not James, who craved active service.

To make matters worse he received news that his report on the Sind to Parliament had been suppressed, leaving the field open to his enemies. It is interesting to note that some time later, in November 1876, an article in the Contemporary Review claimed that the Cabinet of Sir Robert Peel had disapproved of the conquest of the Sind, but had been powerless to prevent it. The whole question of the Sind was debated at length in the Commons without the benefit of his report, and as a consequence he felt it was both incomplete and biased. He was acutely aware of the harm this would do his reputation, and made attempts to establish his version of what had occurred so that, even if it was kept secret, future scholars might have access to it and set the record straight. Ellenborough was recalled to England in May 1844, and was replaced by Sir Henry Hardinge. James, aware of the damage done to him in Calcutta and London, was not hopeful that his fortunes would revive under the new Governor-General, and after six months resigned his post at Nimar and returned to Bombay, intending to go to England.

Calcutta did not acknowledge his resignation immediately, and the delay caused James to miss the mail boat that left for England at the beginning of October 1844. He remained in Bombay throughout October, and yet again his future course was to be diverted. A rebellion against British rule broke out in Southern Maratha, a part of Western India between Bombay and Goa, and a detachment of troops was sent from the town of Belgam to restore order. They encountered stiff opposition. The fort of Samangarh resisted their efforts to take it, and at Budargarh the garrison repulsed them. The insurrection caused the unrest to spread to neighbouring territories, and reinforcements were urgently called for to restore British rule.

James immediately offered his services, which were accepted, and he was put on special duty to the commanding officer, Colonel Wallace.

On October 11 another attempt was made to take the fort at Samangarh, this time with success. James took part and was in the van of the assault, at one stage finding himself isolated among the defenders before his troops caught up with him. Colonel Wallace was unstinting in his praise of the part James played in the assault, not only for his courage and fighting qualities but the experience and guidance he had provided, which, he wrote, contributed significantly to the success of the attack.

It appears however that local grievances ran deep. Administrative reorganisation had resulted in great hardship and discontent; the local army had been disbanded and the military class found itself unemployed. The rebellion continued to spread unchecked. James moved on with Wallace to Kagal, where a local minister, Daji Pandit had become unpopular and had been imprisoned by the local warlord in the fort of Panhala. On the appearance of the British contingent the minister was released and the young Rajah of Kolhapur changed sides and joined the British. The rebel leader responsible for the minister's incarceration, Babaji Ahirakar, took 500 troops and occupied the fort of Budargarh. When this was threatened by the British he moved on again to Panhala, where they took Colonel Ovans, British resident at Satara, hostage. James volunteered to take Ovans' place as hostage, on the basis that Ovans was known and respected by the rebels, and they may trust him to represent their interests in any negotiations, but Ovans would not hear of this. It took the British two weeks to rescue Ovans and capture the stronghold. James once again took a leading part, taking his force up a steep and rugged path to the walls under heavy fire. Having established a position close to the walls, in which they were bombarded with stones, they were eventually able to force an entry.

Despite this heroism, it seems James could do little right in the eyes of the Government at Calcutta. His tactics at Kolhapur and Kagal were questioned, although he maintained that he was acting under the orders of Wallace. At Kolhapur the criticism was that forces had been split when concentration was required, while the amnesty granted the Rajah and his family at Kagal raised all the old questions of James' relationship with local rulers. As James was assigned to special duty the Government could take a somewhat unconventional view of James' actions. He was afforded the freedom to act as he judged best, and was not subject to the same restrictions and instructions that constrained the main commanders, but the disadvantage of having this freedom was that he would be personally criticised for anything the Government did not like. James responded to these strictures spiritedly – perhaps too spiritedly – which further annoyed the Governor-General. James claimed that his heated reply was prompted by the fact that he saw the criticisms as reflecting upon Wallace and his officers, and was merely defending them. However once the full story of the campaign was reported to Calcutta a reappraisal of his actions took place, and he was commended for his part.

Whilst in Southern Maratha he was offered the post of political agent. This was a position considerably less senior than the ones he had occupied in the Sind, and reawakened old grievances. James pointed out that on his return to India he had accepted an inferior position to prove his zeal and loyalty, and had volunteered for active service after his return to Bombay from Nimar. He therefore considered that to accept this inferior post would admit the justice of the treatment he had received. He requested that instead he be permitted to return to his regiment.

On his way back to Bombay James received good news in a letter from his wife. Her health having improved considerably, she planned to leave England on February 1, 1845. This settled James in his decision to remain in India, which was just as well, for no sooner was he back in Bombay than his services were urgently required to quell a serious disturbance in Sawant-Wari, a territory south of where he had recently been. This time the command was his. He was to command a detachment of 1,200 troops, comprised of Native infantry, sappers, artillery and local men. It seems that the fugitives from Kolhapur had been driven south and linked up with 2,000 Wari soldiers under two notorious chiefs, Phund Sawant and Anna Sahib, who ruled over a lawless tract of difficult terrain. They had in the past proved impossible to capture or dislodge because the inhospitable countryside allowed them to use guerrilla tactics.

James immediately took matters into his own hands. Instead of a series of tentative forays, he commanded his full force of 1,200 to sweep forward from Wari towards the forts of Manohar and Mansantosh, driving the rebels down a valley. This required cutting their way through thick jungle, and ascending high, steep passes. In one forced march he covered 46 miles in twenty-four hours and succeeded in driving the rebels out of a series of their villages until he reached the fort at Mansantosh. He ordered a feint at the neighbouring Manohar, and by this ploy succeeded in getting his forces close to the walls of Mansantosh, occupying stockades hastily vacated by defenders. But the fort proved resistant to attack, and for two days James' men sought points of entry. On the third morning they discovered that the defenders had slipped out under cover of darkness, leaving both forts empty.

James lost no time in pursuing the rebels through the jungle again. He drove them south until they reached the territory of Goa, which posed for him a diplomatic problem, as this was under the rule of the Portuguese. Unable to pursue them any further, James entered into delicate negotiations with the Portuguese governor, the result of which was that the Portuguese rounded up many of the insurgents who had entered Goan territory and closed their borders to the remainder. James was therefore able to report a successful conclusion to his campaign, less than three weeks after his arrival in Sawant-Wari. Given the past problems experienced with these troublesome tribesmen, his success astonished Calcutta, and he received great praise from a number of sources, including the Governor of Bombay, Sir George Arthur and the Governor-General, Lord Hardinge. As a consequence he was offered the post of Resident at Satara, which he accepted.

James took up his post on May 26, 1845. This proved to be a very pleasant location when compared with his previous assignments. His wife was with him, and they were able to avoid the severe heat by retiring to the heights at Mahableshwar. The work was not demanding, providing ample time for rest and reflection. His sympathy with the local people and policy of justice and fairness drew favourable reports of his time there. Yet this free time also presented pressures, for he was able to take notice of the arguments over his conduct in the Sind which continued to rumble on. A section of the press, stoked by anonymous writers who attacked him personally, persisted in misrepresenting his actions in the Sind, and fed his sense of injury and unfair treatment.

A book entitled "Conquest of Sind," written by General Napier's brother, had been published. It set out Napier's achievements in heroic terms, and sought to justify the British actions in the Sind. It quoted liberally from Napier's letters. It was also a virulent personal criticism of James, driven by the author's resentment at James' perceived criticism of Napier. James was astounded at the misstatements and unfair accusations: the letters appeared to have been selectively used to demolish his reputation. With time on his hands he set out his reply to this book in the hope that it would receive equal publicity and rebut many of the criticisms. The Bombay Times immediately took up the attack on his behalf, reproducing several passages from Napier's book and highlighting the factual errors and misrepresentations, which were manifest and plentiful. James also erupted in public, addressing a letter of protest to the author of the book, William Napier, which was published in the Bombay Times. This was in direct conflict with a government order forbidding the protagonists to be heard in public, but the body of opinion in both London and India was sympathetic to James. The row persisted, however: a scurrilous article in the Kurrachee Advertiser, which had become the organ for Napier's champions, criticised James heavily and repeated the arguments in favour of Napier. It was plain to everyone that these arguments were seriously flawed and many of the "facts" untrue, and typically James felt sorry for Napier: "Those Curachee articles will positively destroy the poor old man – what a pity there is no one about him with sense to see, and independence enough to tell Sir Charles, how utterly mean and indefensible is such a quibbling mode of avoiding the prohibition of Govt. to publish such matters."[200]

James made an official application to the Government for permission to defend himself. Lord Ripon questioned Napier on the publication of his letters in his brother's book, but Napier disclaimed responsibility for these and the Kurrachee Advertiser articles. Before a decision could be made on James' request extracts of his response to the book started to appear in the Bombay Times, and it was rumoured that private copies of a book by James were in circulation. Soon it was generally available, to the regret of many, who felt it unwise to publicise such painful matters. The dispute was by now so public that there were concerns that it must be harmful to the British position in India to see senior figures in the administration in such conflict. Added to this was the amount of detail about the annexation of Sind that was being aired. James refrained from criticising Ellenborough, which meant that the burden of blame fell on Napier, making his account somewhat unbalanced. But the truth of many of his assertions was plain to see, and he mounted a very strong case on behalf of the wronged Amirs. His book won them many converts. Although his account was received with irritation by the powers in London, an appeal by Napier to have it suppressed was denied. They believed his brother's book to have been written in collaboration with the General, and James deserved the right of reply. A fresh injunction against public vindication of the respective positions was issued.

Later the Governor-General, Lord Dalhousie, was to experience an uncannily similar dispute with Napier. Napier was appointed Commander-in-Chief of forces in India, and resented any interference in his command, particularly from the political branch of the administration. He and Dalhousie disagreed on many matters, and Dalhousie was forced to use his authority to direct Napier. Matters came to a head in 1850 when Napier, having alienated not only the Governor-General but the President of the Court of Directors, was forced to resign. When Napier finally left India he, and his brother, mounted a virulent and sustained criticism of Dalhousie in justification of his own position and actions.

At the end of 1845 news came that a Sikh army had again shown signs of rebelling in the Punjab, and had crossed the Satlej River. True to form, James could not resist the opportunity, and immediately volunteered for active duty in the field. The Commander-in Chief indicated that he would welcome James' participation, but both the Bombay Government and Calcutta opposed his secondment on the grounds that he was needed in his present post. In fact, Napier was participating in the campaign, and there was concern that the two men would again clash. When Sir George Arthur explained this to James, he was furious. Napier, having assembled a force in readiness, was not directly involved but stood ready to support the action. What was more, he argued, why should his quarrel with Napier prevent him from serving in the army as a loyal soldier? The Sikh uprising was swiftly put down without him, though he could not resist writing to Lord Jocelyn urging moderation in victory, in order to avoid provoking further insurrection. He felt that he had found a model for successful occupation of India and was keen to convert others to it.

CHAPTER 9.

RETURN TO BARODA.

Two relatively peaceful and restful years passed at Satara. In May 1847 James was offered the position of Resident at Baroda, a considerable promotion. He described the post as "the highest political situation under the Bombay Government." The new Governor of Bombay, Sir George Clerk, was sympathetic towards James' work in the Sind, and had followed his career since then with interest. James nevertheless wrote to his mother on May 17: "I shall never consider myself righted until I am replaced in political employment under the Government of India, from which Lord Ellenborough removed me, and until the condemnation his lordship recorded against me, respecting Sind, is expunged."[201] Baroda was already familiar to James through his work with the Gaikawar and its people, and he saw this appointment as an opportunity to purge this important territory of rampant bribery and corruption, much of which involved the government itself. The local name for this was khatpat. Successive Residents and regimes had failed to deal with it, and there was a prevailing suspicion that, perhaps, the Bombay Government did not wish it to be tackled. There was also the thought that if the extent of khatpat was unveiled, the details would be highly embarrassing to the British. In fact documents existed in the British files which argued that khatpat was an effective tool of rule. British employees in India were paid very little – a clerk received £5 per annum, the going rate for domestic servants back home – and looked to compensate for this by making what they could on the side. A common saying of the time was: "The good old principles of Leadenhall Street economy – small salaries and immense perquisites."[202]

James was no stranger to khatpat. In 1835 he had prepared a report on Baroda for Sir Robert Grant in which he not only highlighted the extent of the practice and its ill effects, but pointed out that public officials could be, and probably were, swayed in their judgement by bribery. One case that gained prominence was of a British adjudicating officer who found in favour of a contestant in an inheritance claim. He was revealed to have taken bribes, and witnesses to have committed perjury. Although James had brought this to the attention of the relevant authorities the offending officials had either escaped conviction or been given a very light sentence. The Government went to some length to hush up the proceedings. Later, as his first stint in Baroda drew to an end, James had addressed a strong letter to Bombay urging the Government to take action against a corrupt Thakur, only to be put firmly in his place. The implication was that he would be well advised to be less concerned by such matters, and have more confidence in the discrimination and good sense of his superiors.

James was therefore not surprised to find on his return to Baroda that little had changed in his absence. He quickly discovered that his principal assistant, Narsu Pant, a clerk of winning manners and plausible attitude and for many years the confidential agent of the Residency, was a rogue, and that the man he had replaced, Baba Farki, had been perhaps too efficient and effective and had been hounded from office with the passive acquiescence of Bombay. He immediately demanded that Narsu Pant resign. His cause was not helped by the ill health of Sir George Clerk, which forced him to retire, to be replaced by Lord Falkland. A further blow came with the news that his wife's brother, Lieutenant Anderson, had been murdered by the soldiers of Mulraj in part of a Sikh revolt. James immediately volunteered for active service, and wrote to the Resident at Lahore full of ideas for how to tackle the Sikhs. His application to the new Governor-General in Calcutta, James Andrew Ramsay, Earl of Dalhousie, was received favourably, but it was suggested he should apply to his own government at Bombay. Falkland's response to his request was a polite refusal. He wished James to apply his energies to the problems in Baroda. Before James could rectify matters there, and set about tackling the widespread khatpat, his health failed, and he was advised to seek recuperation in a healthier clime. Thus in November 1848, barely eighteen months after his arrival in Baroda, he and his wife left India for Egypt, where it was hoped he could recover.

From Suez they journeyed to Cairo through the desert in a "van" which carried six passengers. On the way they encountered a van travelling in the opposite direction that held Sir Henry Lawrence and his wife, bound for India. Lawrence, three years younger than James, had gained a tremendous reputation in India. He had joined the Bengal Artillery at Calcutta in 1823, and fought in Burma. In 1829 he was appointed revenue surveyor at Orakhpur, and later fought in the Afghan war. He was destined to play a distinguished role in the relief of Lucknow during the Mutiny. The two men knew each other by reputation but had never met, and this was to be a significant coming together of leaders who had given considerable thought to the way India should be ruled. Lawrence was an idealist, and shared James' conviction that the English in India should treat the local populace with consideration and tolerance. A deeply religious man, he believed passionately that it was his duty to help the people he ruled, and to allow them to own property, to develop and prosper. Both held the greatest respect for the other, and Lawrence had resorted to print in periodicals to defend James. They had corresponded previously, and were instinctively drawn to each other. The meeting was to cement a lifelong friendship, and to confirm James in his instincts.

Margaret left in December to return to England, leaving James alone in Alexandria. He used his time there to study Arabic, and to visit some of the ancient sites. He soon regained his health and strength, and after sixteen weeks in Egypt was ready to return to India. He had read with growing concern of the worsening political situation in the Punjab, and felt his duty lay back in India as soon as possible. But whilst in Egypt he received two disappointing letters which reinforced his feelings that the authorities in Calcutta were prejudiced against him. The first was a curt note from the Governor-General's private secretary confirming that his request to join the army in the field had been rejected. It was written in such terms that his sensitivities were bruised. The second was worse. It was a claim from the Pay Department for the refund of Sind prize money which, they argued, as a civil appointment he should not have received. It took the Court of Governors in London to agree that this was a mistaken interpretation before the matter was resolved. His concern at the unfavourable light in which he was held was heightened by the news that Sir Charles Napier had been appointed Commander-in-Chief of the army in India.

These events, and the consideration that his replacement at Baroda held the tenure until May, caused him to delay his return. He resumed his sightseeing, which concentrated on inspecting fortifications. Preparing to leave Alexandria in June, he suffered an attack of acute spinal rheumatism, which caused great pain. To shake it off he took a cruise along the coast to Syria. From there he visited Beirut and finally returned to Cairo in October, restored to health. It was not until January 1850 that he re-embarked on the steamer "Ajdaha" for the return trip to India. In the meantime he had become increasingly concerned that a return to Baroda would not be a politically advantageous move, given his opposition to Government policy. He therefore requested a posting to Nagpur, applying directly to Lord Dalhousie. He argued that to set up home there would enable him to bring out his wife and son and enjoy a period of peace and quiet retreat after so many years of active service. His disenchantment was such that privately he expressed the wish to retire from the service and take up a posting in England, but his financial situation was not good, and he could ill afford to take an inferior position at this time. His request was refused, and he was directed to return to Baroda.

There is a collection of papers which indicates that James used his time in Egypt to good effect. On his return to India he presented these to Government. They consist of a detailed analysis of the fortifications of Alexandria, a political review of the country, a lengthy schedule of the country's military and agricultural resources, its revenues and means of transport, and a strategic assessment of the country's capabilities. Both the Governor General and the Governor of Bombay commended him for the work and the value of the information. James also sent a summary of his findings to a friend and staunch supporter in London, Lord Jocelyn. When he in turn presented it to the Cabinet Lord Palmerston added his voice to the praise, describing the information "most valuable" in the context of the conflict with Russia and Turkey.[203] The gist of this report was later published under the title "Dry Leaves from Young Egypt" in the Gazeteer of Sind.[204]

In April 1850 the debate over the Sind campaign was revived. Sir George Clerk, Governor of Bombay, had assumed responsibility for the Sind in February 1848, and had at once commissioned a study on it in preparation for a visit by him. What he found gave cause for alarm. Despite an efficient military organisation there was considerable evidence of maladministration, corruption and waste. The Sind was a constant and heavy drain on British finances, and the question of costs was therefore a sensitive issue. Even more seriously, many of the deceptions relating to Ali Murad were uncovered. Clerk, who as a Persian scholar could read many of the original documents, was also an administrator of real ability, and with considerable experience of Muslim countries. Alarmed by what he found, not least by the gaps in Napier's report of what had occurred, Clerk appointed a commission to enquire into the original treaties. Aided by Sheikh Ali Hasan, who had arranged much of the negotiations on behalf of Ali Murad, the whole deception was brought to light. James' warnings, his advice to Napier, and his subsequent writings on the subject were shown to be totally accurate, and his position completely vindicated. Napier was once again under criticism. This, added to problems the new Governor-General, Lord Dalhousie, was having with him, led finally to his replacement as Commander-in-Chief. As a soldier he was still very popular, and his departure from India on February 3, 1851 was attended with due ceremony. Lord Ellenborough, sitting in the House of Lords, leapt to Napier's defence but only succeeded in opening old wounds and making himself look ridiculous as inaccuracies and misrepresentations were exposed.

James' return to Baroda in May 1850 contained unpleasant surprises. It appeared that as soon as he had left for Egypt Narsu Pant had reconsidered his resignation, and was still in post. Babu Farki, whom James had recommended as Narsu's replacement, had been made an outcast. Various appeals to Government had resulted in the reversal of James' policies, and the implicit criticism of his actions was not only a personal insult but a dangerous precedent of a challenge to British authority in the person of the Resident. What upset James even further was that the decision to retain Narsu had been made before he left Bombay for Egypt. The Bombay Government had had ample opportunity to consult him and hear the reasons for his recommendations, but chose not to. The implication of this, he claimed, was that khatpat stretched as far as the upper echelons of the Bombay Government. Now he was returning to his post to resume his enquiries, against a background in which his judgement had been questioned and his authority undermined.

James' first act was to submit a long despatch to the Governor of Bombay on June 22, 1850, requesting that the case of Farki be reconsidered, and suggesting that his unfavourable treatment had arisen from his success in exposing corruption among local staff. It did not pull any punches. James started by stating that "I should be wanting in my duty did I shrink from soliciting from Government the revocation of what I consider an unjust decision; formed on a misapprehension of the case." He argued that this arose from "the aid which he had afforded to myself and others, in exposing the depravity of certain native officials...it does appear..that His Highness the Gaicowar must have been influenced...by the representations of [the late Acting Resident – who was Captain French]." Despite James' repeated requests to French for an explanation, and French's assertion that he could explain everything "the late acting Resident declines to afford me the information I requested," saying that he was solely responsible to Government, who had not called upon him to reply. James went on to set out the valuable work Farki had done in uncovering widespread corruption, yet in 1843 he had been dismissed from service by a Mr Remington, then in charge of the Native Agency of Rewa Kanta, where Farki worked. Remington's reasons for his dismissal were that "From the very first I was struck with the high tone he assumed"...and so "I sought his removal at a very early period." James observed: "A prejudice thus appears to have been caused, by (his) independent manner,...so different from the comparatively sycophantish bearing to which...Mr Remington had been accustomed." There followed three pages of details showing the animosity towards Farki from locals who had influenced Remington's judgment, although Farki had served for five and a quarter years "without accusation or taint...with no offence beyond that of an independent bearing." James pointed out that some of the papers submitted to Government in support of Farki's removal appeared false. He finished by pressing for a thorough enquiry to be instituted. The Governor regarded this letter as "intemperate and indiscreet"[205] and saw "no reason whatever for the interference of our Resident between Farki and his Highness of Gaikawar." The despatch was suppressed and filed, so that the merits of James' argument and the tone of his despatch were not available for others to judge.

While these were uncomfortable questions, with direct criticism of other English officials, the main reproof was aimed at corrupt locals who wanted the persistent Farki, who was probing their affairs, gone. This despatch appears hardly the incendiary document it was made out to be.[206] Throughout this affair James showed a strong sense of fair play, and was not afraid to challenge Bombay when he found the British authorities unfair and apathetic to the Gaikawar government. A member of the Bombay Council, Willoughby, dissented from the official view, and his minute on the subject confirmed that the extent of bribery and corruption among the establishment in Gujarat, and especially at Baroda, was notorious. He went on: "It is evident that Lieutenant-Colonel Outram believes, and I have not a doubt honestly and in good faith believes, that Baba Pherkeea [Farki] has been subjected to oppression and ill-treatment for having aided him in bringing corrupt practices to light….so far from considering that officer [Outram]…to have acted indiscreetly and intemperately in submitting this representation to Government, I do not see how, as a man of honour, he could have avoided doing so. I cannot therefore concur in the censure passed upon the Resident…I think the case should…be fully investigated."

James settled into a dull, rather lonely, bachelor existence. There were no women at the station, and although he dined regularly with a couple of friends, he did not spend much time in the army mess. His routine was to rise at 4am, ride until sunrise, breakfast at 9, work until sunset and retire to bed at 9pm. He continued to pursue corruption relentlessly with little support from Government, despite a circular from Bombay issued in the month of his return urging Residents to report any evidence of corruption and make suggestions for its eradication. James submitted five charges against Narsu

Pant, and assembled a "Statement of Facts" which set out the extent of the corruption he believed he had uncovered. He wrote this statement in such a form that it could, if necessary, be submitted to the British Parliament and public. He also prepared an appeal against the Bombay Government to hold in reserve should this be necessary. This latter document was in response to Bombay's decision to appoint a Commissioner to enquire into his findings – an action James saw as critical of him and a way of deflecting his charges.

James' Statement of Facts provoked rage in Bombay. He received a very angry letter with a resolution of the Governor to remove him from office, but giving him the opportunity to withdraw in the manner least offensive to his own feelings, and least calculated to embarrass Government, or affect their amicable relations with the Gaikawar.[207] His response was to request permission to proceed to Bombay on a month's leave with the understanding that his successor would be appointed at the end of that period. He wrote home indicating his intention to leave immediately thereafter for England. His letter to his wife was positive, reassuring her that he was not discouraged by his rejection, and making detailed plans to settle down in London close to India House, "where I may have much to do."[208] He wanted to adopt a low profile, and was not coming home "to agitate, or to induce the Court to censure or annul the measures of the Bombay Government." Nevertheless he expected that a careful perusal of all the correspondence, including the Khatpat Report, would justify his actions and exonerate him of any wrongdoing.

The Khatpat Report was submitted to Government on October 31, 1851, for submission to the Court of Directors. The introduction noted that the doctrine of khatpat was generally accepted throughout the country and that Government treated those servants whose guilt had been established with singular leniency. This, James argued, led to the assumption among the locals that their rulers were morally lax. The body of the report set out in detail the events in Baroda, showing how individual officials had been the recipients of bribes and naming local agents who had attempted to bribe British officials, although there was no evidence that they had succumbed to the temptation. It referred to the case of Baba Farki and Narsu Pant, and remarked "that in reality the Resident, not the accused, was on his trial."[209] Finally the Report set out a number of proposals: that the Gaikawar be requested to co-operate in putting a stop to corruption throughout his dominion; that the Gaikawar dismiss his adviser, Bhao Traimbak, who had been the main obstructer during James' enquiries; that any subjects seeking to corrupt British officials be severely punished; that Baba Farki be rewarded for his services in a substantial and public manner; that Narsu Pant's offences and punishment be published; and that a court be set up at Baroda to try cases of corruption. It is interesting to note that although these proposals were not acted upon at the time – indeed, they were rejected, and not even forwarded to the Court of Directors – in 1854 and 1855 they were, in the main, carried out.

James left Baroda on December 20, 1850. Before he left he addressed a long letter to Government regretting the interpretation which had been placed upon his letter accompanying the Khatpat Report which, he claimed, had done him more harm than the Report itself. This letter had complained that little regard had been paid to the Resident by his official superiors, and this had led to his enquiry and its findings being seriously impaired. The circumstances called for strong, plain language which, he argued was necessary in view of the impairment to Government's credibility. He also pointed out that more than one attempt had been made to poison him.[210] On reaching Bombay he met a number of the members of the Governor's Council, but the Governor himself refused to meet James. The subsequent publication of his own findings under the title "Baroda Intrigues and Bombay Khatpat" includes the sentence: "I deemed it my duty to leave nothing untold which was requisite to enable the Court of Directors (from whom the Bombay Government had withheld my appeals) to judge of the nature and propriety of those official obstructions which had been thrown in my way."[211]

James sailed from Bombay on February 17, 1851, aboard the Achilles. He rejoined his wife in London where they stayed until the middle of summer. The next few months were spent travelling at leisure to Brighton and Paris before returning to London in November. But the idle life did not suit him, and he remained restless. He disliked parties, and shunned the considerable public attention he was given as he was seen as a hero by some and a disgraced villain by others. When at home he spent most of his time working on his recollections of Baroda, doing research or talking to parliamentarians or India Office friends, preparing the ground for justifying his stand. His mother joined the couple in London, and brought a levity to an otherwise rather sombre time in their lives. Without gainful employment the family finances reached a low ebb, and economies were necessary. The defence of his stand in Baroda was an important factor in his future prospects.

The Court of Directors in London responded to the Bombay Government's report on Baroda by supporting the reprimand to James for communicating in terms which were not consistent "with that respect for the Government under which he was serving, which ought to be observed in all such representations."[212] There were dissenting voices, however. Fourteen Directors resorted to print in pointing out that the Court of Directors response concentrated more on the lack of respect in James' letter than the much more serious issue of khatpat, thus approving of the proceedings of the Bombay Government, which must be open to question. It seems that eighteen out of twenty-three Directors objected to the Court's response, but were overruled by the President of the Board of Control, who insisted that the response be sent to India.

Thirteen of these dissenters recorded their protests, the other five leaving town to avoid signing the response.

Discussion was not limited to the Court of Directors. In April 1852 Chisholm Anstey raised the matter in the House of Commons, much to James' consternation. He foresaw that he would be accused of insubordination and lack of integrity in agitating for a hearing, and immediately came forward to disavow any connection with Anstey and reconfirm that he believed this was a subject for the East India Company and no one else. Nevertheless, in October the report on Baroda was published. It took the form of two huge blue-books, so badly organised that it was unlikely that anyone outside of Parliament would read them, let alone take in their findings. By May 1853 no progress had been seen, although friendly Directors of the Court kept reassuring James that papers filtering through from Bombay supported his stand, and would strengthen his case. He was warned, however, that it was unthinkable that a servant of the Company could be publicly seen to score a victory over the Court. So James wrote to the Court asking them to recommend him for a political post in India. He really wanted the post at Baroda back: only this would annul the humiliation and degradation he had experienced, particularly in the view of the local inhabitants. He claimed that his dismissal and the subsequent limbo in which he found himself had resulted in a personal financial loss of nearly £6,000 – a "virtual fine for an offence which was nothing more than the theoretical expression of an opinion."[213]

The Court accordingly wrote to the Governor-General in Calcutta recommending that he be re-employed in a capacity suitable to his talents and services.[214] The letter referred to his representations from Baroda as objectionable but gave him credit for the zeal, energy, ability, and success with which he prosecuted inquiries. James also wrote to Lord Dalhousie offering himself for employment in any part of India, and received a friendly letter that did not hold out any hope owing to other claimants in line for promotion. Lord Dalhousie, whose decision it was to return James to Baroda, wrote a very enlightening note on it on May 22, 1853: "Hitherto the Supreme Government has had nothing to do with Baroda or Col. Outram. In his last letter Sir C. Wood (Pres. of B. of C.) intimates an intention of putting Baroda under me; and he pleads for employment by me of Col. Outram. I said I could not employ Col. O. in India without excluding some one else; and it seems to me hard that one of my officers, as good as he, should lose his reward because Col. O. chooses to quarrel with his own Government and with his bread and butter. Since then I have read a compilation from the Baroda Blue-Book. I think the Government of Bombay shows very badly. And if I get Baroda, the first thing I shall do (as at present advised) will be to put Col. Outram back there. That the Gaicowar, and all Guzerat, and all Western Indians believe in Khutput - that is to say, that they believe the Government of Bombay can be and daily is bribed – is undoubted. That the Bombay Government have confirmed that impression by their conduct about Baroda is clear. That Col. Outram was wholly right at Baroda, except in using disrespectful language, is admitted, and that he is the most conspicuous and most successful enemy of Khutput is notorious. It seems to me, therefore, that the heaviest blow I could strike at Khutput would be to replace its most formidable enemy at its headquarters. If it be considered a slap to the Bombay Government, I can't help it. My concern is the reputation of the British name, not the feelings of the Bombay Government. Moreover, they have no right to regard it as a slap. For they only accused Col. O of disrespect; they turned him out for it; he will have been severely and sufficiently punished by nearly two years' exclusion from office, and the Ct. of D. has itself expressed a wish for his re-employment somewhere. If I take Baroda and put him there, I shall send for him here, in order to explain, and get his explanation, and to give him to understand that we shall get on very well, provided he obeys orders and keeps a civil tongue in his head."[215]

James revered Dalhousie, and told a friend: "that he had had interviews with the Duke of Wellington, with Sir Robert Peel, and other leading statesmen in England, but never felt such awe and a such a feeling of inferiority as in interviews with Lord Dalhousie, who had ever been most kind to him."[216] Meanwhile he was offered, and accepted, the appointment of an honorary Aide-de-Camp to the Governor-General. Although a sinecure, it was seen by James as a sign of authoritative approval of his conduct and support for him from the highest position in the land. This would reinforce his status when he returned to Baroda. Whilst filling this position, he was asked to write a report addressing the possibility of an invasion of India from the west, which was prompted by the probability of a European war and consequent political turmoil. Dalhousie wrote: "By good luck there have been lately two men better able to give an authoritative opinion on that question than any other pair now alive, - Col. Outram and Major Abbott….. I have got a paper from them which is to my mind most conclusive. They show that such a thing as a Russian invasion of India is physically almost, and morally altogether, impossible."[217]

James' first step on the journey back to Baroda was to call on the Governor of Bombay, as that Presidency remained nominally responsible for Baroda. Lord Elphinstone had succeeded Falkland to the post, and James' reception in Bombay was altogether different to the atmosphere at his departure. Elphinstone welcomed James' appointment. Behind the scenes he had been recommending him for advancement. James returned to Baroda on March 19, 1854, and immediately visited the Gaikawar, who was somewhat concerned to see his old adversary. James brought instructions from Dalhousie that the Gaikawar's entourage of officials who had been implicated in Khatpat should be dismissed. The

Gaikawar protested, as many were within his favoured circle, but James held firm and within a month all had gone. News also came that Narsu Pant had died, removing yet another thorn in the flesh of the Resident. Dalhousie noted: "Outram's reception at Baroda has been triumphant. His Minister, a notorious scoundrel, persuaded the silly Guicowar to write a letter to me objecting to the nomination of Outram. I was of course very angry, refused to answer it and desired the Bombay Government to return it to him. When I appointed Outram I demanded the dismissal of this Minister. The Guicowar was, therefore, frightened out of his wits at the thought of Outram's return. However, he received him very civilly - the populace, it is said, cheered Outram, and H.H. is again at his ease."[218]

At this point an unexpected diversion occurred. James was summoned to the Foreign Office on July 3 and told to station himself at Alexandria and await communication from Lord Stratford in Constantinople. Worsening relations with Russia had aroused anxieties over the position of Turkey, and the best officers available for special employment in Turkey were sought out. In fact he was not needed as the alarm subsided. Lord Stratford invited him nevertheless to come to Turkey "for amusement, and to take his chance"[219] but James, anxious to re-establish himself in India, felt that he should proceed there as soon as possible. For the rest of his life he regretted that he had missed the opportunity to participate in the Crimean War.

Elphinstone had strongly recommended to the Governor-General that James be appointed to Aden, where the civil and military responsibilities were combined, and Dalhousie had approved the appointment: "The fitness of the post and the man for each other were so manifest, and the triumph of Outram of being elevated to such a post by the Bombay Government was so great, that I at once said he should have him after he had set matters right at Baroda, and returned there for a short time. Accordingly this will be done. Col. Outram does not seem altogether to fancy exchanging the service of the Supreme Government for that of the Bombay Government again, but I think it is an enormous triumph for him. He owes me a day in harvest, I think."[220] Aden was seen as a key port in the event of war in Europe, and the position was thus of the utmost importance. James accepted, but asked that the move remain confidential until after he had gone to Baroda, as this would weaken the effect of his return. The move to Aden was convenient in one way: his mother was elderly, Aden was much nearer to England and the move would enable him to visit home for two months, going and returning through the continent.[221]

In April Dalhousie wrote to James giving him authority to summon his successor, Major Malcolm, of whom James approved. James had been hard at work studying the affairs of the Yemen and Aden in particular, and was ready to move. He sailed from Bombay on the steamer Ajdaha in June 1854, and reached Aden in sixteen days. His new position was not to be an easy one. Aden had been seized for the British in 1839 after a number of ships had been harassed and plundered by men of the local Sultan of Lahaj. The Yemeni who lived in the interior were hostile, and continually attempting raids on Aden and its garrison of 700 British soldiers. The land approaches to the garrison could not be easily defended, and supplies were frequently disrupted. Several of the garrison had been murdered not far from the fortifications, and it had not been possible to exact retribution.

James drew up an elaborate report of the causes which had brought about the unfriendly relations. He identified defects in the policy towards the Arabs, and suggested that an attempt should be made to win them over. He made contact with the chiefs involved, adopted a firm but conciliatory stance and won their confidence. He conveyed the smack of firm government: promises would be kept, threats would be carried out and treaties would be faithfully adhered to. The Governor-General gave James his full backing, and went further, authorising him to assist the Sultan of Lahaj should he be attacked. James was given licence to use armed force if in his judgement it was required.

James also looked to the well-being of the British troops in Aden. The water supply was polluted and poor, the best wells being in the hands of private individuals. The troops drank what was described as a "strong solution of salt." He appointed a special committee to investigate the whole question of water supply, the upshot of which was that the wells in the hands of individuals who could not prove legal title were made generally available and every soldier received a gallon of fresh water every day.[222] He established gardens by importing seeds and irrigating the gardens from water descending from the nearby hills into the sea. He even considered the feasibility of driving a canal from the Gulf of Aqaba, in Jordan, to the Mediterranean via the Dead Sea, but this came to nothing.

As usual, James had driven himself unremittingly, and he soon fell victim to Aden's enervating climate. By September he was forced to warn Elphinstone that his health was failing, and this was reinforced by travellers calling in at Aden who remarked on his changed appearance. He could not continue to live in Aden, but his ailing health was to lead to his most prestigious posting, and greatest challenge, in his career to date.

CHAPTER 10.

LUCKNOW.

Lucknow was known as the City of Gardens, one of the loveliest and richest cities in India. William Howard Russell of The Times described it as a city of "palaces, minars, domes azure and golden…..long facades of fair perspective in pillar and column, terraced roofs - all rising up amid a calm, still ocean of the brightest verdure. Look for miles and miles away, and still the ocean spreads, and the towers of the fairy-city gleam in its midst. Spires of gold glitter in the sun. Turrets and gilded spheres shine like constellations. There is nothing mean or squalid to be seen. There is a city more vast than Paris, as it seems, and more brilliant. Is this a city in Oudh? Is this the capital of a semi-barbarous race, erected by a corrupt, effete and degraded dynasty? I confess I felt inclined to rub my eyes again and again."[223]

James' standing was now so high that he was offered one of the most important positions in India: that of Resident at Lucknow. This he accepted with alacrity, but not before bringing to Dalhousie's notice the fact that he did not speak Persian, "in which I understand the Resident's transactions with the Court of Oudh are conducted, and a thorough knowledge of which may perhaps be deemed essential to the representative of government at that court."[224] Dalhousie replied: "Oudh has long been in a ticklish state. The 'sick man' may any day be in our hands. With that contingency in view we wish to have the best man at our disposal to fill the vacancy. With one voice we pronounced you to be the man, and to have the best public claims to it, moreover, viewed as a public reward."[225] James wrote home jubilantly: not only was his reputation restored but he had received the whole-hearted support of his Governor-General, who noted: "The Resident at Lucknow has become suddenly ill. This is generally considered the first political appointment under the Government of India. The selection was of consequence. On the whole, adverting to the critical state of that court - to what may any day happen - and to his own personal claims, I have resolved to give it to Col. Outram. His appointment to Aden by Bombay, which I thought would delight him, has disgusted him. He will be right glad to get back under the Government of India. If his star for ten years has been obscured, it has come clear out now, and is in the ascendant towards its zenith.[226]" James' financial situation was improved dramatically by the appointment, and he advised his mother that he would be able to send her considerably more than the £500 per annum he had hitherto remitted. He insisted that she now acquire a carriage and maid with the increased remittance. He was succeeded in Aden by Colonel William Coghlan, who was to enjoy a distinguished career in that difficult post.

James must have felt that his stand against oppressive British rule was being vindicated by the appointment to one of the most sophisticated cities in India. But his residency at Lucknow was not to be a bed of roses, for he was to be a prominent player in perhaps one of the most infamous episodes in the East India Company's rule in India, to which Russell obliquely refers. The province of Oudh, in which Lucknow was the largest city, covered 24,000 square miles. The majority of its population lived from the land, in hovels of mud and thatch. It had been part of the Mughal Empire. Until the British arrived it was ruled by a Nawab, or Viceroy, who derived his authority from the Emperor in Delhi. But as the Emperor's power and influence waned, Oudh became more independent, finally rejecting his nominal sovereignty. The state issued coins struck in the name of the Nawab and on October 9 1813 the Nawab had himself crowned king of his territories. Under the Nawabs it flourished as a seat of luxury and culture. It attracted artists who had lost their royal patronage, and became famous for its music and fine arts. Dance in different forms and various handicrafts came to dictate fashion. It had in the past been a troublesome territory, but had proved to be an excellent recruiting ground for the best native soldiery.

The impression of independence was illusory. As early as 1773 the Nawab had sought military assistance from the British in repelling invaders (the Rohillas), and successive defence treaties had resulted in nearly half the territory being handed over to the British in return for protection. In 1798 British authority extended to actually dethroning a Nawab and replacing him with another, and thereafter the validity of succession was assumed to depend upon recognition by the British. At the beginning of the nineteenth century the British had reduced the Nawab to little more than a vassal. In exchange for control over the territory and revenues of the province, they had permitted successive local rulers to indulge their avarice and amass considerable treasure. In 1814 the Nawab was proclaimed a sovereign prince, although the title was in name only. Further control was ceded to the British in 1837 when a new Nawab, Muhammed Ali Shah, woken in the middle of the night with the news that his nephew, Nasir-ud-din Hyder, the reigning Nawab, had died unexpectedly, was presented with a paper by the British Resident which read: "I hereby declare that in the event of my being placed on the throne I will agree to sign any new treaty that the Governor-General may dictate."[227] This paper was used rather unscrupulously by Auckland to exert progressively greater control over state affairs in Oudh, and to borrow large amounts to finance military operations outside Oudh. Between 1814 and 1842 the Company borrowed nearly £5 million from Oudh, and the interest paid was "absorbed" by court stipendaries.[228]

On the other hand the British presence provided security – Lucknow was the only major Muslim city in north India that had never been walled – and enabled the aristocracy to channel their energies and wealth into the arts and leisure activities. Lucknow grew and thrived; it became a dazzling city of sumptuous palaces, of thriving bazaars and innovative architectural and engineering works. Scholarship also flourished: Lucknow became renowned for its philosophers, religious thinkers and mathematicians. The Nawabs encouraged poetry and letters, and a splendid library was assembled. However the ruler resented British interference, particularly when it involved disciplining subjects who were seen to be corrupt. But, in common with other parts of India, measures to check corruption were not followed up, and by 1847, when Muhammed Ali Shah's second son, Wajid Ali Shah succeeded to the throne, the Oudh court was riddled with malpractice and the people of Oudh had no recourse to a ruler surrounded by his cronies. The government at Calcutta warned the ruler that the mismanagement must stop or the British would need to take more direct control, but the Shah was in a poor state of health, and no improvements were made.

Dalhousie had a reputation as a moralist and improver, who believed he had a mission to interfere in the way India was administered. A Governor-General's minute dated August 30, 1848, states; "I cannot conceive it possible for anyone to dispute the policy of taking advantage of every just opportunity which presents itself for consolidating the territories that already belong to us, by taking possession of states which may lapse in the midst of them....for extending the uniform application of our system of government to those whose best interests, we sincerely believe, will be promoted thereby."[229] He followed this with another telling comment on September 18, in a letter to a friend; "..I have got two other...kingdoms on hand to dispose of – Oudh and Hyderabad. Both are on the high-road to be taken under our management - not into our possession; and before two years are over I have no doubt they will be managed by us."[230]

The Resident at Lucknow between 1849 and 1854 was Major-General William Sleeman. He was appointed with the purpose that he would validate Dalhousie's forgone conclusions. Sleeman was a man of strong and somewhat puritanical views. He campaigned with religious zeal against thagi – the practice of the ritual murder of Indian travellers – and by 1838 had tried a total of 3,266 Thugs, 1,400 of whom were either hanged or transported for life to the remote Andaman Islands. Forty of his sixty-one years had been spent in India. He admired the Indian village communities, but had no sympathy for Indian princes and the way they governed. He believed absolutely in the superiority of British government and the improvements it had brought to India. From the start of his residency he despatched scathing reports of the corruption, depravity, neglect of duty and abuse of authority he encountered at the Oudh court. Convinced that the administration was incorrigibly evil, he urged the Governor-General, Lord Dalhousie, to make him the effective ruler of Oudh. He wanted a council of regency set up, headed by the Resident and composing of Lucknow's leading citizens.[231] Dalhousie had other, weightier matters on his agenda, and a decision was deferred. In 1854 Sleeman was forced to leave Lucknow through ill-health, and his successor was given the task of studying the future for Oudh.

The English East India Company had, as early as 1813 laid down a policy of "subordinate isolation" for Indian states. This policy promised protection for states annexed by the British in return for which they were deprived of the rights to make war or enter into arrangements with their neighbours or employ foreigners. They also had restrictions placed on armaments. The Company undertook to defend them against hostile attack. However the British did not wish to become burdened by the minutiae of local administration, and the princes who ruled were given that authority. Hence the "isolation." Complaints against these princes would not be entertained by the protectors. Dalhousie soon realised that where, in his opinion, an Indian state was not ruled competently, his hands were tied. Indeed, through inactivity he was accused of conniving at misrule and oppression. If he was to possess Oudh, a strong and sound case would need to be made out. In fact Dalhousie had a reputation as something of a despot, and regarded the Indian states as anachronisms. He believed strongly that the entire Indian sub-continent could be shaped into one, modern unitary state.[232]

When taking up the position of Resident in Lucknow, James was able to draw upon the knowledge and experience of the two previous residents, Colonels Low and Sleeman, who were friends of his and still in service in India. They advised him that, at the outset, in order to establish his position in Lucknow as an equal of the ruler, the protocol of his arrival was of great importance. It was thus that, crossing the Ganges at Kanpur, he was met by a lavishly ornamented State carriage drawn by four horses. His process into Lucknow was impressive: a large crowd curious to catch sight of the man who would be most influential in their lives lined the road. At the outskirts of Lucknow he was greeted by a salute from the British artillery, and driven to the Dilkusha Palace where he was received by the heir apparent, the king being too ill to be present. A guard of honour from three regiments, commanded by European officers, attended. All the local nobility was present. The procession involved some three hundred extravagantly dressed elephants and camels. Footmen and horsemen surrounded the attendees, who were adorned with brilliant costumes and jewels. Having met the heir apparent, the two entourages moved off through the streets to a magnificent breakfast at the Shah Manzil, a very elegant palace, before James entered the Residence.

James found that one of his first tasks was to tackle an old enemy: khatpat. Some of the ruler's staff had spread it about that the British could be persuaded to commit acts of favouritism for money. James immediately wrote to the ruler urging the dismissal of these officials, and a royal mandate was obtained to this effect. Although his brief was to ascertain the present state of the province and whether the improvements demanded by the British government had been implemented, the die was already cast. If the improvements had not been implemented, it was "…the settled resolution of government to wait no longer for impossible improvements from within, but at once to shape their measures for the assertion, in accordance with treaty, of the authority of the paramount state."[233] Without any knowledge or experience of Oudh, and a tight deadline to meet, James was forced to rely heavily upon Sleeman's recommendations. He said he was "entirely dependent for my information on what I find in the Residency Records."[234] When Sir Charles Wood became President of the Court of Directors he showed a readiness to support Dalhousie. On October 21, 1853 he wrote to the Governor-General: "Take Oudh by a voluntary surrender, and you will have done a very good deed in India for the people of the country. I am not at all averse to the operation, and only am I anxious that it should be skilfully performed.….One cannot nowadays disregard public opinion, and the Court of Directors is by no means a popular body."[235]

James' full report on the State of Oudh, following upon Sleeman's work, took four months to compile, and was submitted to Calcutta in March 1855. His first finding was to concur with previous opinion that the present ruler was unfit to govern. "His Majesty continues to confide the conduct of his affairs to the same worthless and incompetent characters, to devote all his time to personal gratifications and frivolous amusements, and to manifest the same utter disregard of his duties and responsibilities."[236] An example of this frivolity was cited from a report by one of James' staff, Dr Joseph Fayrer, who spoke Persian and therefore was able to understand more of what went on in the Court of Oudh: "His majesty was

this morning carried in his tonjon to the Mahal, and there
he and So-and-so [ladies] were entertained with the fights of
two pairs of new rams, which fought with great energy, also of
some quails…His majesty then listened to a new singer, and
amused himself afterwards by kite-flying until 4 p.m., when
he went to sleep." James added however that the king was
anxious to co-operate with the British where its interests were
involved. James went on to deplore the state of the province
resulting from this misrule, and reluctantly recommended the
direct annexation of Oudh by the British, admitting that this
was in contrast to his oft-expressed view that states should
be ruled by Indians. But he was so alarmed by the state of
affairs that only direct intervention would suffice. Ominously
for what was to occur later, however, James' report included
the paragraph: "Every agricultural family in Oudh, perhaps
without exception sends one of its members into the British
army….The number of Oudh Sepoys in our service…is
estimated at 40,000."[237] Dalhousie responded by recording:
"A very heavy though very interesting and important paper
has lately come, being General Outram's report on the present
state of Oudh. He has brought together a tremendous bill of
indictment against the Government of that ill-fated land. I
don't think it can be allowed to stand. And I count it internally
a symptom of improving health in myself that the desire to
upset that court before I go has revived within me. It would
make a good wind-up; and if they will let me, I think I could
engage to have the country at our feet - every fort dismantled,
and every man disarmed in three months."[238] Later, James'
enemies were to remark that he had simply regurgitated
Sleeman's views without probing them at all.

What Dalhousie was proposing was very close to
annexation of the state of Oudh. Annexation had become
established policy by the Company, and had accelerated under
Dalhousie. It was laid down that where a local ruler had no
natural heir, the British should annex his domain. Adoption

was not accepted as a substitute for a natural heir; the British saw this as a ploy used by local rulers to get round the edict. (In fact the move by local rulers was often misunderstood. Their religion required a family, which would die out if no natural heir existed, to adopt a son, since it was only through the ceremonies and offerings of the son that the soul of the father could be released from Put (purgatory)). The intentions of the British authorities were revealed in the Blue Book relating to the annexation of Satara: the general principle was "to 'persevere in the one and clear direct course of abandoning no just and honourable accession of territory or revenue; while all existing claims of right are, at the same time, scrupulously respected; a fair and open line of policy with which nobody can quarrel.' Lord Dalhousie indorses this as follows: 'I take this fitting occasion of recording my strong and deliberate opinion that in the exercise of a wise and sound policy, the British Government is bound not to put aside or to neglect such rightful opportunities of acquiring territory or revenue, as may from time to time present themselves, whether they arise from the lapse of subordinate States by the failure of all heirs of every description whatsoever, or from the failure of heirs natural, when the succession can be sustained only by the sanction of Government being given to the ceremony of adoption, according to Hindu Law. The Government,' he continues, ' is bound in duty as well as policy to act on every such occasion with the purest integrity, and in the most scrupulous observance of good faith where even a shadow of doubt can be shown, the claim should be at once abandoned.'"[239]

Annexation policy was originally the policy of the Government and of the Board in London. Secret despatches from London approved any action proposed by Governors-General. Often it was the President of the Court of Directors who suggested annexation in private letters. Sir Charles Wood had his doubts about the wisdom of annexation. He was less concerned about its morality than what was justifiable in Parliament. He initially sought rules and consistency in deciding which states should be annexed. When Dalhousie proposed taking over the government of Oudh, Wood wrote to him: "…I am not prepared to annex Oudh unless you can make out a case beyond question….That we must take Oudh sooner or later I have no doubt; the only question in my mind is the time – opportunity and pretext, and as it is very desirable not to shew a grasping disposition at present I am unwilling to occupy our principality."[240]

Lord Dalhousie, in his report to the Court of Directors, did not recommend annexation, however. He proposed a new treaty that would supersede all previous treaties, leaving the sovereignty intact, but vesting the civil and military administration in the hands of the East India Company. This treaty would provide for the king and members of the royal family by annual stipend, but the residue of revenues from the province would be received by the East India Company. This proposal could be seen to be, in spirit if not in practice, close to the policy of "subordinate isolation" laid down in 1813 by the Company, referred to above. But Dalhousie could have hardly anticipated the reaction in London. This was the age of liberalism, and the belief that Western administration brought the greatest happiness to the greatest number of people. In the 1830's and 1840's Jeremy Bentham, labelled a Utilitarian, led public thinking in Britain on the role of that country in India. He was a firm advocate of strong, central government, and believed that active intervention by the British rulers in India would bring about a fairer, more just and efficient system of government. The liberals believed in representative government, but not yet for India. The prevailing mood in London was one of imperialism. Seizure of Oudh was urged as a moral duty, for the people must prefer British rule. The Lucknow correspondent of The Englishman wrote: "Every day that the annexure of this misgoverned country is delayed, another day of suffering is added to the lot of hundreds, nay thousands, of one of the finest races in Hindustan."[241] Despite reservations, public opinion and press comment lead the Directors and the government to decide upon full annexation "…the only…… course by which our duties to the people of Oudh can be fulfilled – that of assuming authoritatively the powers necessary for the permanent establishment of good government throughout the country."[242] The Times, reporting the appointment of Dalhousie as Governor-General had advised: "His easy task is to level those masses of misgovernment which obstruct the free circulation of prosperity and happiness…and to advance those internal improvements by which such blessings are so materially promoted." Addressing the problems of Hyderabad and Oudh, the article continued that the Nizam of Hyderabad was "morally accountable to us, and we have no more right to disregard the people of Oudh than to ignore the population of India."[243]

A serious consideration of what action to take was the worsening climate of opinion in India. In a letter dated October 6, 1855, Dalhousie wrote: "…we are beginning to be less easy every day, and to feel more and more the need of some great success in this war [the Crimean], whose existence is universally known among the natives, and whose course is universally believed by them to have been disastrous to us. In Oudh matters are in a very uncomfortable state. The violent religious feud which I mentioned to you has been temporarily allayed by the shedding of blood; but the causes of the feud remain unremoved. The Mussulman are in a state of great excitement; the Hindoos are equally furious, equally resolved, and far more numerous. If this feud should again break out, it is impossible to say how far the religious feeling may spread or to what it may not lead. The most inflammatory pamphlets on the Mussulman side are being circulated throughout the country, notwithstanding the seizure of them wherever they can be found. Fortunately Outram is at Lucknow, and the affair is thus in the best hands."[244]

Dalhousie was reluctant to exercise force in carrying out his instructions, and did not seek powers to do so. He believed such a move would be contrary to international law. But attitudes in London were hardening, and at the end of November 1855 the Court of Directors, backed by the Cabinet, authorised him to use force if the king of Oudh resisted. This instruction was received by Dalhousie on January 2, 1856. Time was short, for Dalhousie was due to leave India in March. Hastily he devised a fresh plan: the king was to be offered a new treaty with an ultimatum attached. In return for a liberal pension and retention of all his titles, he was to cede the administration of the whole of Oudh to the East India Company. If the treaty was not signed in three days, the kingdom would be taken by force and the king would forfeit all rights. This would amount to annexation.

James was summoned to meet the Governor-General at Barrackpore. Dalhousie noted on January 13: "General Outram has been staying with me. He croaks a good deal, doubting whether the King will accept the treaty, and whether we shall not be obliged to have recourse to arms after all. This surprised me, until I recollected that heroes have indigestions like other people; and I hope that when he comes out of the doctor's hands, in which he now is, he will take a more cheerful view of our prospects. It is impossible to foretell what the King of Oudh or any other native prince will really do in such a case, but there seems to me every probability that he must, and will, yield speedily. It is, of course, rather an anxious and responsible position in which I stand just now; but I know the cause just and my own motives pure, and I look therefore, with confidence for the blessing which we need not fear to ask."[245] To what extent James' "croaking" was due to his misgivings about the action proposed, we shall never know.

On the 30th James returned to Lucknow on January 30, and at once communicated the Governor-General's intention to the First Minister. The Minister professed to be much surprised and distressed. He protested against the advance of troops as quite unnecessary. Next day James explained fully all the details of the proposed annexation and requested an early audience of the King. In the meantime the Queen mother begged an interview. The old Begum was a very sensible, respectable lady, possessing a good deal of influence over her son, and always using it well, which could by no means be said of royal ladies generally, and especially not of royal ladies at Lucknow.[246]

At 8 a.m. on February 4, 1856 James visited the king in his palace. The king had previously received a letter from the Governor-General informing him of the ultimatum, and was very emotional. He pointed out that he was in no position to oppose the move, and had made arrangements for his troops to be disarmed and his guns dismounted. But he would not sign the treaty or receive a stipend. He would instead go to England and put himself at the mercy of Queen Victoria. James, supported by the king's advisers, urged him to sign the treaty, but the king refused, saying he no longer had any authority. James then gave him three days to change his mind, after which he would have no alternative but to assume the government of the province. After consultation with his advisers, the king yielded to the inevitable. On February 7, James called a meeting with the minister and chief officers of state in Oudh, and announced the assumption of government by the English East India Company. The king was deprived of his sovereignty, local government dismantled and a new administration substituted. Military resources were to be under the control of the Resident. James was appointed chief commissioner and his officers were deployed to take charge of the individual districts of Oudh. Thus "subordinate isolation" was set aside on the grounds of the ruler's incompetence, and full annexation, leading to direct rule by the Company, was instigated. It later emerged that James had offered the king's mother a bribe to induce her to persuade him to sign the treaty.

In the Oudh Blue Book James is recorded as writing: "His Lordship in Council will have gathered….that I promised that lady an annual stipend of one lakh of rupees, provided that the King would accept the treaty."[247]

James Mill, father on John Stuart Mill, the famous writer and economist, had been an important influence on Indian policy during his time at the India Office in London, from 1819 to 1836. A disciple of Bentham, he believed that a "hideous state of society" existed in India, "dissembling, treacherous, mendacious."[248] He opposed the zamindar system, believing these officials to be parasites, and proposed that the British should act as landlords and each peasant should be a direct tenant.[249] Dalhousie, influenced by Mill, made it plain that he wished the institutions of traditional leadership which existed to be expunged altogether. Chieftains in the rural villages were traditionally regarded as the landlords (taluqdars), and before annexation the state of Oudh had looked to them for revenue collection from the land, but unfortunate experience elsewhere in India led the British to discard this system in Oudh, and look to the zamindars, hereditary rent collectors under the old Mughal system. This stripped the taluqdars of much of their possessions and influence, which sowed the seeds for later reaction from this powerful group. The local officers sometimes ignored this injunction and preferred to deal with the taluqdars. Oudh had seen the taluqdars growing rapidly in stature; in 1800 there were said to be 17 private fortresses in the state, but by 1849 this had grown to 246.[250] Annexation was not the moment to test their strength, however. It will be seen later, when the sepoy uprising occurred, that Oudh was one of the most recalcitrant states, where the so-called mutiny spread far wider than just the soldiers. The taluqdars were to play a leading role in this resistance.

By February 19 Dalhousie was able to report that everything was proceeding smoothly. As yet not a shot had been fired - except by mistake. Some of the King's troops had seized their officers for arrears of pay and the troops opened fire on them. Some of the mutineers were killed, which procured the speedy surrender of the hostage officers. He went on: "As I anticipated, Outram's nervousness all evaporated when he entered on the scene and drew near the time of action. They all describe him as quite changed - calm, but fierce as a lion. Already the letters which are received show that he has at once established that remarkable influence over the goodwill and ready service of his officers which has always characterised his relations with those subordinate to him. On his part he writes to me in great delight with the prompt and cheerful acquiescence of Civil officers, ordered off into the jungles just as they had arrived from a long dak journey, without kit, without servants, and with the prospect of depending entirely on the villages for food and shelter at the first. It is a fine service, - no wonder it creates great results."[251] Ever the loyal soldier, James had obeyed his orders and carried out the unpleasant task to the best of his ability.

The king moved to Kanpur, and was seen to be far from well. He was now fully convinced that he would not reach Calcutta alive but was ashamed to return.[252] Dalhousie retired on March 1, and was succeeded by Lord Canning. Before he left, he wrote to Queen Victoria that she now "has five million more subjects and £1,300,000 more revenue."[253]

Many commentators have remarked that the annexation of Oudh was the spark that ignited the sepoys' rebellion. The best of the Bengali army were recruited from Oudh, and in spite of the patent misrule by their king, they remained loyal to their state, and the local people. The annexation was seen as usurping local authority, and a real sense of loss of control over the territory and its administration. James reflected the unrest in his communications with the new Governor-General, Lord Canning, reminding him that upon annexation he had requested reinforcements. He hastened to reassure the Governor-General that he was on top of the situation: "…I now feel more confident of averting the evils which must have resulted from a course which at one time it appeared very probable they would pursue. But I must confess I should have been glad had your Lordship allowed one, if not both, the proposed regiments of the Kings Guards."[254] It is a pity the extra troops were not provided, as it may have made a difference to the events of the following year.

His wife joined him in January 1855, but saw little of her husband during the ensuing months. He worked from before dawn to dusk, and took little time off for recreation. Margaret was also kept fully occupied. She was launched into a sea of gaiety and formidable entertainments, very different to the quiet life among the wild Bhils that she had expected when she sailed from England to become her cousin's bride. She rose to the occasion however, and by all accounts made a beautiful and dignified hostess. She wrote to James' mother: "They gave a ball to me the evening before last at which I took cold and have completely lost my voice. It is the race week and I have much to do with gaieties of different kinds, and we have a large party this evening that I fear I cannot attend. I have to give a ball next week, and all these gaieties seem quite out of my line...."[255] Her description of a dinner hosted by the king brings vividly to life the pomp, splendour and confusion of that extraordinary time: "We all enjoyed it as being a little out of the common style, and we had fireworks, nautches, illuminations, a very bad dinner, and bad headaches at the finale. The dresses and jewels were most gorgeous, and except for the crowds of natives standing round the table would have looked very magnificent. The King was unwell and did not come, but his eldest son presided - a fine lad of fourteen. The Royal family were the only people admitted at table. The Minister sat behind the Prince, and after dinner two hookahs were brought in, one for James and the other for Lord Lothian, but no one else was allowed to smoke. Lord Lothian made awful faces over his. I wish you could have seen it, though the heavy native scents and impure air would soon have upset you, and the going there was formidable. Such troops of elephants, carriages, horsemen and natives all in pell-mell confusion. My carriage was nearly upset, but the Doctor who took charge of me got me out (James had to go in state), and some gentlemen gave me theirs. You have no idea of the noise and confusion of all the native shows."[256]

After annexation the Residency became a bustling centre for the civil and military officers who poured into Lucknow before taking up their posts, often in rough rural districts. Among their many duties – organising courts, the police, the post and road communications – the most important was revenue collection. The lack of suitable accommodation outside of Lucknow necessitated many officers' wives remaining in the residency until they could join their husbands. Margaret Outram performed the essential duty of hostess to this passing traffic, and remained very busy. Amid the bustle, good news came from Calcutta. In his last despatch before returning to England, Lord Dalhousie was able to inform James that he had been knighted. Dalhousie was responsible for recommending the knighthood: his letter of recommendation dated September 20, 1855, refers to "the brilliant record attached to his name" and goes on: "I do not hesitate to express my opinion that General Outram has not received the reward that was his due."[257]

James knew Dalhousie's successor, Lord Canning, slightly having met him several years previously. No sooner had Canning taken office than James' health failed again. Pressure of work and mental stress had brought on acute rheumatism of the neck and shoulders, and signs of brain problems. There was no alternative but to seek relief in England. His wife did not return with him, as he fully intended returning to his position in Lucknow before long. She moved to the hills to see out the hot weather, accompanied by her son, Frank, who had recently arrived in India as a qualified member of the Indian

Civil Service, while James travelled to Calcutta. Canning wrote: "He [James] just arrived from Oudh, dreadfully shattered in health; he only takes his six months leave, but there is not a chance that he can return. His place is a most difficult one to fill."[258]

In his last discussion with Canning before embarking, James expressed his concerns about unrest among local troops, a manifestation of which had occurred with trouble in Bengal. He urged the Governor-General to strengthen the garrison at Allahabad, which he identified as a sensitive spot. (Geographically Benares and Allahabad were situated in the middle of a narrowed band of the country where anyone controlling the two cities would effectively control passage north and south). Henry Lawrence subsequently made a similar suggestion. The fort at Allahabad was guarded by sepoys and was therefore vulnerable to any insubordination. So concerned was James that as he passed through Kanpur he arranged for 200 European troops to stand in readiness to be despatched to Allahabad as soon as Calcutta agreed. Had their suggestion been acted upon, the course of the Indian Mutiny in 1857 might have been very different.

James' journey to England was leisurely, to say the least. He proceeded from Egypt along the Mediterranean coast, visiting Beirut, Smyrna, Constantinople, Greece, Malta and Italy. He sought remedies for his ailments in Italian spas, but to little avail. He reached England some two and a half months after leaving Calcutta and was confined to his house for some days under medical treatment. His rheumatism was particularly painful. He was then able to visit his mother and sister in Edinburgh, during which he nearly lost his life. A servant had left the gas turned on in a gas fire and allowed the flame to go out. His mother smelt the gas and raised the alarm.

Recuperation at Brighton seems to have restored James' health fully, for his subsequent letters to his mother were much more cheerful and energetic. He also wrote to Viscount

Canning saying he was perfectly recovered and proposed returning to India in December.[259] How ill he had been, and how much of his positive cheerfulness was a front, is laid open to question by the following account of Colonel Sykes, an East India Company director. When Sykes visited him, James is reported to have said: "I am glad to see you, for it may be the last time." He indeed looked ill. Sykes replied: "I am sorry for that, for I had come to tell you that we had decided to offer you command of the expedition to Persia." "What! Persia? I'll go tomorrow," exclaimed James.[260] He was about to turn 53.

CHAPTER 11.

PERSIA.

Britain had become very concerned about Persia's friendship with Russia, and the potential threat to India from their combined forces. In 1837 a large Persian army, encouraged by Russia, invaded the west of Afghanistan and besieged the regional centre and stronghold town of Herat. Alarmed by this incursion, the British attempted to persuade the Persians to withdraw, and when that had no effect despatched a task force to the Persian Gulf and occupied Kharag Island close to the Persian coast. Supported by cruisers, this task force represented a real threat to the Persian mainland, and the Persians withdrew from Herat. But further attempts to occupy Herat were to follow, and in 1839 a token force from the British naval force landed at Bushire, where the Persians fired upon them. Re-embarking on the Wellesley they joined the garrison on Kharag. These incursions were followed by the resumption of diplomatic relations in 1841. A precondition to the withdrawal from Kharag was stipulated to be a commercial treaty, which was duly signed on October 11, 1841. Kharag was consequently evacuated, but relations between the two countries remained cool, to say the least. The British government recognised that the proximity of Russia and its size would mean that it would always hold greater sway over Persia, and indeed between 1842 and 1844 this relationship continued to expand.

In the aftermath of the Afghan disaster Britain needed to be at peace with Russia, and persuaded the Russians to replace confrontation with co-operation. In return for assistance in restraining Persia, Russia was rewarded by Britain not objecting to Russia consolidating its position on the Caspian

Sea, in Georgia and Caucasia. This co-operation worked well for a time: the two countries "managed" Persia and prevented any further incursions into Afghanistan. This happy state of affairs lasted until the onset of the Crimean War, which found the two countries at each other's throats.

By the end of 1853, relations between Persia and Britain were at a low ebb. Repeated threats by Persia to occupy Herat, the westernmost province of Afghanistan, provoked vigorous protests from the British. Whilst assuring the British that they had no intention of taking Herat, the Persians first attempted to woo the rulers at Herat with presents borne by emissaries, then when that did not work, mounted an expedition which succeeded in capturing Herat in October 1852, imprisoning several Afghan leaders. The Shah of Persia gave orders for Herat to be annexed, and appointed Syed Mohamed Khan governor of the province. Threats and protests by the British led to negotiations in which Persia undertook to withdraw, but managed to delay any action by continually changing the terms of the agreement. Finally a partial withdrawal took place.

The British representative in Teheran was treated with a distinct lack of the diplomatic niceties, and the Shah's communications with the British were less than civil. The tension and ill-feeling were such that the British envoy in the Persian capital was forced to withdraw to Baghdad. Although Persia would have liked to remain neutral in the conflict between Russia and Britain, the Shah was coming under great pressure from the Russians to march into eastern Turkey. The Indian government deterred Persia from entering the Crimean War by rapidly despatching a warship to the Persian Gulf, and re-occupying the small island of Kharag with a view to blockading the port of Bushire. As a consequence Persia remained neutral throughout the war. But the Russians encouraged the Shah to help them in Afghanistan by re-taking Herat. Believing the British still to be preoccupied in the Crimea, the Shah complied, and a military expedition of 9,000 men under the Shah's uncle, Prince Murad Mirza, retook Herat on October 25, 1856. But the Crimean War was soon to be over, settled by the Peace Treaty of Paris, and Britain could turn its attention towards this new challenge.

Negotiations commenced in Constantinople, with the British demanding that the Persians leave Herat, but without success. On November 22 the leading negotiator, Lord Stratford, issued an ultimatum requiring the vacation of Herat, a new treaty in which Persia would renounce any interest in Afghanistan and conclude a new treaty of commerce with England settling all outstanding financial disputes between the two countries. Meanwhile on November 1 the Governor-General of India, Lord Canning, issued three proclamations of war against Persia. The Persians rejected the Constantinople proposals, and turned to Paris, hoping to enlist France as an ally. The declaration of war was not popular back in an England tired of conflict and concerned at the cost of the Crimean War, and anti-war demonstrations were held in a number of cities.

Although Lord Canning was very reluctant to commit forces to Afghanistan again, the British could not afford to allow the Russians and Persians to keep Herat and use it as a foothold to further gains. The British had two options: either they could march through Afghanistan and lay siege to the fortress of Herat, or send a mixed naval and military force to the Persian Gulf as discouragement. Canning enquired whether the Afghan army under Dost Muhammad "could do anything effective towards relieving Herat – and if so, how, & with what aid." Dost Muhammad replied that the Afghan army would have to be raised to 50,000 men with 100 guns, half of which would have to be supplied by the British. Canning immediately abandoned the idea. He calculated that whilst the Afghan army would have been occupied with Herat, the rest of the frontier southwards would have been weakly defended, and the siege carried on by newly raised, undisciplined troops.[261] It was decided to follow the latter course, and move up the Persian Gulf. A substantial task force was assembled in India.

Within days of receiving the offer to assume command in Persia, James was on a ship bound for Aden, declaring himself fully cured, and explaining at length to Canning that he felt himself more needed in Persia than back in India, where affairs were more stable. On December 3, 1856, the Governor of Bombay announced that an expeditionary force was on its way to Persia. It comprised 5,670 fighting men, of whom 2,270 were Europeans, 3,750 followers, 1,150 horses, 430 bullocks and a fleet of 8 war-steamers of the Indian navy, 7 hired steamers and 30 sailing ships. James arrived in Bombay on December 22. On the 27th news reached him that General Stalker, in charge of the expeditionary force, had occupied the fort at Bushire on December 10 and two days later had dislodged the Persians from the stronghold of Reshire. But it was not until January 15, 1857, that James was able to leave Bombay. An administrative error delayed him: before leaving England he had been promoted to Lieutenant-General, but the rank was restricted to India. This meant that, technically, he was of lower rank than Major-General Stalker, and therefore in a rather awkward position if he assumed command of the expeditionary force. Confirmation of his rank outside India arrived on January 12. With him he took the formidable 78th Highlanders, who had been stationed at Pune. Formed in 1793 by Lord Seaforth, and known familiarly as the Seaforth Highlanders, this regiment had an illustrious history, having served with distinction in many of the hot spots of the British Empire.

By January 27, accompanied by reinforcements, James was in Bushire. He commanded a very strong expeditionary force. One of the divisions under his command was led by Brigadier-General Henry Havelock, of whom more will be heard later. He had recommended James as the ideal man to lead the expedition, and was delighted to be serving under him. The cavalry division was commanded by another man who was destined to serve with distinction in India: Brigadier-General John Jacob. He and James were to become close friends. Jacob's Scinde Irregular Horse corps was to become famous throughout the sub-continent. A stickler for detail, Jacob chose only the best men to serve in his regiment, and drilled them to near-perfection. Their discipline was legendary. Highly mobile, they could be ready to move within minutes, and later were to play an important part in maintaining tight control over the borders of Sind.

Stalker advised James that the Persians had fortified the river stronghold of Muhamra, and that storming it would be difficult and dangerous. His scouts also reported a Persian force close to the coast. The men ousted from Bushire had moved inland and joined up with five regiments assembled under Shujah'u-l'Maluk, reputed to be the best general in the Persian army, in an entrenched camp at Burasjun, forty-six miles from Bushire. His force now constituted a total of 8,450 cavalry and infantry, and he had orders to recover Bushire. James wrote to the Governor-General that it had become apparent that the enemy were concentrating a far greater force than it had hitherto been supposed they possibly could accumulate and it was evident to him that unless checked they would soon be in a position to attempt the recapture of Bushire.[262] He resolved to meet this threat immediately, lest it gather momentum and encourage the help of the local inhabitants. Securing Bushire with a detachment of troops reinforced by sailors from the warships, James marched inland 46 miles in 41 hours through swamps, driving sand, rain storms and freezing nights, reaching the enemy's position on the morning of February 5. This they found abandoned. Hearing of his approach, the Persians had retreated in some haste, leaving tents, equipment and some ammunition behind. There was nothing to keep the British at the deserted camp, so James turned round and prepared to return to Bushire. Shortly after midnight a sharp rattle of musketry alerted them to an attack from the rear, the skirmish lasting until dawn. When it became light James was able to observe between 6,000 and 7,000 Persians with some guns to the north-east in battle order. Artillery and cavalry were swiftly brought into position supported by two lines of infantry. The opening salvo from the British artillery inflicted heavy damage, and was followed by a successful cavalry charge. By 10 am the Persians were in full retreat leaving some 700 men dead in the field. James reported that the number of wounded could not be ascertained, but it must have been very large. The remainder fled in a disorganised state, generally throwing away their arms, which lay in the field in vast numbers, and only the lack of cavalry prevented their total destruction and the capture of the remaining guns.[263] James was not present throughout this battle, for whilst approaching the Persian position in pitch darkness the night before, his horse fell and rolled over on him. He was stunned, and recovered only in time to take his place at the head of his force shortly before the close of the action.

Within two days the force was back in Bushire, having endured another difficult march in incessant rain. In his report to the Governor-General he related: "As we were exposed, during the six days occupied in this expedition, to frequent heavy rains, the troops suffered much discomfort in bivouac, and still greater hardship on the march, owing to the heavy, spongy nature of the ground they traversed -all which they bore with admirable cheerfulness and fortitude. The shoes of the greater portion of the infantry were literally drawn off their feet in struggling through the mud; and those which remained were rendered so utterly unserviceable, that I have had to issue a new pair from the stores to every European and Native infantry soldier. This I have done gratis, and I trust it will meet with your lordship's approval."[264] It did, and the government reimbursed him with the cost.

This experience convinced James that it would be difficult to attack the Persians by pushing inland from Bushire. It would call upon all the military experience at his disposal, and a resolute commitment. On February 13 he wrote to Canning: "If war is to be carried further into the interior of Persia than Shiraz, it must be with European troops – the Sepoys holding the low country and posts of communication up to Shiraz."[265] He estimated the Persian force before them at 27,800 infantry and 2,000 horse with 85 guns. Canning replied: "Your announcement that for operations beyond Shiraz all the additional force must be European, has startled me. I do not question the soundness of the opinion – still less the prudence of acting upon it; but it transforms the war into one to be waged, not in part only, but whole and absolutely from England. The prospect of such a war must be looked steadily in the face by the Queen's Govt, and I much doubt whether they will consent to encounter it."[266]

It was agreed that to occupy the head of the Persian Gulf offered much better strategic options. Muhamra, 30 miles from the sea on the north bank of the river Karun, was an important city that was well stocked with supplies and transport, and could be reached by sea, avoiding the tribulation of arduous marches through inhospitable territory. If James could capture Muhamra, defended by 10,000 men, he would be well placed to move inland from there. But Bushire needed to remain secure, threatened as it was from inland, and James was forced to wait for reinforcements. The remainder of Havelock's Second Division had arrived on March 6, and they formed the advance contingent. News also came that Jacob's Sind Horse had embarked at Karachi on March 1. Satisfied that Bushire was secure, James set sail on March 18, leaving General Stalker to defend Bushire.

His progress was hampered by strong north-westerly gales. Shortly before James left, unfortunately General Stalker shot himself and was much mourned. It was said that he committed suicide "in mortification at his supersession by Outram."[267] James had been very aware of the effect that his supersession of Stalker would have on a proud soldier. On taking up his appointment James wrote to Edmonstone, Government Secretary in Calcutta: "I know not whether General Stalker would wish to continue with the army after I have taken command; but should he choose to do so, I might placed him in command of Bushire…Serving under me would be less galling, I hope, to Stalker, inasmuch as we have been intimate friends ever since we entered the service together, on the same day, thirty-seven years ago."[268] Later, on February 15, he wrote to Elphinstone: "From General Stalker I receive the most hearty support, and I have indeed every reason to be most grateful to him. Not content with seconding me in command, he insisted on my being his guest and sharing his tent."[269] James was thus not prepared for Stalker's suicide, and it remains a mystery. Curiously, two days later Commodore Ethersley, commanding the naval squadron, also committed suicide, leaving one to wonder whether there were other reasons for these eminent men to take their own lives. An officer of the 78th Highlanders, with the advance party, wrote: "No cause, save over-anxiety, and an oppressive sense of their respective responsibilities, could be assigned as a reason for their rash acts."[270]

Stalker's place was taken by Brigadier-General Jacob, accompanied by his famous Sind Horse. By March 21 the steamer Feroze, with James aboard, was at Shat- u-l-Arab, at the head of the Gulf, 174 miles from Bushire. Vessels which had preceded the Feroze had grounded on the bar at the mouth of the river, and it was only on the morning of March 26 that the force could move forward. The Persians, in anticipation of an attack, had been strengthening their position at Muhamra. Huge earthworks 20 feet thick and 18 feet high with casemented embrasures had been erected at the junction of the Karun River and Shat-u-l-Arab and heavy artillery installed there. The banks of the river were covered by dense date groves, providing excellent camouflage for riflemen. To reach Muhamra by water an attacking force would need to run the gauntlet of this barrage before landing troops. James decided that the only way of getting through was to take on the batteries, so he brought up four armed steamers and two sloops. The leading steamer was the Berenice, which carried the redoubtable 78th Highlanders and 200 Sappers. He was able to transport the troops in small steamers towing boats, a total of 4,886 soldiers, 400 horses and two artillery batteries. He and his staff had a lucky escape when the steamer they were on, the Feroze, grounded on a sandbank and was rammed by the following sailing ship, which had a shallower draft. The roof of the large deckhouse fell in, but only one officer was superficially injured, On entering the Euphrates they anchored three miles from the southernmost battery, opposite the village of Harteh. From there they concentrated their fire on the land batteries. So accurate was the navy's fire that within forty-five minutes only three or four of the enemy guns were still firing and soon after they succeeded in silencing the enemy artillery altogether. An eye-witness provided a graphic picture of the scene: "The ships, with ensigns flying from every mast-head, seemed decked for a holiday; the river glittering in the early sun-light, its dark date-fringed banks contrasting most effectively with the white canvas of the Falkland, which had loosened sails to get into closer action; the sulky-looking batteries just visible through the grey fleecy clouds which enveloped them; and groups of brightly-dressed horsemen flitting at intervals between the trees where they had their encampment."[271] By nine in the morning the rendezvous flag was flying from the Feroze's masthead, and the troops advanced in small steamers and boats.

The risks to the invading force were great. Crammed together on the decks of the boats the infantrymen presented easy targets from guns no more than a hundred yards away, but though considerable damage was done to the boats and ships (300 musket balls were counted to have lodged in the Feroze alone) there were surprisingly few casualties. The Persians withstood the attack for 3 hours, their embrasures being steadily reduced to rubble by the naval artillery. By the time James landed two miles above the northern point, to his disappointment he found that the Persian army had disappeared. Sixteen guns together with several magazines of ammunition, stores, tents and baggage, were all abandoned in their flight. Even uneaten meals were discovered abandoned in the haste to depart. The Persian army was estimated to be 13,000 strong. Lack of cavalry prevented James from pursuing the retreating army, although a party of Sind Irregular Horse, sent out to reconnoitre, came upon their rear guard retreating in good order, but leaving equipment strewn along the road. Muhamra was thus taken without a shot being fired by the army other than the artillery barrage, and this city did indeed prove to be well stocked. Ample supplies of flour, wheat and barley were found as well as some fine guns and copious quantities of ammunition. The British casualties totalled 10 men and one officer killed. The rapid success of this campaign came as something of a surprise to Lord Elphinstone in Bombay. He had been advised by the captain of a French frigate that the Persian batteries were so formidable that the British must expect to lose two or three ships in any attack! Indeed, as they sailed up river the fire from the banks had been heavy, but the ships were well protected and casualties were minimal. James narrowly escaped being hit when a musket ball hit the hookah in front of him.

The Persian army retreated to Ahwaz, 100 miles upstream. James lost no time in pursuing them. An armed flotilla of three small steamers, the Comet, Planet and Assyria, three gunboats and 300 British infantry moved up the river with instructions to ascertain the position. If the Persians showed signs of making a stand at Ahwaz, the flotilla was to return without taking them on, but if they showed signs of retreating, the party was to land and destroy magazines and stores. James shrewdly reckoned that the Persians, having fled from Muhamra, might see the flotilla as an advance party of the main force, and this was precisely what happened. The force reached Omeira on March 31, hoping to prevent the Persians becoming entrenched at Ahwaz, but they learnt there to their disappointment that the enemy had reached Ahwaz, and were busy digging in on the right bank of the river, opposite the town. At 10 a.m. on April 1 the British landed on the left bank near the town of Ahwaz. Surprisingly it was defended by a mere 500 men and 30 horse, and they had no trouble taking the town and destroying the military stores. Observing Ahwaz to be lost, and believing as James had hoped that this was the advance guard of a much bigger British force, the Persian army decamped in some haste. Between 9,000 and 10,000 men had retreated in the face of 300! The effect on the local inhabitants of seeing such a small force defeat the might of the Persian army with guns and cavalry in abundance, was profound.

The war was effectively at an end. On the day the expedition returned to Muhamra from Ahwaz James received news that peace with Persia had been concluded on March 4. The terms of the treaty were extremely favourable to the British: the Shah of Persia renounced all claim of sovereignty over Herat or any other Afghan province, and in future England was to act as friendly mediator over any quarrel between Persia and Afghanistan. In a letter written on April 23 James was confident of total victory. He complained that the peace tied his hands, and saved the Prince's army from unconditional capitulation, which must have followed the advance to Ahwaz (if not to Shuster itself). He believed that the inhabitants of Shuster and Dizphool would probably have risen against their oppressors at the approach of the British as they had scarcely any musket ammunition left with which to defend themselves.[272]

To have left Persia immediately would have been impolitic: the British needed to see that the terms of the treaty were being adhered to, and that the Persians were serious about peace. Muhamra was not the most healthy place to stay, given the searing heat and primitive living conditions, but a survey showed it to be the best available. James was occupied with making living conditions as pleasant as possible for his troops. In addition to adequate quarters, he brought in mosquito nets, books and games, and improved the food provisions. They expected to be there for at least three months, but in April instructions arrived from Bombay summoning back as many European troops as could be spared. Leaving Colonel Jacob in command with a small garrison at Bushire, satisfied that the Persians were sufficiently convinced of the British military superiority not to provoke more conflict, James made arrangements for his army to return to India, and finally left Persia on June 17, reaching Bombay on the 26th. Such was his reputation and popularity that, unbeknown to him, the 78th Highlanders, on leaving Muhamra, organised a special celebration to cheer their commander as they departed.

On July 11 Lord Clarendon wrote to James from the Foreign Office in London conveying the Queen's approval of "the zeal, judgment, and ability which you have shown throughout the whole of the operations"[273]and conferring upon him the Grand Cross of the Bath. The Indian authorities were quick to endorse these plaudits. The Times published an article drawing attention to what had been achieved: "We have struck a blow at Persia; we have invaded her territory; we have evidently frightened her out of her wits, and let her know what we can do….The expedition has done its own work – written its own peace; and happily some of its text is much more recent than that of the treaty before us….Sir James Outram has been the real negotiator, and no one can mistake or forget what he means."

The campaign had been very demanding physically, and James would have been entitled, after his long and debilitating illness, to enjoy his success in a relaxing post somewhere. But he was about to face his sternest challenge yet.

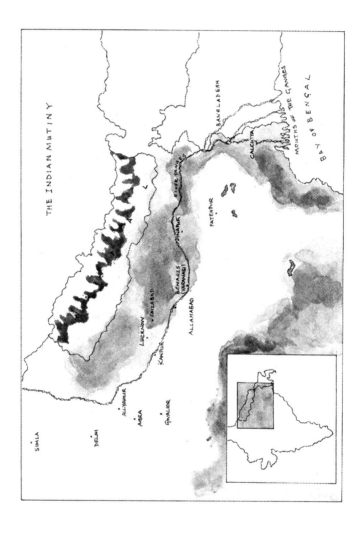

CHAPTER 12.

THE INDIAN MUTINY.

The reason that the troops had been recalled to India so rapidly became immediately evident, for in their absence what the British were to call the Indian Mutiny had erupted. The Indians still object to the term. The idealists see it as the first stirrings of the independence movement that was to lead to freedom after the Second World War. It can hardly be called that, bearing in mind that the uprising was confined to only part of India, and the remainder of the country remained calm, with the Indian regiments staunchly loyal to their British officers. But it was more than merely a handful of regiments rebelling. It quickly spread to the surrounding countryside, with a wide diversity of men joining in. Many of the worst atrocities were performed by unruly mobs that were not part of the army.

The causes of this sudden uprising were complex. Ostensibly the trigger point was the introduction to the Indian Army of the new Enfield rifle, which used waxed cartridges. These cartridges were rumoured to have been coated with pigs' fat. Riflemen were required to tear the waxed paper with their teeth, and Muslims refused to touch pigs' fat with their lips, and therefore were not prepared to use the cartridges. Their British officers insisted the cartridges were safe. The rank and file, their fears stoked by trouble-makers that spread the rumour that it was all a plot to break their religious beliefs, stubbornly resisted. There was a danger that examples would be made of soldiers refusing to use the cartridges.

There were many other reasons for unrest and ferment, probably one of the most serious being the activities of Christian missionaries, whose zeal in attempting to convert the natives was much resented, and seen as a threat to traditional religion and values. Missionary work in India was not a late development. As early as 1792 Charles Grant, whose son was to become President of the Court of Directors, saw missionary work as social rather than theological. He spoke of the need for moral improvement, in which context Christianity would be very useful to the Indians. He and like-minded Evangelists hoped for the rapid transformation of Indian society, whose deficiencies they attributed to immaturity.[274] In a tract written that year he noted: "Upon the whole...we cannot avoid recognizing in the people of Hindostan a race of men lamentably degenerate and base, retaining but a feeble sense of moral obligation."[275] As the nineteenth century progressed, British attitudes changed. From being liberal and laissez-faire about Indian society, more strongly–held opinions emerged. There was widespread repugnance at the alien practices of sati (the tradition whereby bereaved wives were required to have their lives ended) and female child killing, and the perceived depravity practised in the rulers' courts. Disapproval of child marriages was considered by the Indians interference in the religion to which they strongly adhered. The assertive Christians saw it as their duty to convert these barbarians, and set about their task aggressively. This initially provoked bewilderment among Indians, then resentment, and finally fear and anger. The missionaries were suspected of aiming to destroy the caste system, and wishing to bring Indians within a uniform Christian ethics system.

It is also likely that in such a vast country local discontent and grudges took diverse forms, and were harnessed under the promptings of the ringleaders into rebellion. Although the mutiny has been widely portrayed as an uprising by the sepoys of the Bengal Army, the rebellion was more widespread and popular than that. Loss of lands, power and authority turned local rulers against the British. In addition the English East India Company had used its political power to erode the indigenous Indian economy. The developments they introduced – railways, the telegraph, Western education – created suspicion in the minds of the masses, who saw these as a means to convert them to Christianity. Finally, the administrative system was mistrusted, and refusal to consider Indians for positions of authority and trust was resented.

Several commentators have remarked upon the fact that the British were caught by surprise when the uprising occurred. They should not have been. There had been a number of small reactions in isolated barracks for decades previous to 1857. Often the cause was pay. Although many of the sepoys came from good families of high caste, they were paid a pittance. They received between 7 and 9 Rupees per month, out of which they had to pay for food, uniform and transport of baggage. At times when the Company's finances were strained, attempts were made to reduce pay, and that caused resentment and resistance. 1857 was one of those occasions.

The uprising came as no surprise to James, who had been concerned for some time, particularly with the discipline of the Bengal army. On April 27, 1857 he wrote to Lord Elphinstone: "The mutinous spirit so extensively displayed in the Bengal army is a very serious matter, and is the consequence of the faulty system of its organisation, so different from that of Bombay, where such insubordination is scarcely possible; for with us, the intermediate tie between the European officers and the men – i.e. the native officers – is a loyal efficient body, selected for their superior ability and gratefully attached to their officers in consequence. Their superior ability naturally exercises a wholesome influence over the men, among whom no mutinous spirit could be engendered without their knowledge, and the exertion of their influence to counteract it; whereas, the seniority system of the Bengal army supplies neither able nor influential native officers - old imbeciles merely, possessing no control over the men, and owing no gratitude to their officers, or to the Government, for a position which is merely the result of seniority in the service. I pointed this out to Lord Dalhousie once, who told me he had seriously considered the matter, and had consulted some of the highest officers of the Bengal army, who, one and all, deprecated any attempt to change the system, as a dangerous innovation. Whatever the danger, it should be incurred, the change being gradually introduced; for, as at present constituted, the Bengal army never can be depended on." [276]

James, with more thought, broadened his reasoning in a letter to Dalhousie dated March 27, 1858, when the rebellion had almost run its course, and he was in Lucknow: "The abolition of suttee, the abolition of infanticide, the introduction of vaccination, the law to legalise the remarriage of Hindu widows, the promulgation through our colleges of the facts of astronomy, geology, etc., so opposed to the priestly cosmogonies of the country, the dissections practised in our medical schools, the attempts to establish female seminaries, and to elevate the moral and social position of the female sex, with many other of our efforts to do good were pressed upon the attention of the army and the masses as so many deliberate assaults on the outworks both of Mahomedism and of Hinduism. And the simple, superstitious, credulous Sepoys were told that the time was rapidly approaching when the grand coup was to be struck – when by some piece of Jadu [magic] the accursed Christians, whose sorceries enabled them to communicate in a few minutes between Lahore and Calcutta, through the medium of a mysterious wire, would at once uncaste the whole Hindu population and outrage all their holiest traditions and feelings. These efforts to prepare the way for a military mutiny and a popular insurrection were much aided by the unsettled state of the public mind, which had been for some time looking forward with vague expectancy to some commotion in which a Saviour, or Avatar, would appear. Such I believe to have been the elements of the storm, and I cannot but regard the greased cartridges as the means through which Providence was pleased to baffle the conspiracy. They precipitated the mutiny before it had been thoroughly organised, and before adequate arrangements had been made for making the mutiny a first step in a popular insurrection. We hear much of the annexation policy of Lord Dalhousie, and more especially the annexation of Oudh having caused the mutiny. To my apprehension all the facts of the case are utterly opposed to such an hypothesis."[277]

John Lawrence was on record as agreeing with this assessment. Nevertheless it is clear that the revolt centred on Oudh, and that among the most notorious leaders were the taluqdars who had been deprived of their power and lands by the annexation. In particular a deep sense of grievance had built up among the men from Oudh and Bihar who formed the mainstay of the Bengal army. Sent on distant, dangerous missions for inadequate remuneration and no advancement, these men felt betrayed and resentful. A large proportion of this army was of high-caste origin, Brahmins and Rajputs unused to subordination. Meanwhile the successful expansion of empire had fostered over-confidence among the British, who failed to notice the signs of disaffection in their previously devoted native regiments.

There was no doubting the breadth and seriousness of the uprising. Starting on May 10, 1857 in Meerut, where Indian soldiers killed all their British officers, it rapidly spread. Delhi was seized. The savagery was gruesome; wherever there were British enclaves the inhabitants were put to the sword, with no man, woman or child spared. There were stories of great gallantry, and many sepoys attempted to remain loyal to their regiments and officers, only to be overwhelmed by the bloody frenzy gripping the mutineers. Unprepared for the violence, uncomprehending in their assessment, the British officers could not believe that their loyal soldiers, who hitherto had been seen as children in a large collective family led by their officers, could betray them so. This led to a delayed response, and placed British rule in India in serious jeopardy.

At this point Lord Canning cabled Lord Elphinstone: "Write to Sir James Outram, that I wish him to return to India immediately, and the same to General Jacob – we want all our best men here." His personal reminiscences at the time record: "Outram's arrival was a godsend. There was not a man to whom I could with any approach of confidence entrust the command in Bengal and the Central Province."[278] James reached Bombay on June 26, where there was an urgent summons for him to travel on to Calcutta. While in Bombay he studied the progress and nature of the rebellion in some detail. It was of vital importance that it did not spread to the Bombay Presidency. The Bombay government proposed to increase the strength of its native regiments in readiness. James' official letter to Elphinstone recommended that instead two supernumerary companies should be raised for each regiment. This would provide the opportunity to promote native commissioned and non-commissioned officers, rewarding loyalty and good service, and consolidating their allegiance.

James reached Calcutta on August 1, where he met Canning. The Governor-General had thought long and hard about how to use James's skills to best effect. He contemplated appointing him to his Council, but concluded he would be best used in the field, and put him in charge of the country between Calcutta and Lucknow. He was appointed to the command of the Dinapur and Kanpur divisions. Whilst in Calcutta he stayed at the Governor-General's Residence, where Lady Canning was unimpressed: "The steamer arrived and brought Sir J. Outram…We have squeezed him into the house by Dunkeld giving up his sitting room ….He is a very common looking little dark Jewish bearded man, with a desponding slow hesitating manner, very unlike descriptions – or rather the idea raised in one's mind by the old Bombay name the 'Bayard of the East', and the Bombay saying of this year 'a fox is a fool and a lion a coward by the side of Sir J.O.' He never can have done things Sir C. Napier accuses him of, but he is not the least my idea of a hero."[279] James had never been considered to be Jewish before!

One of the prime targets for the mutineers was Lucknow. The British annexation of the Kingdom of Oudh was bitterly resented, both by the taluqdars and the sepoys. Oudh was a major recruiting source for the Bengal army, which was now in widespread mutiny, and Lucknow was the principal city. James's successor there, Coverley Jackson, although an able administrator, had a violent temper. He quarrelled with his subordinates and constantly complained of them to the Governor-General, and communicated less and less of the important affairs of the province. Finally Canning's patience gave out and he was replaced with Sir Henry Lawrence, a most fortunate choice given the turbulence that was about to test the province. The importance to the mutineers of Lucknow was recognised by Lawrence, who swiftly took measures to protect his position in the Residency, which he prepared to resist a siege. Huge stores of provisions were stockpiled, and the garrison church converted into a granary. On June 7 Lawrence summoned all the women and children in the Division, which included the out-posts, into the Residency. As discipline broke down across the territory, those men who could find their way back to Lucknow followed.

It was not long before violence erupted in Lucknow. The 7th Oudh Irregular Infantry refused to bite their cartridges, and threatened to kill their officers. Prompt action by Lawrence, who charged them with European troops, forced some to flee and the others to lay down their arms, but although order and security was restored to the Residency, it soon came under siege. Thousands of Muslims assembled outside their mosques and marched through Lucknow, looking for Christians to attack. Any British residents who lived and remained outside the walls of the Residency quickly moved into the heavily fortified compound, which became the focal point of conflict.

Another major city with a strong British military presence also came under siege at this time. Kanpur, with a population of 60,000, was situated on the trunk road between Delhi and Benares and on the banks of the Ganges, providing a port navigable from Calcutta a thousand miles away. It was a vital link in the chain of British-occupied locations. Help was urgently needed, as it was unlikely that the garrison there could hold out for long against overwhelming opposition. Unlike Lucknow, Kanpur did not have a fortified Residence to shelter the defenders. When the Indian soldiers did mutiny there on June 6, therefore, the British garrison was unusually vulnerable.

At Allahabad, 120 miles away, Brigadier-General Henry Havelock, back from Persia, prepared to march to the relief of Kanpur, which stood between Allahabad and Lucknow, and needed to be secured before he could advance to Lucknow. He commanded a European army of only 1,200, plus 150 Sikhs and a couple of troops of irregular native cavalry, and the road to Kanpur was reported to be strongly defended by the mutineers. Havelock had served in India for 34 years, and had a distinguished military record, notably while under the command of James in Persia. But the fact that he had been granted his first command at the age of 62 suggested that he was not that highly thought of by his superiors. An intensely religious man who had embraced the Baptist faith, he had a reputation for being stern and unbending, and somewhat cautious. But on this occasion he was conscious of the need for urgency, and on July 6 he left Allahabad in torrential rain. An advance party under the command of Major Renaud reported back that the enemy was moving towards Havelock in great strength, and after four days the two armies made their first encounter, at Fatehpur. Although the fighting was fierce and the mutineers vastly outnumbered Havelock's force, they were soon routed and swept before the advancing British. At each town along the road the scene was repeated: large numbers of mutineers would resist the advance but would break and flee in the face of determined infantry and accurate artillery. The 78th Highlanders once again distinguished themselves by the ferocity of their fighting and their pride, although most of the British soldiers fought in a semi-inebriated state after copious supplies of rum were provided. When confronted by the rebels in a strong position in one of the villages with a heavy gun which resisted initial attempts to silence it, Havelock recalled: "The 78th were ordered to charge and take the gun. I never saw anything so fine. The men went on, with sloped arms, like a wall; till within a hundred yards not a shot was fired. At the word 'Charge' they broke just like an eager pack of hounds. And the village was taken in an instant."

Finally Havelock reached the outskirts of Kanpur on the 17th, to be faced by a local warlord, Nana Sahib, with a force of 5,000 and eight guns drawn up in crescent shape outside the city. Nana Sahib was the adopted son of Peshwar Bajirao II, the Maratha ruler, who had lost power and prestige under British rule. A cavalry contingent was sent forward to simulate a frontal attack on the mutineers, while the main body of infantry circled through a grove of mango trees to attack from the left flank. The ploy was successful and the enemy was soon in retreat, but not without some stiff resistance. A long day finally came to an end with the British force on the edge of the Kanpur maidan, and the enemy fleeing. Kanpur had been won.

But Havelock was too late to save the unfortunate garrison there. Among the many stories of atrocities committed during the Mutiny, the siege of Kanpur, stands out as a tale of particular horror. The large British garrison under the command of the ageing Major-General Sir Hugh Massy Wheeler had not believed that the four Indian regiments there numbering in all about 3,000 men would cause any trouble. Consequently no serious preparations had been made to resist a mutiny. When these soldiers mutinied, they were quickly joined by local inhabitants and the forces of Nana Sahib. For nearly three weeks the British garrison, protected only by rather pathetic earthworks hastily thrown up, resisted a horrific pounding from the surrounding rebels. On June 25, with little hope of a relieving force reaching them in time and resistance all but expended, with considerable casualties, Wheeler agreed to surrender to Nana Sahib on the basis that the remaining British would be allowed to leave unharmed by boat. However once they were embarked on the river the treacherous rebels opened fire, killing most of them, including Wheeler. Only a very few escaped to tell the tale. Worse still, surviving women and children were rounded up and incarcerated in cells within Nana Sahib's residence. They were slaughtered later in particularly gruesome circumstances, leading to rumours of atrocities. This led to blood-lust among the British forces intent on avenging their countryfolk. Discovering the dreadful truth about the betrayal of Wheeler and the murder of the women and children, the relieving force took harsh revenge on the townsfolk and any rebels they could lay their hands on.

On July 22 Havelock began to move his force across the Ganges in preparation for a march on Lucknow. Troops and supplies were ferried across in small boats, in torrential rain. This operation took 5 days to complete. Soon the already meagre force was diminished by the ravages of cholera and dysentery. Fighting was fierce, with pockets of mutineers resisting Havelock's progress all the way. Casualties mounted, with no reinforcements imminent and with only 600 effective European troops left, Havelock was forced to turn back. On August 13 he recrossed the Ganges and settled down to await the promised reinforcements. The troops available to Havelock could barely defend Kanpur, and the country between the two cities of Kanpur and Lucknow was in the hands of the mutineers. The hard-pressed garrison at Delhi had sent urgent requests for help, while a strong army of 5,000 mutineers with twenty or thirty guns at Gwalior threatened both Kanpur and Lucknow. The Residency at Lucknow continued to hold out, but this position was becoming critical. Should this fall, the mutinous resources released would spread to other key points, including Allahabad and Benares [now Varanasi], on the Ganges.

On August 6 James started up the Ganges, accompanied by Colonel Robert Napier of the Bengal Engineers, who acted as his military secretary and chief of staff. James wrote to Elphinstone that he took up a mountain train, but that no artillerymen were to be had, and therefore he must extemporise a crew for the guns as best he could from among the sailors and soldiers.[280] James had at his disposal only two incomplete regiments, together with Havelock's men near Kanpur. James mustered those men who could (reluctantly) be released from stations en route to Kanpur. He proposed to ferry as many as he could up the river by steamers, towing "flats." The monsoon season was at is height and the Ganges was flowing strongly down towards the sea, so progress was likely to be slow. Progress was further hampered by civil authorities that, concerned with their own problems and unable to see the larger picture, diverted resources to their own needs along the way. Quite apart from the need to relieve the besieged cities, James was conscious that the ships he was using were urgently required back in Calcutta. He determined to land at Benares and proceed by land from there, joining up with Havelock at Kanpur. He let it be known that his intention was to continue beyond Benares by river, so that any leaks in intelligence would mislead the enemy. This misinformation was also conveyed to Havelock, who believed that James intended to relieve Lucknow from Faizabad. Kanpur was coming under increasing pressure, and may have to be abandoned. Havelock was in urgent need of help.

With so many problems to overcome, James had little time for personal considerations, but he was very concerned about his family. His wife and son had been at Allyghur when the mutiny occurred, and it was from there that she wrote to him on May 19: "We are all quiet and safe here, and our Sepoys are behaving admirably, though the state of excitement, both amongst natives and Europeans is still very great, and we feel very sad and weary. Frank was ordered out with an escort to drive back some of the Delhi villagers who had come to plunder in the district, and I am thankful to say that they immediately went off, and Frank returns, D.V., tomorrow morning. He showed much of his father in his behaviour on the occasion, and was full of vigour and anxiety for the duty…. Two nights ago, just when we were going to bed, the servants came in and said a fire had broken out in the lines. This of course was terrible news and kept us so anxious all night (though it proved only to be an empty bungalow) that I came over yesterday to the Judge's family and am now with them."[281] But her reassurance was short-lived. On June 2 she wrote to James's mother: "Our Sepoys at Allyghur followed the general example and mutinied, and we had to fly for our lives, leaving everything to be burnt and destroyed. I had to mount up behind Frank on horseback, and twice tumbled on my head, then had to run without my shoes. My feet were fearfully skinned." She reached Agra fort in safety, and wrote from there: "This place is comparatively safe, unless matters get worse and worse. The panic is dreadful, people flock to houses which are best defended and I am now in a bungalow next the Barracks, without carpet or mat, and scarcely any furniture, with three ladies and a child sleeping in the same room and the gentlemen in the next. We eat, dress, and all, in one room, and the heat, anxiety (for every night attacks are expected) are very wearing."[282]

A month later Margaret wrote again to James that they remained safe at Agra, although not without regular alarms.

On one such occasion Frank "buckled on sword and pistols, and said he would ride to Cantonments (where the soldiers and gentlemen were, the women being all here) and see what was going on. He had not been gone long when the alarm was given and the troops ordered out. We heard nothing of what was going on till about 3 o'clock, when cannon commenced. The action was visible from the high bastions, but I could not go in the sun; indeed I was too miserable. The firing continued without the least cessation for an hour, then there was a little lull, and it began again, and so on till a retreat was sounded. The anxiety particularly after this was intense, wounded men pouring in, and it was not till the last that I heard Frank was safe, with a slight wound. Upwards of a hundred, out of six hundred, were wounded, and forty-six killed."[283]

Slow but steady progress was made up the Ganges. James was at Dinapur on August 19, preoccupied with deploying his limited forces. He needed to balance the urgency of moving troops up to Kanpur as quickly as possible with the demands of local garrisons along the way, who were mindful of protecting their own positions. On August 20 he wrote: "As I am resolved to make my way to Lucknow from Benares, through Jaunpore, passing up between the Goomtee and the Sye….I must collect all the few Europeans that can be rendered available, and shall be obliged, therefore, to withdraw the 100 men of the 90th left at Buxar, which town must hold its own until the Madras Regiment comes up (due in a week at furthest, I should think)….Please don't let out my proposed plan of advance on Lucknow, it being an object to make it believed I purpose taking the Faizabad route."[284] The 90th Regiment was already ahead of him, going to Benares, but unaccountably was recalled and met James coming up the river. An epidemic of cholera on board delayed progress for a further twenty-four hours as it was necessary to disembark the men while the boats were fumigated and cleansed.

By August 28 James was at Benares, recognising that a direct route to Lucknow from there would be quickest but most hazardous, and would leave Havelock exposed at Kanpur. The distance from Benares to Lucknow was 150 miles, and the Commander-in-Chief in Calcutta wrote to James pointing out the difficulties of taking that route, which was blocked by several bands of mutineers. Havelock was considering a retreat to Allahabad, and the suggestion was made that should James contemplate joining Havelock at Kanpur their combined force may be strong enough to force a way through to Lucknow. The news that Havelock was under pressure accelerated the movement of troops in the advance. With the briefest of rests, James pushed on.

James reached Allahabad on September 1. He was dismayed by the chaos he found. He drew this to the attention of Canning: "...the very disorganised state of the Allahabad, Tuttehpore and Kanpur districts...which appear, as far as I can learn, to be almost without any civil Government, beyond the immediate influence of the garrisons of Allahabad and Kanpur."[285] James, although preoccupied with the logistics of his march, had noted that the attitudes of the local population varied greatly as he passed through. He wrote a thoughtful letter to Lord Canning on September 13, addressing the treatment of these locals, and suggesting that "the time has arrived, I think, for your Lordship to decide how the native soldiery who are committed to no overt act of atrocity, are to be dealt with."[286] He pointed out that many of the native soldiers had not committed acts of atrocity, but were nevertheless fearful of the British reaction. Many had been pressed into service by the mutineers, but had returned to their villages peacefully when confronted. He went on: "Unless these men receive an assurance that they will remain in our service, with the present pay and privileges, their minds will naturally be imbued with doubts as to their future fate, rendering them yet liable to seduction.....
Might it not my Lord, now be proclaimed, that upwards of 4

months having elapsed since the outburst of the rebellion, the Government is satisfied that those regiments which thro' so long a period have withstood the menace and temptations by which they have been incessantly assailed by their disaffected comrades, are proved to be true and trustworthy servants of Government...that those regiments will be retained in the service, with all the privileges and advantages heretofore enjoyed, and be rewarded for their fidelity... that Government has made this announcement now that all India is convinced of the speedy re-establishment of its power." He went further, and proposed that those sepoys who had deserted, but could prove that they were not actively involved in the rebellion, should be interviewed and re-enrolled if found to be innocent. James proposed that such a board for interviews be set up in Fatehpur, and that the Hindus, who so far had shown more moderation than the Muslims, be encouraged to take the side of the British. Amid the violence and retribution which was to follow, the blood-lust of the British intent on indiscriminately avenging the slaughter of innocent women and children, James' thoughtful appraisal of the actual situation, and the direction to be taken to secure the future, shines out like a beacon.

The garrison at Allahabad was reduced to the minimum in order to strengthen James' contingent, and 1,448 men set out for the 127 mile march to Kanpur. James was hoping that further reinforcements, already embarked upon the Ganges from Calcutta, would catch up with them, for the reports reaching him were of very large numbers of mutineers in his way. Progress was again slow; James wrote: "The 90th having been cooped up on board ship and in river boats for five months past, is quite unequal to double marches, I find, a very large proportion being knocked up by this first march of fourteen miles."[287] He was concerned that they would not be fit to fight on reaching Kanpur: "I propose...to pursue the ordinary ten marches to Kanpur, which will delay this detachment's arrival at Kanpur till the 15th, instead of the 11th, as I proposed."[288] Havelock agreed.

The progress of the relief force was being closely followed in England, but not without criticism. The press reflected impatience at the time being taken to move towards Lucknow, and the Globe accused James of vacillation. Dalhousie, in retirement in Edinburgh, reflected: "I don't know how to get 'The Globe.' But as to Outram - his past history would certainly negative a charge of vacillation. At Lucknow in 55-56 he was nervous beforehand but he did not vacillate when the time for action came. A year may have changed him - and if he is vacillating now, he must have changed in that time."[289]

At Kalogan on September 9 James heard from Havelock that the Residency at Lucknow was hard pressed, with provisions only until the 28th. James replied that he was confident they could reach Lucknow by then, despite a high number of casualties from the 90th Regiment due to illness and fatigue. "We are getting better, as the 90th grow more accustomed to their shore legs."[290] But before the relieving force could reach Lucknow, they had to clear the way to Kanpur. James received news that some 400 mutineers were occupying the opposite bank of the river to where he was, and threatening his flank. So he despatched Major Eyre with 100 Europeans, mounted on elephants, with two guns, to confront them. They were joined at a neighbouring village by a squadron of Irregulars. In fact the number of the enemy had been significantly understated, but Eyre succeeded in driving them into the river and all but annihilating them.

When James learnt that he would be joining Havelock, he was faced with a problem of protocol. He was still the man in overall charge of the province of Oudh despite his absence in Persia, and he outranked Havelock. Indeed, Havelock learned from the Gazette of August 5 of the appointment of James to the military command of the united Dinapore and Cawnpore Divisions.[291] But Havelock was the commanding officer in the field, and had been fighting there for some time. For James to take over would be awkward, and he felt the honour of relieving Lucknow should go to Havelock. He immediately announced that he had no intention of superseding Havelock, would waive his rank for the occasion and accompany Havelock to Lucknow in the civil capacity of Chief Commissioner of Oudh, tendering his military services as a volunteer. This prompted the Governor-General to write in the warmest terms of the "truly handsome and generous proposal."[292] For indeed it was just that. James' journal shows that he believed that, with the relief of Lucknow and the fall of Delhi, the mutiny would be all but over. He believed that this military campaign would be the last significant action he would see. Therefore any further honours coming his way would have to be earned on this campaign, and he was unlikely to gain significantly if he was not the Commander-in-Chief. Moreover, the treasury of the Residence at Lucknow was likely to be declared prize-money. It amounted to a considerable sum – between 23 and 32 lakhs of Rupees – but his share as a civil volunteer would be very small. Thus, he wrote, he was depriving himself not only of all honours but "of the only means of support for the declining years of a life the chequered vicissitudes of which have afforded no opportunity of making any provision for the requirements of age."[293] An Indian historian, R.C.Majumdar, lends his voice to the praise of James' gesture "with his characteristic magnanimity which is unparalleled in the military history."[294] Dalhousie reflected: "You will remember that I always expressed a conviction that Outram would not supersede Havelock. His conduct has been generous, chivalrous, radiant with true nobility, but only like himself…..Outram was actually appointed to the command of the Cawnpore and Dinapore divisions, including Oudh. He waived that military rank and served under his own Brigadier. Though General of Division and Chief Commissioner for Oudh, he served under him as a simple trooper, and resigned to him all the public honour and all the exquisite personal pleasure of rescuing the glorious band at Lucknow. A more magnanimous act was never done."[295]

As James approached Kanpur, the correspondence between him and Havelock increased. Havelock occupied the right bank of the Ganges; to move on Lucknow he would need to take control of the left bank. The enemy was building up its strength on the left bank by adding men and guns. James wrote that if Havelock could have a bridge in place by the time he arrived, they would lose no time on the march towards Lucknow. "I quite agree with you in thinking our surest and best plan is …for me to cross the Ganges some miles below Kanpur, march up the opposite bank, and turn the enemy's entrenchments, while you cross by the bridge thrown directly over to the islands."[296] The building of the bridge was more difficult than James envisaged, for the ground was marshy and no obvious crossing point presented itself. Enemy troops were seen to be moving down the bank in anticipation of this crossing as Havelock commenced bridge-building. The first stage was to establish a bridge to an island in mid-stream, which could be occupied and defended while the remainder of the river, the dangerous part, was bridged. This was achieved without mishap in three days.

On September 14, having heard of Havelock's success in bridging the Ganges, James changed his plans. "As little or no opposition to your crossing is now expected, the detour I proposed to make at the opposite bank to take the enemy's works in reverse, may be unnecessary; and as the Oudh side is said to be a swamp, it is as well to avoid the attempt to operate that way…I shall, therefore…join you at Kanpur."[297] Although he was to hand over command to Havelock when they met, James could not resist adding detailed advice on how the advancing columns should be organised! James reached Kanpur on September 16, and wrote to Colonel Inglis, commanding Lucknow: "All the troops have now come up – the bridge getting ready, and no time will be lost. Cannot of course fix the exact day."[298] He advised against the Lucknow garrison becoming over-confident and carrying out raids as "it is not unlikely the enemy may have a strong body concealed near you, ready to make a rush upon your works in the expectation that they may be left weakly guarded, as their last chance of getting at you."[299] In fact he had discovered to his dismay that the bridge was not yet complete, reaching only to the island in mid-stream. There was still much to do before Lucknow could be relieved.

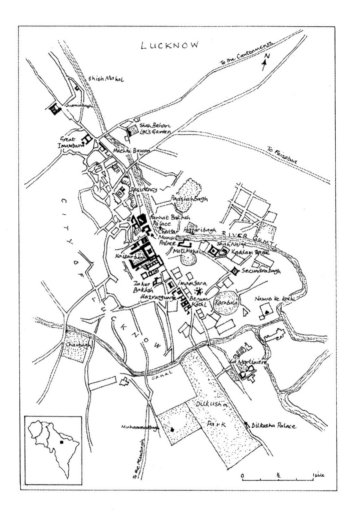

CHAPTER 13.

THE RELIEF OF LUCKNOW.

From the start the relationship between Havelock and James did not run smoothly. A sign of this can be seen in James' letter to the Governor-General's Military Secretary dated September 17: "Lest the newspapers should misrepresent the fact of a body of troops, which Havelock had put in orders to cross the river yesterday morning, having been countermanded after my arrival...as an interference on my part involving delay in our advance, I beg you will have the kindness to explain to Lord Canning and Sir Colin Campbell what are the real facts of the case."[300] Havelock had proposed constructing a boat bridge over which troops and guns would be transported to protect the construction of the permanent bridge from the island. James felt that without shelter in the swamp the men there would be vulnerable to enemy fire, and that it would be better to hold them back while the bridge was completed and only deploy them should the bridge come under attack. Havelock agreed, saying this was his original plan but that he had been overruled by the engineers. In a letter to the Governor-General dated September 18 James expressed some frustration at the slow progress: "I regret to say, bridging the Ganges has proved a more tedious work than I was led to expect. Instead of being completed in one day, as the engineer officers hoped, this is the third since its commencement; and it cannot be completed till the evening, if then."[301] The two men were, temperamentally, opposites. Havelock was cautious, conservative, slow to action; James, as we have seen, was impetuous, daring, sometimes foolhardy.

Having gained control of the island, Havelock built his bridge to the left bank without resistance, the enemy retreating without much of a fight. The crossing of his troops ensued, and heavy guns and baggage also moved across. This enabled the two forces to combine in their thrust towards Lucknow. By September 20 James was camped on the left bank of the Ganges. His first act on entering the province of Oudh was to issue a proclamation offering clemency to anyone who lay down their arms and joined the British. He explained this to the Governor-General: "Under any circumstances, such an intimation would [open] the door to those who are not irretrievably committed beyond the pale of mercy; but it is particularly called for at this juncture, to counteract the effect of the strenuous endeavours now being exerted at Lucknow by the rebel leaders, to draw all classes to their cause by representing that all who have in any way borne arms against the British are equally certain to meet the fate we award to the mutineers who fall into our hands; consequently that nothing is left for them but war to the death against the English."[302]

The army which advanced into Oudh numbered 3,179 soldiers in total. Of these the cavalry numbered 109, the artillery 282, Sikh infantry 341 and Native Irregular Cavalry 59. The remaining 2,388 were European infantry. The rainy season was not yet over, and they marched in a persistent downpour through flooded fields. On the third day, at Mangalwar they encountered a vast horde of mutineers in a strong position, supported by twelve guns. Without hesitation, giving the enemy no time to prepare, the British attacked, James to the fore. Within minutes their enemy was put to flight, and pursued along the road to Bashiratganj. James reported to the Governor-General that the rebels along the road were in full flight before the British force that had marched twenty miles that day, and fourteen miles the day before. Their retreat was too precipitate to enable them to destroy the Bunnee Bridge. Only four guns were taken, but many had been cast into wells, and only four passed the Bunnee Bridge. Firing in Lucknow was distinctly heard, and royal salutes by the 24-pounders were fired by the advancing force to announce their approach.[303]

James cut a somewhat cavalier figure as a volunteer. He was described thus: "Outram, in the temporary character of a cavalry volunteer, developed an eccentricity in the choice of his weapon. He wore a sword, but he never drew it. His arm was a stout gold-topped malacca cane, which he was wont to wave about his head in a demonstrative fashion, putting it to purposeful use…..He rode a gigantic Australian horse which had a clumsy, bison-like manner of galloping, but withal such a turn of speed that the square-shouldered compact man on its back was ever well out in the forefront of the rush."[304]

At Bunni, which they reached on the second day, they were surprised and pleased to find that in their haste the retreating mutineers had not destroyed the bridge over the unfordable River Sye, and the defensive positions commanding the bridge had been abandoned. The British force thus made speedy progress towards their objective, but as they neared Lucknow, for the first time they met fierce resistance. The enemy guns kept up a constant barrage on their positions, and attempts to probe forward at various points were met with ferocious fire from infantry. Losses were suffered when the enemy cavalry circled round to the rear and attacked the baggage train. James, who despite his civil position could not resist becoming involved in command, counselled caution. He assessed the enemy's strength such that any vulnerability shown by the British would be taken advantage of, and it would be rash to leave a rear guard exposed. Therefore any attack should be carefully planned and cautiously executed. They set up camp in the Alambagh, enclosed gardens on the edge of Lucknow, which they were able to occupy after a sharp skirmish.

The occupants of the Residency were thought by now to be in dire straits, with their rations all but exhausted and the enemy at the gates, pouring shot into the compound and attempting to undermine the fortifications. The importance of the position at Lucknow was such that it seemed the eyes and ears of the world were trained on the unfolding saga. News that Henry Lawrence had been killed by an exploding shell came as a blow to the advancing army, and a shock to the British public. Colonel Inglis, in charge of the Residency since Lawrence's demise, reported that he hoped to hold out until September 25, the next day. This lent urgency to the relief party.

Early on the morning of September 25 the advance commenced in earnest. James played a large part in the planning, his knowledge of the city and its environs providing invaluable intelligence. The obvious approach to the Residency was via the main road from Kanpur, which led in a direct line for a mile and a half to the gates of the Residency, but this was known to be defended "by entrenchment behind entrenchment, and battery upon battery."[305] The narrow road led through the heart of the city, and any approach would be vulnerable to musketry in the surrounding houses, many of which were loopholed. The second route involved a detour to the right by the Dilkusha palace and park, allowing the troops to approach down either bank of the canal and then the river Gumti to a site facing the Residency. This had the advantage of avoiding the most heavily defended part of the city, and providing a possible escape road to evacuate the residents. Havelock favoured this route. The disadvantage was that incessant rain for three days had left the earth near the river very soft and muddy, which would make progress difficult. James had reconnoitred the ground on September 24 and reported that it would be impossible to move even light artillery across it. The third route was a compromise between the other two: it was to force a bridgehead at Charbagh bridge, left of the road from the Alambagh, then move right to the main road, avoiding the Dilkusha bridge, which would be heavily defended and difficult to take with a frontal assault. A left turn onto the main road would lead to the Kaisarbagh and an approach to the Residency through the Baillie Guard Gate. The engineers' office in Lucknow had drawn up this proposal, and James was in favour of it, even though it meant some tough fighting close to the Residency. Havelock still favoured a wide detour but James held to his view adamantly, and Havelock yielded.

The advance started with the first brigade, led by James, moving towards the Charbagh bridge under heavy fire from guns and muskets in the long grass and sugar cane on either side of the road, circling to the right to clear the Charbagh garden, and then advancing from the canal bank to ring the defenders of the bridge under flanking fire. Meanwhile the Fusiliers directed a frontal assault, storming the Charbagh Bridge, capturing the enemy batteries and occupying the surrounding houses. Havelock commanded the second brigade, which followed the first. Across the bridge they pressed forward through the narrow lanes, making better progress than they expected. When they reached the Moti Munzil they came under severe fire from the Kaisarbagh. This building was a vast warren of apartments, courtyards and parterres that offered excellent cover and movement to its defenders. From there onwards every yard was hard won; every house seemed to be occupied by armed defenders laying down withering fire.

Half a mile from the Residency progress was halted. The British realised that to proceed further they would have to fight from house to house, working their ways through the palaces that lined the streets, as the fire directed into the road was ferocious, and heavy losses were being sustained. Darkness was approaching, and the troops were feeling the effects of an exhausting day. James proposed a short halt to enable the rear-guard with heavy guns to catch up, but Havelock was anxious to press on. He was conscious that at any moment mines could breach the Residency walls, and any delay would demoralise the residents whose hopes had been buoyed up by the sound of fighting. This could lead to desertions from the natives within the Residency. Havelock also believed that the success enjoyed so far should be capitalised upon, and the enemy not given a chance to regroup. Once again the differences arising between Havelock and Outram became apparent. Sensitive to his reputation, James wrote later to the Commander-in Chief: "I trust that you will forgive me for bringing a small personal matter to your private notice which has caused me some slight annoyance, for such consideration as you may think it deserving of. I perceive from the published despatch of Sir Henry Havelock, describing the operations connected with his entrance into Lucknow for the relief of the garrison, the lamented General therein states that; after taking the Chattar Munzil, we held a conversation, at which I recommended that we should remain where we were, while he advocated pushing on at once, and adopted the latter course. It seems to me that a dispassionate peruser of the above passage would infer that the relief of the garrison was due to General Havelock's adoption of his own views in preferrence to mine, and I therefore wish to explain that I proposed a halt, of only a few hours' duration, in order to enable the rear-guard, with which were all our heavy guns, the baggage, and the doolies containing our wounded, to come up, by which time the whole force would have occupied the Chattar Munzil in security, which we were then holding, and from which we could have effected our way to the Residency....General Havelock pushed on without waiting for the rear-guard, which was consequently cut off for two nights and a day, not effecting its entrance to the entrenchment until the morning of the 27th, and then only at a heavy sacrifice of life."[306]

A letter from one of the officers in the Lucknow garrison confirmed the situation as described by James: "Consider the plans, and bear in mind the circumstances of the case. Generals Outram and Havelock both believed that the garrison was on its last biscuit; and they had been unable to bring with them any provisions beyond the few days' rations the men carried in their haversacks. They came not to reinforce, but to extricate us. Their object, therefore, was not so much to accelerate their advance to our position as - with the least possible sacrifice of those precious lives on which the safe removal of the garrison must be, in a great measure, dependent - to open and keep open such communications with the Residency as should enable us to be withdrawn with our sick and wounded, women and children. In this view, the concentration of the entire relieving force, under the shelter of the palaces, appeared to Sir J. Outram preferable to pushing on at once, and leaving the rear-guard behind; and he thought it more advisable to open communications with the Residency….Though General Outram afterwards 'concurred' in General Havelock's determination to push on without the rear-guard, and to take the street route, instead of that through the palaces, he retained his own opinion to the last. But, as he had voluntarily placed himself under General Havelock, it would have been unbecoming in him to persist in setting up his judgment in opposition to that of his commander. He yielded; but, in doing so, craved permission to lead what he knew must be a fearfully perilous advance. I scarcely understand what General Havelock meant to express when referring to his anxiety to let the garrison know that succour was at hand."[307]   Havelock had in fact publicly committed himself to be in the Residency before nightfall. James later reflected: "Then my temper got a little the better of me and I replied: 'Let us go then, in God's name!' I have often since asked myself whether I should not then and there have resumed command."[308]

So the advance began again, Highlanders and Sikhs in the van, with Havelock and Outram leading them. From every house and balcony came a stream of fire, which the advancing army found difficult to return as the houses crowded in upon them. For nearly a mile the ordeal persisted. Losses were heavy, but the soldiers did not flinch, and finally a shout went up as the gates of the Residency came into view. With renewed vigour, the soldiers charged through the fire to the gates of the Residency. At their head rode James, but his horse balked at the embrasure guarding the Residency, and he and his horse were heaved bodily across it by the triumphant Highlanders following him.

Of the relieving force of two thousand, approximately five hundred were killed or wounded. James received a flesh wound in the arm early in the day, but although he suffered some loss of blood continued until the Residency was entered. Just in time it appears, for "Since we have obtained access to the exterior of the entrenchments, we find that the enemy had completed six mines in the most artistic manner – one of them from a distance of 200 feet – under our principal defensive works, which were ready for loading, and the firing of which must have placed the garrison entirely at their mercy. The delay of another day, therefore, might have sealed their fate."[309] Needless to say, the welcome these gallant soldiers received was overwhelming. James renewed acquaintance with many old friends in the Residency, including his brother-in-law, Lieutenant J.C.Anderson, Commanding Engineer Officer.

The officer commanding the garrison, Brigadier Inglis, wrote a graphic report of the defence of the Residency: "…the troops have ever undergone greater hardships, exposed as they have to a never-ceasing musketry fire and cannonade. They have also experienced the alternate vicissitudes of extreme wet and of intense heat, and that, too, with very insufficient shelter from either, and in many places without any shelter at all. In addition to having had to repel real attacks, they have been exposed night and day to the hardly less harassing false alarms that the enemy have been constantly raising. The insurgents have frequently fired very heavily, sounded the advance, and shouted for several hours together."[310]

James was able to report that since joining the garrison many thousands of the enemy had deserted the city, and the late king's son and his court had fled to Faizabad.[311] For a short period the resolve of the rebels wavered. It turned out that there had been loss of heart in other parts of Oudh, with James' proclamation of mercy having some effect. But then the rebel troops were rallied by the Begam and Maulavi in Lucknow, and came together to renew the siege of the Residency. They were joined by remnants of other factions dislodged elsewhere by the advancing British forces. It dawned upon Havelock and James that far from relieving the Residency they had incarcerated themselves in an isolated position, without fresh supplies. James was shocked at the damage done to the compound, where many buildings were smoking ruins. The relieving force had added 1,000 men to the garrison, and set new problems in the Residency.

As will have been observed from James' comments prior to the final push, the rear-guard had remained behind in the city and needed to be rescued. On the morning of September 26, with Havelock in poor health James resumed command, and sent out reinforcements to defend the heavy guns. Under cover of darkness that night the wounded and camels were brought into the Residency while the guns and wagons were withdrawn to a safe position. In the next two days the position was consolidated by occupation of all the palaces between the Residency and Kaisarbagh, to use for accommodating troops. From there they were able to do some damage by mounting sorties on enemy positions, destroying guns and reducing the pressure on the Residency. Havelock commanded the troops occupying the palaces and outposts, but it was very difficult to sustain communications with the force stationed at the entrance to the city in Alambagh. James wrote that with a view to the possibility of adopting the Kanpur road as his line of communication with Alambagh, Major Haliburton, 78th Highlanders, "commenced on the 3rd to work from house to house with a crow-bar and axe."[312] It was now urgent that word was conveyed to Kanpur to send reinforcements. James requested men from Delhi, which had been subdued, to strengthen the contingent at Kanpur.

He reported to the Commander-in-Chief that the insurgents were too strong to move anyone from the garrison. The sick, wounded, women and children, amounted to upwards of 1,000.[313] One enemy battery continued to fire upon the Residency, and its capture became a necessity. On October 2 the battery was stormed and the guns destroyed with the loss of two men killed and eleven wounded, James discovered to his relief that although medicines and hospital stores were virtually exhausted, the stores of provisions remaining had been underestimated, and this lifted the pressure somewhat on the besieged. It transpired that Sir Henry Lawrence, before his death, had foreseen a crisis, and squirrelled away grain in a number of different locations within the compound, some of which had been overlooked. Shortly after their arrival an underground swimming pool packed full of grain was discovered. By October 6 the rebels outside the walls had increased noticeably, augmented by irregulars from other parts of the region, including Delhi, which had been recaptured by the British. James wrote that their position was more untenable than that of the previous garrison because they were obliged to occupy the neighbouring palaces outside the entrenchment to accommodate the Europeans in positions that the enemy was able to mine from cover of neighbouring buildings. There was still no communication with the town, and little prospect of procuring provisions.[314]

It was apparent that the detachment at Alambagh was in no better position to move. It could not be withdrawn to Kanpur with its sick, wounded, 200 elephants, camels, and wagons, without being greatly reinforced; and such reinforcement would enable it to hold on where it is, in its fortified post. The moral effect of maintaining troops there, and gradually reinforcing that post, it was hoped, would give them an advantage.[315] By October 8 the Alambagh contingent had run out of supplies and were slaughtering cattle in order to subsist. However on the same day a convoy under Major Brigham arrived from Kanpur, carrying supplies. This enabled the garrison there to send back the elephants and camels "which are so necessary for our future supplies."[316] The elephants reached Kanpur safely on the 12th. James continued to urge that reinforcements be sent from Kanpur, concentrating the numbers at Alambagh. He wrote to Captain Bruce, commanding the Kanpur garrison: "I don't think the Kanpur garrison should be less than 350 effective Europeans, and that of Futtehpore 150….you could hardly afford to send more than 200 or 250 Europeans in addition to the return escort of 100 which took back the elephants."[317]

James remained concerned about the position of the local Oudh people. He instructed Bruce on no account to send any police into Oudh. Their presence would confirm the belief that the British intended forcibly to destroy caste.[318] James continued to publicise the proclamation of amnesty, instructing Bruce that those who signed it did so on the understanding that they would have to stand the consequences if it was proved that they had sided with the rebels.[319]

James requests for help were heeded. A column from Delhi under the command of Sir Hope Grant moved south and reached Fatheghar on October 8. Sir Colin Campbell had arrived in Calcutta three months previously to assume overall command of the army. There he had waited for reinforcements from the Cape of Good Hope before moving up country by rail to Kanpur, which he reached on November 3. Whilst at Kanpur Campbell learnt that the Gwalior contingent of mutineers, noted for their bravery and ferocity, were marching towards Kalpi with the objective of linking up with Nana Sahib and the remnants of his force from Dinapore. James suggested that Campbell should consider Lucknow a secondary objective as it was of vital importance that the Gwalior contingent should be destroyed, but Campbell rejected his advice.[320] Leaving

500 European soldiers to defend Kanpur, he moved forward to the Alambagh outside Lucknow. His progress throughout this manoeuvre was cautious to the point of being tardy. Campbell was notorious for his cautiousness, and had earned the nickname among his troops of "Sir Crawling Camel."[321]

James, hearing of Campbell's arrival, immediately sent a series of letters preparing the ground for him, and advising him of the most appropriate route to take from the Alambagh to the Residency. It was clear that he was most anxious for the relief column to arrive, but it appeared to have taken an extraordinary length of time to reach Alambagh. It had apparently only left Kanpur on October 22, and was harassed all the way to Alambagh by mutineers who were fully aware of the relief column and its importance. It reached the Alambagh on October 27, where it found Hope Grant waiting. Campbell's total force numbered 4,200 men, facing an estimated 60,000 entrenched rebels. But he recognised the urgency of his mission and advanced, reaching the Dilkusha, a huge palace built in the style of a cross between a French chateau Palladian villa that had been used as a hunting lodge, on November 14. After a two-hour running fight he set up his headquarters in Martiniere, a Christian boys' college also built in the grand style as a palace for, ironically, visiting Europeans.

From there the advance was along the river bank for about a mile before taking to narrow lanes in a sweep to the right. This was in accord with James' advice: "The direct advance… via Charbagh, and the main street…should not be attempted, very formidable opposition being prepared on the other side of the Charbagh bridge, the bridge itself being destroyed, and the passage strongly fortified."[322] Like the original relieving force they came under fierce fire as they approached the Residency. The final stand of the rebels was made at Moti Mahal, close to the walls of the Residency. Once they were dislodged the battle was won. While Campbell was advancing James seized the opportunity to extend his position along the river front to an adjacent palace, the Chattar Munzil. On the open ground between the two buildings, with stray bullets still whistling through the air, took place the historic meeting of Campbell, Outram and Havelock commemorated by the famous painting now hanging in the National Portrait Gallery, London (and featured on the cover of this book). The relief had been accomplished. Unfortunately, pockets of rebels remained, and in their journey to the Moti Mahal four staff officers were hit – young Henry Havelock (General Havelock's son), Napier, Sitwell and Russell.[323]

The conflict was not over, and any movement of residents out of Lucknow remained very dangerous. James was destined to play a leading part in the endgame that was about to unfold.

CHAPTER 14.

THE END OF THE MUTINY.

Campbell's strategy was to keep up the pressure by pounding enemy positions with his artillery and make rapid raids upon individual strongholds, leading the rebels to expect a frontal attack. While their attention was engaged the women and children were evacuated from the Residency together with the wounded, treasury, guns, stores and prisoners. At midnight on November 22 the garrison quietly withdrew, leaving the Residency deserted. Not a shot was fired during this operation. They were led through five miles of heavy sand, the weak and ill drawn slowly along in carts by horses. More than once they came under ill-directed fire. After an hour they reached the Secundrabagh, where Campbell welcomed them. They reached the Dilkusha, which had been secured by the cavalry on the previous day, on the afternoon of the 23rd. They were followed, silently by the soldiers from the Residency, ordered not to march in step so that they would not be heard. From the Dilkusha they were moved to safety. The diary of a lady evacuated that night, Mrs German, described the scene vividly: "The whole army marched except a few to keep the Dilkusha for a short time. One thousand sick were taken in doolies and 467 women and children in any kind of conveyance that could be got for them – doolies were not even allowed to ladies who were hourly expecting their confinement. Sir Colin said the wounded men must be first thought of as they had saved our lives. Never shall I forget the scene – as far as the eye could search on all sides were strings of vehicles, elephants, camels, etc. The dust was overpowering. We went across country to avoid the enemy – our road lay over cultivated fields and such ups and downs it was a wonder how the vehicles got over them."[324] Not a man, woman or child was lost that night throughout the withdrawal through more than 40,000 mutineers. James received the credit for what was a brilliant manoeuvre, receiving later as a result the freedom of the city of London, but he protested long and hard that it was Sir Colin Campbell's plan, and he had merely carried out his orders.

James was now eager to counter-attack, believing that the Kaisarbagh was vulnerable, and that its capture would enable a reasonably modest force of 600 men to hold the city. Campbell disagreed, being apprehensive that such a move would expose his men unnecessarily, and detract from the more defensive strategy of occupying a strong position outside the city to hold it in check and concentrate on subduing the rest of Oudh. "I conceive that a strong moveable division outside the town, with field and heavy artillery in a good military position, is the real manner of holding the city of Lucknow in check, according to our practice with the other great city of India," he wrote to the Governor-General, "Such a division would aid in subduing the country hereafter, and its position would be quite sufficient evidence of our intention not to abandon the province of Oudh."[325] Campbell withdrew to the Alambagh, leaving James at the Dilkusha to supervise the movement of the women and wounded to Kanpur. Sadly Sir Henry Havelock, worn out by dysentery and the strenuousness of the campaign, died at this stage. He was buried in the Alambagh with full military honours, all the senior officers attending. James ordered that the grave be well hidden to escape detection, and precise measurements were taken to ensure it could be found later.

The Commander-in-Chief was coming under increasing criticism for the cautious tactics that he was employing. Anxious about British subjects besieged by the mutineers, and impatient at the lack of progress, the authorities in England brought increased pressure to bear on the Governor-General, and Sir Colin Campbell. Interestingly, Lord Dalhousie, when Governor-General, had written in April 1855: "I hope there is no chance of Sir Colin Campbell getting high command. He was always a very gallant fellow, most attentive to his men, active, hale, and well-spirited. I dare say he will now make a good divisional officer; but I have known and heard much of him, and I do not believe him capable of high command."[326]

Campbell was conscious that his resources remained stretched, and communication difficult. Cautious to a fault, his first inclination was to withdraw completely from the province, thus preserving his army intact, and providing maximum protection for the retreat of the non-combatants. This was in contradiction to James's view, and Canning supported him in a letter to Campbell dated November 18: "I will not say that it (the full withdrawal) ought not to take place, because it may be a necessity, but I look with apprehension to the consequences and would sacrifice a good deal to avoid it...I thought it possible that although the whole column might be required to bring away the garrison in safety, a portion might return and occupy some safely tenable spot in Lucknow as a sign that we did not abandon possession. Do not think that I am forgetting that in our present condition in the Central Provinces, Political consideration must give way to Military. All I desire is to impress you with the importance of keeping a foot in Oudh, if it can possibly be done."[327]

Accordingly Sir Colin Campbell left Alambagh on November 27, leaving James in charge with instructions to stay there until circumstances permitted the recapture of Lucknow. This was easier said than done, for they still faced a huge enemy force of 120,000 troops with more than 130 guns, who gave them little rest. The difficulties of his position were spelt out in a report James made in February 1858: "The position assigned us was within a mile and a half of the suburbs of Lucknow. Our advance posts were within gunshot range of the outworks of a vast city, swarming with hosts of mutinous sepoys…with many thousand city badmashes, the armed and turbulent scum of a population of 700,000 souls, and with numerous bands of feudal retainers of the chieftains and great zamindars of Oudh, whose normal state for the last fifty years has been one of warfare."[328]

James' main force was camped in open ground straddling the Kanpur road, protected by field works stretching in a circle for eleven miles. They were not connected by continuous trenches. The Alambagh enclosure had been fortified but could only accommodate a small garrison. His right flank was protected by a detachment occupying a dilapidated old fort at Jalalabad. He found any form of attack difficult, for he faced the outskirts of the city where cover was freely available in the houses. The country outside the city was also dotted with small villages which afforded cover, and the ability for the enemy to get quite close to the Alambagh without being detected. James' brief was to act defensively, and only to strike when the opportunity presented itself. The enemy that faced him now realised, from the retribution exacted by the British elsewhere, that they had nothing to lose in opposing James. He had at his disposal 4442 men, of whom 540 was stationed at Bunni, 12 miles distant preserving the rear and keeping a vital bridge open. The fort at Alambagh contained 600 men, Jalalabad 450. The remainder were positioned on the plain, poised for action when not on convoy duty to and fro from Kanpur, 45 miles away, which was their only source of supply. He was fortunate to have an experienced and highly skilled team of officers who had seen action successfully in a number of arenas, and were very cool under pressure. He also had the "glorious" 78th Regiment, who had been with him in Persia, and with whom he had a strong affinity.

James was of the opinion that Lucknow was vulnerable, and could be taken with a determined push. The withdrawal of the main British force meant that no attack would be planned at least until the next cold season, and he argued that in the circumstances his force could be stationed just about anywhere in Oudh without losing face, for they would still be seen to be holding sway in the province. He was concerned about their vulnerability at Alambagh, and argued for more resources. But James was at last learning diplomacy: he wound up his letter to Campbell by saying he was only advocating retreat if an attack on Lucknow was not imminently contemplated. The general staff did not rule out an attack at the right moment, so James settled down to wait.

On December 22 the enemy made a major move. They had been erecting batteries in front of his position, and manoeuvring on the plain. James' intelligence- gathering alerted him to a move against his rear, and he was prepared when it came. His spies had informed him two days previously that the enemy planed to surround his position in order to cut off supplies, stop foraging expeditions and intercept communications with Bunnee. James accordingly despatched a force to Guilee, which took up a position between that village and Budroop, about a mile away. On the evening of the 21st James heard that the rebels had been reinforced, and that their strength amounted to about 4,000 infantry, 400 cavalry, and 8 field guns [there were actually 4, which were all captured]. Having ascertained that a space of about half a mile intervened between their position and the gardens skirting the canal and the Dilkoosha, he moved out at 5a.m. in the hope of surprising them at daybreak. But the main body of the enemy was already on the march. A brief skirmish ensued resulting in the rebels losing four horse artillery guns, ammunition, elephants and baggage, and some fifty or sixty men before they retreated back into the city. James noted: "This will, I think, deter the enemy from again venturing beyond their defensive works."[329] There were signs that some of the leaders in Lucknow were beginning to waver, but at the same time the force was being augmented by numbers pouring in from other towns as the British dislodged the mutineers. Lucknow was fast becoming the focus for conflict between the two sides, and the defensive position at Alambagh was seen as protection against insurgents falling on Kanpur again.

On January 12 a frontal attack was made against the Alambagh with huge numbers of men. Once again James had been informed of the planned attack, and was ready for it. About sunrise large masses of the enemy were seen on the left front, and they gradually spread round the whole front and flanks of the British position, extending from opposite the left rear outpost to near Jellalabad on the right, a distance of at least six miles. There were estimated to be at least 30,000 men.[330] They were, however, unprepared for the severe artillery barrage that opened up on them across the whole front, and were soon in disorderly retreat. Throughout the day attacks were made on selected points of the British defence: first the right, near Jalalabad, then the left, then the middle. On each occasion the mass of infantry, supported by field guns, was driven back with withering and accurate fire which caused huge losses. By four in the afternoon the enemy had disappeared and returned to their original positions. James' total casualties were six wounded.

Further sporadic attacks were attempted, but with less intensity, and were repulsed, the enemy suffering significant losses again. James requested reinforcements from Campbell, who arranged to send the 34th Regiment and four 24-pounder siege guns. This strengthened his hand greatly, and when on February 25 another full-blooded attempt was made to break through the British ranks, he was able to strike hard and successfully head-on, inflicting heavy casualties and putting the enemy to flight. The mutineers' losses were estimated at between 400 and 500 dead, while James lost 5 men killed and 35 officers and men wounded.

This was in effect the enemy's last throw of the dice. They realised that James was well equipped to defend the Alambagh, and concentrated their efforts on building up the defences of

Lucknow. This gave the British a welcome breather from the incessant attacks. But morale had held up remarkably well. A flavour of the esteem in which James was held by his men came from Forrester's Selections: "Sir James had a cheery word for officers and men at each post, generally some small compliment – such as a regret that the enemy would not come on, because you're always so well prepared – and his visit seemed a welcome one everywhere. As you know, he could be uncommonly irate on provocation…I was told that when he did 'let out' at any one, especially a youngster, he was not comfortable till he had made it up by some kind word or deed, and that as often as not a 'wig' ended by the offer of a cheroot – a valuable gift at the Alambagh. His holster was stuffed with these luxuries instead of a revolver, and he dispensed them right liberally."[331]

Sir Colin Campbell had at last mustered the resources to bring overwhelming force to bear on Lucknow. Reinforcements had been pouring into the country through Calcutta: the 64th and 78th Highlanders from Persia, the 90th Scottish regiment from Hong Kong, the 93rd Highlanders from Cape Town (diverted from their journey to China) and three regiments of Highlanders from Malta taking the overland route across the Suez isthmus. They were joined in November by the 8th Hussars, hastily summoned from England. Campbell had been required first to defend Kanpur, then to transport the many families rescued from Lucknow back to Allahabad, using a large supply of carts, and then to subdue Fatehgarh and recover the Do-ab. But by mid-February he had freed up enough men, carts, artillery and other resources to feel confident enough to march on Lucknow. He left Kanpur on February 28 with 17 battalions of infantry, 28 squadrons of cavalry, 54 light and 80 heavy guns. He had arranged to rendezvous with Brigadier-General T.H. Franks, who was coming up to Lucknow from the south with 3 European and 6 Gurkha battalions and 20 guns, and with Maharajah Jung Bahadoor, who was approaching from the south-east in command of 9000 Nepalese troops and 24 guns. By the time they assembled at the Alambagh the army comprised 20,000 men and 180 guns.

James was in favour of attacking from the west and taking the enemy defence from the rear, which would have the added benefit of preventing escape. Campbell, who decided to attack the defenders of Lucknow from two directions, rejected this. James, with a large and crack force would start the attack from the further side of the river Gumti, where it looked as though the enemy had neglected to build up their defences. When progress was made in this sphere the main force would head on through the Dilkusha and Martiniere. James crossed the Gumti on March 6, easily repulsing enemy attacks. Campbell wrote: "This duty was ably performed by Sir James Outram, who pitched his camp …after a skirmish of his advance guard, in front of the Chakkar Walla Kotee [Chakarwala Kothi or Yellow-house]. On the 7th he was attacked by the enemy, who was speedily driven back. Having reconnoitred the ground on the 8th instant, I directed Sir James Outram to arrange his batteries during the succeeding night, and to attack the enemy's position."[332] The Chakarwala Kothi commanded an iron bridge above the Residence. James strengthened this position before directing his fire on the Kaisarbagh and main street. "All this was carried out…with the most marked success."[333]

Campbell's main force crossed the canal and on March 11 prepared to attack the Begum Kothi that was captured after two hours of fierce fighting. By March 12 Campbell had brought forward sufficient support to reinforce James with heavy guns and mortars which were also turned on the Kaisarbagh. By the 13th the cross-fire directed on this stronghold forced the enemy to flee, and on the 14th Campbell, whose main force had fought its way forward until it could storm the building, entered the Kaisarbagh. James now proposed that he cross the iron bridge and circle around behind the Residence to cut off the retreating enemy, but Campbell refused his request unless he could cross the bridge without losing a single man. This James could not guarantee, and a golden opportunity to round up the mutineers was lost. His job done, James led his force back over the Gumti and was able to march almost unopposed up to the Residency. "Vast numbers of the enemy having been seen crossing the stone bridge from the city…..His Excellency ordered me to press our movement. I immediately ordered the advance, and took possession of the Residency with little opposition, the 23rd Fusiliers charging through the gateway, and driving the enemy before them at the point of the bayonet."[334] The Residency secure, James moved on to take the Machi Bawan and the Imambara.

Campbell was full of praise for James's role: "It was a matter of real gratification to me to be able to entrust the trans-Goomtee operation to this very distinguished officer, and after that had been conducted to my perfect satisfaction, to bring him forward again to put the finishing stroke on the enemy, while the extended position of the town was of necessity held by the troops who had won it. My thanks are entirely due to him."[335] By March 19 the recapture of Lucknow was complete. Unfortunately the mistakes made during the final days of the campaign enabled most of the rebels to escape into the countryside where they continued to cause trouble throughout the province. Most notably, during an attack on the strongly-held point of Musa Bagh to the north-west of the city, a cavalry brigade commanded by Brigadier William Campbell, an inexperienced officer recently arrived in India, was instructed to pursue and cut up the enemy forces as they retreated, but failed to do so, and an estimated 9,000 troops escaped from Lucknow. Had James' plan to circle behind the enemy and thus cut off their retreat been adopted, these blunders might have been avoided. The commanders came in for considerable criticism for these lapses, despite the success of the relief campaign.

James was requested to stay at Lucknow. On March 14, 1858 Lord Canning issued a proclamation which, with few exceptions, confiscated all the estates in Oudh. As Chief Commissioner of Oudh, whose task it was to issue the proclamation, James objected to its severity. He urged Canning to grant pardons to the taluqdars and to restore their old possessions. He argued that Oudh depended upon this leading land-owning class to maintain good order in the province, and to treat them harshly would be counter-productive. Canning felt that to treat them generously would be rewarding the very people who had led the rebellion in Oudh, but mindful of James' knowledge of Oudh, tempered his decree a little: "I have flatly refused, but have added a sentence to the proclamation which will make it clear that though confiscation of proprietary right in the soil is the general penalty, restitution of it is the reward for coming in and behaving well. I am not surprised at these councils coming from Outram, who is kind and generous to a weakness."[336]

The proclamation required that private armies be disabled, cannon confiscated, and fortresses pulled down. The taluqdars stood to lose everything, and were close to revolt. The proclamation led to a storm of protest in London, and James predicted that its effects would be disastrous. Without the land-owning class on his side, the government of Oudh would be impossible. He maintained that less than a dozen landowners had actually borne arms against the British. In fact James had set out his position in a long letter to Lord Dalhousie on January 7, 1858. This letter mainly reiterated his explanations for the sepoy rising, but then went on to address the position: "Some people argue that the hostility of the population of Oudh is a proof of the impolicy of the annexation of the province. To this I would reply that the mass of the community are not hostile. The agricultural classes are at heart with us to a man. That the principal landowners are in arms, I must reluctantly admit. But even their disaffection, I confidently affirm, is not owing to their annexation in se, but to that unhappy system of settlement which was carried out against my wishes and warnings, and I am sure contrary to those of your Lordship, by which the entire body of these men were entirely ousted from their possessions….. Before too hastily condemning the conduct of the rebellious Oudh Zamindars, it should be borne in mind that not a man rose."[337]

James could have pointed out that Canning himself had in the past referred to the taluqdari system as "ancient, indigenous and cherished." Robert Montgomery, the Oudh chief commissioner, who described the taluqdari as a necessary element in the social constitution of the province, and saw them as possessing "superiority and influence" supported him.[338] Under pressure from James, Canning promised indulgence and a "liberal" review of the claims of all those who capitulated without delay, and James made the most of this concession. The passage inserted at James's behest read: "To those amongst them who shall promptly come forward and give to the Chief Commissioner their support in the restoration of peace and order this indulgence will be large; and the Governor-General will be ready to view liberally the claims which they may thus acquire to a restitution of their former rights."[339] James was to exploit this amendment to the limit: in October 1859 Canning himself presided over a durbar at which 169 sanads – rights to hold land – were issued to taulqdars.

James' objections to the proclamation, and his success in moderating the effects, were to be recognised by the liberal element in England. In 1906 Harcourt Butler wrote: "How come it that thoughtful men on all sides now are asking why the government of Oudh has been so strikingly successful? Where, they ask, in India can be found more true happiness and ease under British rule, more solid progress, more unquestioning loyalty? Where such smooth relations between the rulers and the ruled, between the party of order and the party of change? Where a like measure of agrarian peace? Where a more effective combination of old sanctions and young aspirations? What are the peculiar possessions of the province, what institutions, what particular foundations or superstructure, to which it owes its great and growing reputation?"[340] The answer, he wrote, was the preservation of its landed aristocracy, the ancient, indigenous and cherished system of the country. He believed the right way to rule India was through the natural leaders of the people. As it turned out, this credo contained a good degree of rhetoric, for the taluqdars were actually reduced to nothing more than landlords by the proclamation.

The proclamation was destined to bring Canning considerable trouble. Bitter debates in both Houses of Parliament threatened the very structure of rule in India, and led to the resignation of Lord Ellenborough. No other act by Canning invoked more severe criticism of him. Not only James, but Sir John Lawrence was against it. The Times correspondent, Russell, wrote: "…if this Proclamation goes forth 'pure et simple', the duties of the Commissioner will become all but impossible…Time must elapse ere Oudh be ours. It turns out unhappily that the fall of Lucknow has by no means secured the submission of Oudh, as Lord Canning must have supposed it would when he hurled his bull from Allahabad…I have not heard one voice raised in its defence."[341] Karl Marx wrote in the New York Tribune on June 7, 1858: "The great point of this controversy is, what is the exact position which the zamindars, talookdars or sirdars, so called hold in the economical system of India? Are they properly to be considered as landed proprietors or as mere tax-gatherers?…Lord Canning's opinion as to the light in which the conduct of landholders of Oudh in joining in the rebellion ought to be viewed does not appear to differ much from that of Sir James Outram and Lord Ellenborough. He argues that they stand in a very different position not only from the mutinous Sepoys, but also from that of the inhabitants of rebellious districts in which the British rule had been longer

241

established. He admits that they are entitled to be treated as persons having provocation for the course they took; but at the same time insists that they must be made to understand that rebellion cannot be resorted to without involving serious consequences for themselves. We shall soon learn what the effect of the issue of the proclamation has been, and whether Lord Canning or Sir James Outram was nearer right in his anticipation of its results."

On March 20, after the proclamation had been issued, James gave his first opinion: "The Proclamation has not been attended hitherto with the slightest effect, although the city itself is beginning to be populated, not however I fear from the inducements held out by your Lordship, but in consequence of the Proclamation issued by the Commander-in-Chief that the town would be bombarded if the inhabitants did not open their shops." Later, in defence of his position, Canning quoted from a letter he received from James, dated January 15, 1858: "The lands of men who have taken an active part against us, should be largely confiscated, in order among other reasons, to enable us to reward others in a manner most acceptable to a native. But I see no prospect of returning tranquillity, except by having recourse for the next few years to the old Talookdaree system."[342] James claimed that Canning was quoting him out of context.

During this period James kept up a voluminous correspondence with his mentor, Lord Dalhousie, now resident in Malta. Dalhousie noted on April 9: "Another long series of letters to and from Outram has come to me, but I have not read them yet. Unhappily, Outram's facility with the pen is as extreme as his difficulty of verbal expression. Accordingly, on every provocation, or any pretext, he rushes into writing. He sheds his ink as readily as he does his blood, and sometimes as much to his own loss. In his correspondence with the Bombay Government…. he began by being completely in the right, but he wrote himself into the wrong. Accordingly, when I put him back to Baroda, I never justified the language that had caused his removal from thence. All I said was that the punishment inflicted by the Bombay Government had been over-severe; that he was then adequately punished, and should be relieved from further penalty. He would never have gone wrong with me; but even with me, and probably always, his pen would be his evil spirit. As soon as Lucknow falls, I understand he is to come down into Council, and there his pen may range round any limits without challenge."[343]

In the Punjab, Sir John Lawrence was very perturbed at the turn of events. He wrote home: "The Oudh Proclamation, in the first instance, was calculated to do harm rather than good; to bind all men into one desperate confederation against us. To tell men that all their lands and property were confiscate, to allow them no 'locus parentiae,' was to drive them to despair. What made it also the less reasonable, was that we should never have carried it out. Why not then, when beating down all opposition with one hand, hold out the olive branch with the other? I understand that the Proclamation has since been modified, and I trust it is the case."[344]

True to form, Ellenborough had already entered the fray. As a member of the Court of Directors he had participated in heated discussions on the question of the Proclamation, but on April 19 took it upon himself to write to Canning voicing personal criticism. This letter was then laid before the Lords and published in the Times on May 6. He rehearsed the arguments used by James and Lawrence, but tellingly and damagingly went on: "We are under the impression that the war in Oudh has derived much of its popular character from the righteous manner in which, without regard to what the chief landholders have become accustomed to consider as their rights, the summary settlement had in a large portion of the Province been carried out by your officers." This was tantamount to accusing the Indian Government of stealing the land. He went on: "We must admit that, under the

243

circumstances, the hostilities which have been carried out in Oudh have rather the character of legitimate war than that of rebellion, and that the people of Oudh should rather be regarded with indulgent consideration than made the objects of a penalty, exceeding in extent, and in severity, almost any which has been recorded in history as inflicted upon a subdued nation….We desire that you will mitigate, in practice, the stringent severity of the degree of confiscation…We desire to see British authority in India rest upon the willing obedience of a contented people."[345] Immediate concerns were raised that the publication of this letter, with its insinuation of illegal confiscation, would inflame resistance in Oudh. Queen Victoria, when advised of the letter, remarked: "It is a great pity that Lord Ellenborough with his knowledge, experience, activity and cleverness, should be so entirely unable to submit to general rules of conduct."[346] Shortly thereafter, Ellenborough resigned.

It was time for James to move on. He wrote to Canning on March 20: "My health although in a critical state has not yet failed, as the constant and active excitement sustains me. But I cannot hope that it will last under the sedentary occupation, now before me, under which it broke down at the same season two years ago. I trust however that I may be released as soon as possible, for as my policy is so strongly disapproved, I cannot discharge my duties either with confidence or zeal nor do I know how I can be of real use."[347]

His mission successfully completed, his thoughts turned to his wife.

CHAPTER 15.

AN OFFICE JOB.

Word arrived that Margaret had escaped safely from Agra. She wrote to James' mother on Jan 26 1858 from a camp 36 miles south of Agra: "Dear Frank and I are so far on our way down south. He is to accompany me as far as Allahabad, and I go on to Calcutta. I have not heard from James for some time, but all the news from Alambagh is right, and we must hope and trust it will soon be over."[348]

James' reward for his sterling work was a seat on the Governor-General's council in Calcutta as military member, which meant leaving Oudh. He was relieved to do so. His health was not good, and the requirement that he carry out the terms of a proclamation with which he profoundly disagreed, was odious. James met Lord Canning at Allahabad as he journeyed south. In spite of the difference of opinion over the proclamation James was cordially received and invited to be the Governor-General's guest there.

There were still those who were critical of James. In 1857 John Bruce Norton had written: "To the student of the East India Company's character, the career of Sir James Outram is not less instructive than that of Sir Charles Napier. It affords an admirable illustration of what awaits those who will do the Company's bidding, be it what it may; as that of Napier shews what will be the result of their displeasure. The two men could scarcely be placed in more complete antagonism…. Sir James Outram vilified Sir CharlesNapier in the public prints; in vain the latter tried to bring him to a court-martial; he was too powerfully protected….Sir James does the dirty work in Oudh with the most cheerful alacrity; he is rewarded with the command of the Persian expedition. What he might have done, if there had been an opportunity, I cannot say; but the most fulsome paeans have been sung over the most trumpery affairs there. He jeopardized his army by an expedition into the interior for no sensible object, and was only extricated by the darkness of the night and the faint-heartedness of the enemy from a most perilous position....The most flaming order has just been published by the Governor-General, and the fortunate Outram, with all Napier's charges against him as yet unanswered, is, it is said, named Provisional member of Council."[349]

It was clear that James and Campbell had not always seen eye to eye. There were critics who considered the faults to be James'. An unpleasant and unjustifiable rumour was circulated suggesting that James had sought a Victoria Cross. It was not considered good form for a senior officer so to do. A letter from James to Dalhousie at the time reveals James' version of the story. Dalhousie wrote: "[Outram writes] that no answer was given [by Sir Colin Campbell] at all except on the passage regarding the Victoria Cross. On that Sir Colin says he does not think the Cross was meant for any one but those who could not, from subaltern rank, have the Bath. But he adds that he has made known to the Duke of Cambridge Outram's 'request' for the Cross. Outram very naturally replies that he is much annoyed by Sir Colin having done so. He had never 'requested' the Cross; he had never meant the passage of a private letter to be repeated; he had never wished to ask for an honour, for, if asked, it ceases in his eyes to be an honour even if it comes. To this there is no reply from Sir Colin. Though the letters are controversial I think you will see that Outram has much the best of it at all points, and that the Commander-in-Chief's treatment of him has been very unhandsome, to say the least of it."[350]

Waiting at Calcutta for James was his wife. She wrote to James' mother on April 29: "James arrived all safe a few days ago, and was looking remarkable well after all his labours. He is in good spirits and I trust the climate here, which is moist, will agree with him. He has taken his seat in the Council, and has a great deal to do. I have so many visitors to receive…and now there are so many invitations and distractions of that kind as well as other business, that my letters will be very short. James is of course, made much of just now, but to have him safe and well is enough. We have indeed been highly favoured, and Frank is safe too, I trust, at Allahabad…..I feel now a little reconciled to Calcutta, and recovering old feelings, but in common with most of those who have been spectators of the late horrors I feel utter disgust and dislike to the vanities of common life, and I fret over the prospect of gaieties, etc., in which I cannot feel a part."[351]

It was clear that in the aftermath of the mutiny the Indian army would need to be drastically reorganised. The Charter Act of 1833 had stripped the Company of its commercial character by introducing free trade doctrines and compelling it to give up commercial monopolies, but had extended its charter as an administrative body to April 1854. The provincial governments were stripped of their legislative powers, and although the Presidencies of Bombay and Madras remained, it was clearly stated that the Governor-General was the lawmaking authority for the whole of India. Although there had been criticism of the Company's failure to make improvements since 1833, Parliament had decided to extend the Charter indefinitely. One of the movers of this extension, Lord Russell, later commented that he had wanted the extension so that the Company's rule could be terminated in 1858, and the Crown could assume direct rule.[352] A distinguished committee met in London in 1858 to consider what should be done. Their first decision was to end Company rule in India; all military forces would be taken over by the Crown. It introduced a large degree of centralisation into the authorities in India. The Government of India Act of 1858 established the sovereign authority of the Crown, and provided for a secretary of State and a Council of India. The Governor-General was replaced with a Viceroy, representing the Crown. The President of the Board of Control became Secretary of State for India, and the new Council of India, established to advise the Secretary of State, combined the roles of the Board of Control and Court of Directors.[353]

The new government would never again give its support to the Evangelical project of Christianisation. Policy henceforward would be to govern with, rather than against, indigenous tradition. Another major reform was the dropping of Dalhousie's doctrine of lapse. Canning proclaimed on April 30, 1860 that he proposed to give an assurance to "every Chief...that on failure of natural heirs, his adoption of a successor...will be recognised."[354] This was aimed at strengthening Britain's direct rule through strong attachments by local rulers, who could now see a perpetuation of their reign. Effectively it was also establishing self-rule in certain matters, as Wood acknowledged: "It is not by the extension of our Empire that its permanence is to be secured, but by the character of British rule in the territories already committed to our care, and by practically demonstrating that we are willing to respect the rights of others as we are capable of maintaining our own."[355] James must have approved of these sentiments, and reflected how different the outcome of the Sind campaign would have been had they prevailed at that time.

Henceforward the only British cavalry and infantry would be part of the Royal army, enlisted for service anywhere in the world.[356] The strength of the force in India should number around 80,000 Europeans, double that present in 1857, and higher than most witnesses to the Committee had recommended. The Indian Army, part of the British army under the Crown, commanded by British officers, was seen as separate and distinct from the Company's force. In 1856 the proportion of British to Indian troops was 1:9, and the Committee felt it should not be less than 1:4. Finally a ratio of 1:2 white to Indian troops in Bengal and 1:3 in Madras and

Bombay was settled upon, and by the time the reorganisation was complete in 1863 the numbers were 62,000 British troops to 125,000 Indians.

Almost all the serving officers in India were firmly against the proposal, with James among the most vocal. He received strong support from Sir Bartle Frere, a great humanitarian, Chief Commissioner of Sind, a member of the Governor-General's Council, and later to be Governor of Bombay. He argued that if we could only hold India by a foreign army of occupation, we had no business there at all.[357] British rule was only justified if there was a large measure of consent. James believed the Indian army should be totally trusted if it was to function properly, and this meant arming sepoys with rifles equal in effectiveness to those of the British. He argued for a significant improvement in their living conditions, but maintained that a merger was not feasible. But change was in the air: the British government was determined that lessons would be learnt from the Mutiny. Moreover, with hard-headed Victorian commercialism, it had calculated that the high incapacity rate through illness in India (an average of 4,830 would die each year and 5,880 be hospitalised) was costing £1 million per annum, as it cost £100 to recruit and train a soldier in India. The regiments were reshaped and drastically reformed, so that by 1861 the amalgamation was a fait accompli.

As military representative on the Council, James was concerned with the morale of the British army. An incipient mutiny of troops at Barrackpore was firmly repressed, but there was no denying the dissatisfaction running through the ranks. The soldiers were concerned about changes in their terms and conditions, rights and privileges, in which they had no say. A particular concern was pension rights. The British government had assumed control of the army, and enlisted men were required without option to transfer to Her Majesty's service from the English East India Company. Many argued that this was illegal, and asked to return to England. Others accepted cash bonuses and transferred. As the Prime Minister, Palmerston, had indicated that discharge would be acceptable, Canning conceded the point, and there arose a steady demand for repatriation. Of the total strength of the British army in India, in excess of 15,000, 10,116 took their discharge and returned to England.

One of Canning's last acts before his retirement as Governor-General was to recognise the achievements of the heroes of the mutiny. The idea for a new Order apparently originated with Queen Victoria, and was inaugurated at Allahabad as the Star of India on November 1, 1861. Among those receiving the honour was James who, along with Sir John Lawrence, was invested by the Queen herself in London.

James served as a member of the Supreme Government from May 1858 until July 1860. These were among the most tranquil and settled years of his life. He and his wife shared a house at Garden Reach with an old friend, Le Geyt of the Bombay Civil Service. It was normal in Calcutta to entertain frequently, and as James did not care to go out at night, much of the entertaining took place at home. His health was not good, and consequently he did not travel much. However he worked hard and conscientiously, becoming something of a focal point for anyone with a grievance. He took up any complaint which he felt was justified, fearlessly, stepping on officials' toes from time to time. He seems to have made his peace with Lord Canning, however, and the two rubbed along well. He also found an opportunity, at a dinner given by the Engineers for Colonel Robert Napier, who had been appointed to command a division of the Expeditionary Army to China, to praise Charles Napier, whom he said he respected and esteemed. He attributed the differences that had grown up between them to "the indiscretion of partisans who came between."[358] The queen, at Lord Ellenborough's suggestion, conferred a baronetcy on him together with a yearly pension of £1000. In January 1859 he was granted the freedom of the city of London.

As he had started in India, so he continued to help his mother financially. Her will, written in 1858, several years before her death, shows the extent of his help. "My noble, noble son, with the generous dutiful feelings few have equalled, ever since he went to India, remitted to me for many years £200 per annum. Though my own income only yielded that sum it sufficed for me, and I never touched my son's donation, but had it accumulated to a large sum, which, with little savings of my own, I foolishly embarked in Railways, hoping to make a fortune for my son which his own generosity would never permit himself to do. A panic came - my whole funds were lost - but my dearest son went on in his glorious career, and for some years I have accepted from him £400 per annum, which I have had placed at interest, and at my death I wish this money, all I possess, to be placed to his account, or account of his wife and child."[359]

James continued to reflect on the aftermath of the Mutiny, and on Oudh in particular. He obviously thought deeply about the need to plan the future, and to provide local, native rulers with greater latitude. In a letter to Captain Eastwick dated May 2, 1858, James set out his thoughts on this topic: "By the aid of its existing landed aristocracy this may easily be done. And I think that even the most fanatically keen admirers of the North-West Province and Punjab systems are now inclined to admit that it is worth trying whether the universal laws of social progress do not hold, as regards India --whether the revenue of the State may not be maintained, and the happiness of the masses promoted, as satisfactorily under a system which recognises the legitimacy and advantages of capital and of baronial landlordism, as under a system which tends to reduce the entire population to the dreary and ever-sinking level of a demi-pauperised peasant proprietary."[360]

As a man of action James quickly became frustrated with his desk job. His disillusionment showed in another letter to Eastwick, dated July 17: "Since I have been behind the curtain, however, I have come to the conviction that the Council is as useless a drag here as in the subordinate Presidencies, and really as little efficacious for good as a check against evil. For instance, in those political missions the propriety of which have of late been most questioned, i.e. the Oudh proclamation, the negotiations with Nepaul, and the first dealing with the European soldier's disaffection, the Council had no voice whatever.....and [I] should be glad, on personal as well as on public grounds, to see the Councils abolished at once, a great saving being thereby secured at no injury to State interests. Of this I feel so conscious that I have some scruples to draw my large salary."[361]

He did achieve something while in office: appalled by the ravages of alcohol among the army, he established Outram Institutes in a number of garrisons and cantonments to promote temperance with the injunction: "Give them in our canteens shade and coolness….in the daytime, abundant illumination in the evening, light unadulterated beer to any extent they choose to pay for…and supplement ….by compelling our canteen-keepers to furnish fresh, strong, delicious coffee, genuine and well-made tea, and good and cheap ginger beer, lemonade and soda water…just in the same proportion shall we win our soldiers from the love of alcohol."[362]

In April 1860 his health gave serious cause for concern, and when a relaxing sea trip to Singapore had no effect there was no alternative but to return to England. He left Calcutta on July 20 after a series of ceremonies that celebrated his career, heaped praise on his head and recalled his achievements. A subscription was raised in Bombay to present him with a suitable testimonial, which succeeded in raising £1000. He was also granted an annuity of £1000 per annum by the Court of Governors of the East India Company. Even the bestowing of a pension on James was not without controversy, for one Governor, a Mr Lewin, said that "in his opinion Sir J. Outram had erred most grievously in the course that he had pursued with respect to the annexation of Oudh. If, instead of bending to the views of Lord Dalhousie, Sir J. Outram had declined being a party to that proceeding, he would have entitled himself to the unqualified approbation that the motion contained. Entertaining these opinions, he moved as an amendment 'That the conduct of Sir J. Outram with regard to the annexation of Oudh disentitles him to the unqualified approbation expressed in the resolution.'"[363] Fortunately for James, Mr Lewin failed in his objection.

James sailed as far as Marseilles and continued overland in leisurely fashion via Paris, reaching London on August 29. He was not well enough to go on to Edinburgh to see his mother, but settled into his quarters in Brighton. His wife had come back to London in 1859, and now joined him. She was shocked by his appearance and the deterioration that had taken place in the nine months since she had last seen him. On December 26 he was able to attend a ceremony in the Guildhall in London to have conferred upon him the freedom of the city. However he was not well enough to attend the banquet in the evening. In March 1861 a public meeting was held to raise funds for a statue in London (which stands today on the Victoria Embankment) and a duplicate in Calcutta, where it stands on the maidan. An illuminated testimonial was presented to him with a series of artistic silver centre-pieces, signed by 127 subscribers including the Prime Minister, Lord Palmerston.

James felt the need to move to a milder climate and in the winter of 1861/62 he and his wife spent several weeks in Nice. Yet he did not rest entirely, but occupied himself by taking up the causes of several friends. The mistral blew strongly after Christmas, and the cold wind brought on bronchitis, necessitating a move to Pau. Here he died, on March 11, 1863, his wife and son at his bedside. His mother had died a few days earlier. On March 25 crowds flocked to Westminster Abbey to see him buried among the heroes of his country. The funeral was attended by the great and the good, including Lord Clyde, Sir John Lawrence, the Earl of Dalhousie and Sir George Clerk, the ex-governor of Bombay who had formed a life-long friendship with James. But perhaps the most poignant and significant attendants were a party of sergeants from the 78th Regiment of Highlanders, who had travelled a considerable distance to be there, having obtained special leave from their regiment. They asked to carry the coffin from James' house to the Abbey, but the distance was too far for such a weight, and they contented themselves with marching beside the hearse. They had been in the forefront of fighting with James in the Sind, in Persia and at Lucknow. They knew their general well, and were better equipped than anyone to know his worth.

The Times obituary is worth quoting: "James Outram was an illustration of what can be done by a strong-minded, truth-loving, honest, and valiant nature in such an arena as India affords. Because he had neither rank nor fortune, he stood in that press of self-reliant men from which the hand of patron or politician could pluck no favourite. He took his place among his peers in the race when there was a fair field and no favour, and he came to the front and bore himself so well that his distanced rivals echoed the applause which greeted the winner."[363]

EPILOGUE.

The British Empire was the largest empire the world has ever seen. At its height it governed around a quarter of the world's population, and ruled the seas. It has always been a source of amazement that such a small island came to assume such a dominant position. It arose initially out of economic necessity: Britain lacked essential raw materials, and had to shop abroad. Its leaders learnt to look and think outside Britain's borders. The search for materials, and wealth, led to massive emigration.

India has been described as the jewel in the crown of the British Empire. With its vast resources and great manpower it was more valuable to Britain in the nineteenth century than the rest of the Empire put together. In 1700 India's share of total world output was estimated at 24%, (Britain's was 3%). It certainly played a prominent part in the development of the Empire, and provided a cascade of wealth and resources that helped Britain to expand throughout the world.

The Industrial Revolution in Britain changed this country irrevocably. It is estimated that per capita wealth doubled in value between 1801 and 1851. Not only did it alter society radically, with the rapid development of industrial cities, but it changed attitudes as well. The confidence born of scientific and engineering advances, the economic power afforded the country, made the British feel that they were destined to lead the world. The Evangelists, not only certain in their faith but believing they had a duty to take it to non-believers, promoted the view that their idea of morality was the right one. In India this led to the imposition of British ideas and values, a campaign to foster Christianity, and a desire to improve the lot of subject people.

Yet, at the heart of this movement, there was confusion. Liberal thinking in Britain believed in personal liberty; but the prevailing view for a large part of the nineteenth century was that such liberty was not appropriate to other parts of the empire, where care, protection and guidance were more appropriate. Few at the time questioned the morality of what was being done in Britain's name. In India this led to a stiffening of attitudes by the British, and an arrogance towards the subject people which was bound to cause resentment. The importance of India led to a growing political involvement from Britain and greater attention from the press. Local officials lost the scope for personal initiative. Equally importantly, it slowed the pace of development and change towards self-rule. As the nineteenth century gave way to the twentieth, the Boer war, then two successive world wars, eclipsed the preoccupation with India. Only briefly, at the time of Independence after the second world war, did India regain its place on the front pages.

Looking back over this period from the twenty-first century, we have the benefit of historical perspective. Not only can we see clearly the rise and fall of the British Empire, but we can assess the attitudes that prevailed in the nineteenth century in the context of developments since. The decline of organised western religions, the move towards egalitarianism, the emphasis on racial equality and the recognition of the merits of diverse cultures are merely a few of the significant changes which have occurred. It has therefore been interesting to review the life of an influential individual who devoted his life to a career in India, who did not always subscribe to the collective wisdom of the time, who really did "make a difference."

At the beginning of the book the question was asked: was James Outram too good to be true? The answer has to be yes. His career was punctuated with setbacks, many of his own making as he sought to argue his corner, often in a forthright and undiplomatic manner. His lack of social graces and an inability to express himself skilfully told against him. Critics saw him as a minor official incapable of rising above the mediocre. Whilst his military record was of the highest order, and rarely challenged, his political judgement was called into question at crucial times: in the Sind, at Lucknow. It would have been impossible for a man of such humble background and inadequate training to have met every expectation that such a testing and demanding country as India would have posed him, and for that reason Goldsmid's biography only told one side of the story.

Undoubtedly James was a brave, successful soldier whose achievements led to him being recognised as one of the leading military men in India. Ultimately his success as a leader was recognised, and he was accorded great honour, and finally a position on the governing council of India. Although he died a relatively poor man, he can justly claim to have been accepted by the great and the good of Britain – not bad for a lad from the provinces.

What is interesting is to place his life in the context of the times. Along with a handful of far-seeing statesmen – Elphinstone, Metcalfe, the Lawrence brothers, and latterly Bartle Frere – he believed that in time India would come to be ruled by Indians. He saw that by giving the indigenous people local responsibility, by allowing them to shape their own destiny, he could achieve a great deal more than by ruling with an iron fist. As attitudes in Britain evolved, his approach came to be recognised more and more. Yet he did not and could not win every argument – frequently he was censured by his superiors and overruled.

What made a man with a mediocre education, poor social skills and modest intellect, such an iconoclast? We have seen how the British Raj was shaped by the British aristocracy, by a system of patronage backed up by an established programme of education and training through the English East India Company colleges. Part of this programme centred on the principles of Plato: the British were "guardians who ruled in the light of their own vision of the Good and the Beautiful."[352] James was not part of this system, and possessed no advantageous social connections. He was in many ways an outsider. Perhaps his humble background, his exclusion from inner circles, led him to sympathise with the Indian subjects, and see more clearly than others their needs and aims. That he achieved so much was partly because he refused to toe the Company line, thought outside the conventional lines, and had the courage to pursue his individual approach. In so doing he opened the eyes of many British officials to what was possible in India, and gained a growing public following in Britain as the liberal political climate that developed in the mid-nineteenth century brought his efforts into focus.

It is rare these days to read much of the events of the nineteenth century in India. The subject has been done to death. But perhaps the story of a very singular man, his triumphs and failures, his unusual approach to the problems of India which can, in the twenty-first century, be appreciated much more easily than they were one hundred and fifty years ago, will help provide a reassessment of the British Raj.

GLOSSARY OF INDIAN TERMS.

Amir	A nobleman. A Muslim of high rank.
Bagh	A park or garden
Batta	An allowance in addition to pay; subsistence money.
Begum	Wife of a Nawab, normally from an aristocratic family.
Brahim	The priestly caste.
Desai	Ruler of a paragana or province; revenue officer of a district under the native government; a hereditary petty chief of a province in South India.
Dak	The mail-post.
Dang	Areas below the ghats; a tribe of Rajputs inhabiting the forested districts of eastern Malwa.
Diwan	Chief Minister or Prime Minister of a state.
Doolies	Palanquins held by four people in which old and sick people are carried to reach hilly areas.
Durbar	An Indian court, or audience chamber.
Feringi	Foreigner
Ghas Dana	Military contribution. Grass and grain for the horses or a contribution towards it.
Jemadar	A native Indian officer below subahdar in rank.

Khalsa	Institution founded by the Sikh Guru Gobind Singh to instil new life into the Sikhs in order to safeguard their religion in 1764.
Khan	A surname hailing from Persia or Pathan descent from Afghanistan.
Khatpat	Taking a bribe.
Minars	Minarets.
Nawab	An aristocratic Muslim belonging to the ruling class.
Nayak	A leader, a chief in general. Also a corporal in the Anglo-Indian army and a title borne by tribal leaders of hilly areas.
Palankeen	A light litter for one person borne on poles on men's shoulders.
Pir	A Muslim holy man.
Put	Pergatory.
Rajah	King.
Rajputs	Warrior class of Rajasthan who founded kingdoms and were known for their chivalry.
Sahib	A suffix to a name meaning "sir."
Sardar (or Sirdar)	A cavalryman. A Silkh is called by this title.
Sepoy	Soldier.
Shikargah	A place where hunters assemble after or during hunting.
Taluqdar	An officer administering the administrative division below district level.

| Thakur | A feudal lord in Rajasthan; a chief in Bengal. Also used to indicate respect for the person. |
| Zamindar (zemindar) | A tax-farmer responsible for collecting revenue from Com |

ORIGINAL PAPERS CONSULTED.

British Library: Outram Papers.
                    Secret Letters from India.
                    Parliamentary Blue Books.

West Yorkshire Archive Service (WYAS).

Derby Local Studies Library (DLSL).

NEWSPAPERS AND PERIODICALS.

The Times, London.

The Bombay Times.

The Gazette of Sind.

Kamataka State Gazette

BIBLIOGRAPHY.

Butler, Harcourt	Oudh Policy; the Policy of Sympathy - 1906.
Durand H.M.	The First Afghan War.
Featherstone D.	Victorian Colonial Warfare: India- Blandford, 1992.
Ferguson, Niall	Empire - Penguin 2003.
Fisher Michael (ed.)	The Politics of the British Annexation of India - OUP 1993.
Forbes A.	Havelock – Macmillan, 1897.
Forbes-Mitchell W.	The Relief of Lucknow – The Folio Society, 1962.
Forrest G.W.	The Indian Mutiny – Low Price Publications, 1902.
Germon Maria	Journal of the Siege of Lucknow – London. (no date)
Goldsmid F.J.	James Outram – Smith Elder, 1880.
Hibbert C.	The Great Mutiny: India 1857 – Penguin, 1978.
Holmes Rice T.A	A History of the Indian Mutiny, - London 1898.
Holmes Richard	Sahib: The British Soldier in India - Harper Collins, London, 2005.
Hopkirk P.	The Great Game – OUP, 1990.
Hunt Capt G.H.	Outram and Havelock'sPersian Campaign. - G. Routledge & Co. 1858.
Hutchins F.G.	The Illusion of Permanence: British Imperialism in India – Princeton UP.

James, Lawrence	Raj – The Making of British India - Abacus 1997.
Keay J.	The Honourable Company: A History of the English East India Co. – Harper Collins, 1991.
Lambrick H.T.	Sir Charles Napier and Sind – Clarendon Press, 1952.
Lawrence, Rosamond	Charles Napier - John Murray, London 1952.
Lee-Warner, Sir W.	The Life of the Marquis of Dalhousie - Macmillan, London 1904
Low D.A.	Lion Rampant. Frank Cass - London. 1973.
Maclagan M.	Clemency Canning - Macmillan, London 1962.
Majumdar R.C.	An Advanced History of India - Calcutta. The Sepoy Mutiny and the Revolt of 1857 - Calcutta 1973.
Mason Philip	A Matter of Honour - Jonathan Cape 1974.
Mason P.	The Men Who Ruled India – W.W.Norton, 1985.
Metcalf, Thomas R.	Ideologies of the Raj - Cambridge UP 1995.
Mill, James	The History of British India - 1840.
Moore R.J.	Sir Charles Wood's Indian Policy - Manchester UP 1966.
Moorhouse G.	India Britannica - Collins 1983.
Napier W.	History of Sir C. Napier's Administration of Scinde.
Napier W.F.P.	Conquest of Scinde – T.&W.Boone, London, 1845.

Norton, John Bruce	The Rebellion in India - Navrang, New Delhi 1857.
Outram Col. J.	The Conquest of Scinde.
Outram Lt-Gen. J.	Outram's Campaign in India.
Outram M.F.	Margaret Outram 1778-1863 – John Murray, 1938.
Outram Major J.	Rough Notes of the Campaign in Sinde and Affghanistan – Navy & Military Press, 1840.
Pemble J.	The Raj, Indian Mutiny and Kingdom of Oudh – Harvester, 1977.
Richards D.S.	The Savage Frontier - Macmillan, London 1990.
Robb, Peter G.	Evolution of British Politics towards\ Indian Politics, 1880-1920 - Manohar, New Delhi 1992.
Robinson J.	Angels of Albion – Viking, 1996.
Schofield R.B.	Benjamin Outram – Merton Priory, 2000.
Stanley, Peter	The White Mutiny - Hurst 1998.
Stokes, Eric	The English Utilitarians and India - Oxford UP, Delhi 1959.
Trotter L.	The Bayard of India - J.M.Dent 1909. Key's Sepoy War.
Trevelyan C.E.	On the Ed,ucation of the People of India - London 1838.
Wink A.	Land and Sovereignty in India - Cambridge 1986.
Wood, Stephen	Movements for Temperance in the British Army - London U 1984.

Woodruff, Philip	The Men Who Ruled India: The Guardians - Schocken, New York 1954.
Yapp M.E.	Strategies of British India - Clarendon Press, 1980.

NOTES.

[1] Stokes: The English Utilitarians and India P38.
[2] Richard Holmes: Sahib P185.
[3] Yapp: Strategies of British India P473.
[4] Outram: The Conquest of the Scinde.
[5] The Private Letters of Lord Dalhousie P255.
[6] Ibid P279.
[7] James, Lawrence: The Raj; the Making of British India P151.
[8] Robb: The Evolution of British Policy towards Indian Politics P2.
[9] James: The Raj P152.
[10] Robb P4.
[11] Trevelyan C.E.: On the Education of the Indian People P192-195.
[12] Holmes, Rice T.: A History of the Indian Mutiny P278.
[13] Schofield R.B.: Benjamin Outram P2.
[14] DLSL, Tilley Biog. Notes, W.Stevenson to F.D.Outram 21 Jan 1909.
[15] Schofield P192.
[16] Outram M.F.: Margaret Outram P102.
[17] Ibid P109.
[18] Ibid P326.
[19] Ibid P120.
[20] Ibid P122.
[21] Ibid P152.
[22] Goldsmid: James Outram Vol. I P15.
[23] Trotter: The Bayard of India P5.
[24] Goldsmid P22/23.
[25] Outram M.F.P150.
[26] Ibid P151.
[27] Ibid P151.
[28] Quoted in Goldsmid Vol. I P17.
[29] Goldsmid P 51; Outram M.F. P152.
[30] Mason, Philip: A Matter of Honour P189.
[31] Moorhouse G.: India Britannica P41.
[32] Wink A.: Land and Sovereignty in India P39.

[33] James P8/9.

[34] Quoted in Mason: A Matter of Honour P188.

[35] Stokes P72.

[36] Outram M.F. P156.

[37] Mason: A Matter of Honour P190.

[38] Holmes: Sahib P267.

[39] Outram M.F. P160.

[40] Ibid P162.

[41] Goldsmid P40.

[42] Ibid P43.

[43] Kamataka State Gazetteer, ed. Dr Suryanath Kamat P272.

[44] Quoted in Goldsmid Vol. I P115/116.

[45] Goldsmid P59.

[46] Mason Philip: The Men Who Ruled India P94.

[47] Ibid P95.

[48] Goldsmid Vol. I P61.

[49] Outram M.F. P168.

[50] Report to Col. Robertson from Dharangoan dated Sept. 1
– quoted in Goldsmid Vol. I P74.

[51] Goldsmid Vol. I P75.

[52] Outram M.F. P171

[53] Ibid P172/3.

[54] Ibid P174.

[55] Ibid P182.

[56] Ibid P181/2.

[57] James Outram's Journal P81.

[58] Goldsmid Vol. I P87.

[59] OIOC, L/Mil/5/435 quoted in Stanley, Peter:The White Mutiny
P47.

[60] Ibid P49.

[61] Letter to Outram's mother quoted in Goldsmid Vol. I P95.

[62] Outram M.F. P251.

[63] Quoted in Goldsmid Vol. I p122

[64] Ferguson, Niall: Empire P119.

[65] Ibid P136.

[66] Ibid P143.

[67] Goldsmid Vol. I P125.

[68] Ibid P128.

[69] Ibid P131.

[70] Ibid P132.
[71] Ibid P133.
[72] Outram M.F. P239.
[73] Ibid P241.
[74] Ibid P247.
[75] Ibid P244.
[76] Ibid P246.
[77] Ibid P248.
[78] Ibid P250.
[79] Ibid P253.
[80] Ibid P254.
[81] Ibid P255.
[82] Goldsmid Vol.I P140.
[83] Ibid P143; June 7, 1838.
[84] Ibid P148.
[85] Richards D.S.: The Savage Frontier P4.
[86] Yapp P225.
[87] Ibid P201.
[88] James P90.
[89] Richards P11.
[90] Outram, James: Rough Notes P3.
[91] Ibid.
[92] Yapp P259.
[93] Outram, James: Rough Notes P12.
[94] Goldsmid Vol. I P158.
[95] Rough Notes P31.
[96] Ibid P34.
[97] Ibid P50.
[98] Conquest of Scinde – JO P30.
[99] Rough Notes P86.
[100] Goldsmid Vol. I P169.
[101] Letter dated May 16, 1839 quoted in Goldsmid P171.
[102] Quoted in Moore R.J: Sir Charles Wood's Indian Policy P151.
[103] Yapp P268.
[104] Ibid P269.
[105] Rough Notes P120.
[106] Ibid P121.
[107] Ibid P129.
[108] Ibid P130.

[109] Goldsmid Vol. I P191/2.

[110] Ibid. P192/3.

[111] Rough Notes P160.

[112] Ibid 161/2.

[113] Ibid P164.

[114] Ibid P165.

[115] Ibid P166.

[116] Ibid P171.

[117] Ibid P173.

[118] Ibid P175.

[119] Ibid P188.

[120] Goldsmid Vol. I P210.

[121] Ibid. P211.

[122] Outram Letters quoted in Trotter L.: P64/65.

[123] Goldsmid Vol. I P213.

[124] Ibid P214.

[125] Conquest of Scinde P33.

[126] Quoted in Goldsmid Vol. I P216/7.

[127] Ibid P218/9

[128] Ibid P230.

[129] Ibid. P238.

[130] Ibid P240.

[131] The Conquest of Scinde P37.

[132] Yapp P300.

[133] Trotter P71/2.

[134] Goldsmid Vol. I P281.

[135] Hopkirk: P273.

[136] Ibid P275.

[137] Yapp P426.

[138] Norton, John Bruce: The Rebellion in India P63.

[139] Goldsmid Vol. I P248.

[140] Ibid P266.

[141] Yapp P434.

[142] Ibid P479.

[143] Goldsmid Vol. I P277.

[144] Ibid P278.

[145] Ibid P278-280.

[146] Ibid P285.

[147] Lawrence, Rosamond: Charles Napier P62.

[148] Ibid P98.

[149] Goldsmid Vol. I P286.

[150] Ibid P288.

[151] Lawrence, Rosamond P98.

[152] Lambrick H.T.: Sir Charles Napier and Sind P60.

[153] Conquest of Scinde P61.

[154] Fisher, Michael H.: The Politics of the British Annexation P228.

[155] Conquest of Scinde P59.

[156] Ibid P52.

[157] Lambrick P68.

[158] Ibid P73.

[159] Ibid P74.

[160] Ibid.

[161] Goldsmid Vol. I P289/90.

[162] Ibid P289.

[163] Ibid P294.

[164] Lambrick P80.

[165] Goldsmid Vol. I P291.

[166] Ibid P293.

[167] Ibid P296.

[168] Ibid P297.

[169] Correspondence Relative to Sind No.8 – T.R.Harrison, London.

[170] Secret Letters No. 433.

[171] Conquest of Scinde P

[172] Ibid P111.

[173] No. 10 Supplementary Blue Book on Sind.

[174] Goldsmid P308.

[175] Conquest of Scinde P278/9.

[176] Goldsmid Vol. I P311.

[177] Ibid.

[178] Lambrick P118; Life of Napier Vol. II P304/5.

[179] Ibid P120.

[180] Dalhousie's Private Letters P182.

[181] Goldsmid Vol. I P313-316; Commentary P476-480.

[182] Conquest of Scinde P290.

[183] Ibid P305.

[184] Ibid P293.

185 Ibid P327.
186 Ibid P357.
187 Ibid P373.
188 Ibid P396.
189 Lawrence, Rosamond P124.
190 Lambrick P149.
191 Majumdar R.C.: An Advanced History of India P638.
192 Goldsmid Vol. I P329.
193 Lambrick P214; Life of Napier Vol. ii P338.
194 Quoted in Mason: The Men Who Ruled India P194.
195 Goldsmid Vol. I P331.
196 Yapp P489.
197 Lambrick P243.
198 Goldsmid Vol. I P353.
199 Ibid P354.
200 Lambrick P261.
201 Trotter P105.
202 Quoted in Ferguson; Empire P260.
203 Goldsmid Vol. II P42.
204 Gazetteer of Sind Vol. A P125.
205 Goldsmid Vol. II P46.
206 Suppressed Despatch of Col. Outram in the Case of Baba Fudkee – BL.
207 Goldsmid Vol. II P55.
208 Ibid P56.
209 Ibid P59.
210 Ibid P61.
211 Trotter P118.
212 Goldsmid Vol. II P68.
213 Ibid P72.
214 Ibid P73.
215 Dalhousie: Private Letters P254/255.
216 Outram M.F. P261.
217 Dalhousie: Private Letters P289.
218 Ibid P295.
219 Goldsmid Vol. II P76.
220 Private Letters P295.
221 Letter home, quoted in Goldsmid Vol. II P83.
222 Ibid P91.

[223] The Times November 1858.

[224] Trotter P127.

[225] Lee-Warner: Life of Dalhousie Vol. II P319; Letter of Sept 4, 1854.

[226] Private Letters P321.

[227] Pemble J.: Angels of Albion P82.

[228] Ibid P85.

[229] Documents & Speeches on the Indian Princely States, edited by Adrian Sever, Delhi, 1985.

[230] Private letters of the Ministry of Defence P33/4 – London, W, Blackwood 1910.

[231] Pemble P101.

[232] Stokes P249.

[233] Trotter L.: Kay's Sepoy War P129.

[234] Fisher M. P283.

[235] Lee-Warner: Life of Dalhousie Vol. II P316.

[236] Goldsmid Vol. II P107.

[237] Lee-Warner; Life of Dalhousie Vol. II P321.

[238] Private Letters P344.

[239] Norton J.B. P67.

[240] Moore R.J. P162.

[241] Quoted in Pemble P107.

[242] Blue Book P234-236.

[243] Life of Dalhousie Vol. I P97.

[244] Private Letters P347.

[245] Ibid P365.

[246] Ibid P368.

[247] Blue Book P291.

[248] Mill J.: The History of British India: Vol. II p195, 166/7.

[249] Low D.A.: Lion Rampant P51.

[250] Quoted in Low P82.

[251] Private Letters P370.

[252] Outram to Governor-General March 22, 1856. WYAS Leeds.

[253] Private Letters P369.

[254] WYAS Leeds WYL250/9/Vol24/2.

[255] Outram M.F. P264.

[256] Ibid P265.

[257] Goldsmid Vol. II P131..

[258] Maclagan M.: Clemency Canning P48.

[259] WYAS Vol. 24/24.

[260] Goldsmid Vol. II p130.

[261] Canning to Outram 27/1/57, WYL250/9/Vol54/3.

[262] Goldsmid Vol. II P150.

[263] Ibid P154.

[264] Ibid P157/8.

[265] WYAS WYL 250/9/Vol 25/4.

[266] Ibid Vol 54/8.

[267] Maclagan M. P54.

[268] Quoted in Goldsmid Vol. II P137.

[269] Ibid P161.

[270] Hunt G.H.: Outram and Havelock's Persian Campaign P232.

[271] Hunt P250.

[272] Letter to Murray quoted in Goldsmid Vol. II P180.

[273] Ibid P185.

[274] Hutchins F.G.: The Illusion of Permanence P10.

[275] Quoted in Moorhouse P87.

[276] Goldsmid Vol. II P187.

[277] Life of Dalhousie Vol. II P356.

[278] MaclaganP118.

[279] Ibid P122.

[280] Trotter: Kaye's Sepoy War P151/2.

[281] Outram M.F. P284/5.

[282] Ibid P288.

[283] Ibid P294.

[284] Outram's Campaign in India 1857-1859 P218; letter to E.A.Samuells.

[285] WYAS WYL250/9Vol.2514b.

[286] Ibid.

[287] Outram's Campaign in India P253.

[288] Ibid P254.

[289] Dalhousie's Private Letters P389.

[290] Outram's Campaign P260.

[291] Forbes A.: Havelock P168.

[292] Goldsmid Vol. II P218.

[293] Ibid P221/2.

[294] Majumdar R.C.: The Sepoy Mutiny & the Revolt of 1857, Calcutta 1973 P477.

[295] Private Letters P389.

[296] Outram's Campaign: letter to Havelock P278.
[297] Ibid P291/2.
[298] Ibid P294.
[299] Ibid.
[300] Ibid P301.
[301] Ibid 305.
[302] Ibid 307.
[303] Ibid P12; from Baga Gunge, 22/9/57.
[304] Forbes A. P181.
[305] Outram's Campaign P230.
[306] Ibid P18/19; letter from Alambagh 2/1/58.
[307] Ibid P21/22.
[308] Forbes A. P198.
[309] Outram's Campaign P25.
[310] Ibid P39.
[311] Ibid P309.
[312] Ibid P46.
[313] Ibid P312.
[314] Ibid P320.
[315] Ibid P321.
[316] Ibid P326.
[317] Ibid P337.
[318] Ibid P338.
[319] Ibid
[320] Hibbert P336.
[321] Ibid P334.
[322] Outram's Campaign P363.
[323] Goldsmid Vol. II P270.
[324] Mrs German's Journal P128.
[325] Outram's Campaign P378.
[326] Private Letters P340.
[327] Quoted in Maclagan P149.
[328] Outram's Campaign P128.
[329] Ibid P136.
[330] Ibid P140.
[331] Trotter P187.
[332] Outram's Campaign P158.
[333] Ibid P159.
[334] Ibid P168.

[335] Ibid P161/2.

[336] Letter from Canning to Lord Granville 16/3/58 quoted in Maclagan P182.

[337] Lee-Warner: Life of Dalhousie Vol. II P370/1.

[338] Quoted in Metcalf, T.R.: Ideologies of the Raj P47.

[339] Maclagan P185.

[340] Butler H.: Oudh Policy: The Policy of Sympathy.

[341] Maclagan P185.

[342] Ibid P207.

[343] Private Letters P413.

[344] Maclagan P187: letter to R.D.Mangles, 6/5/58.

[345] Quoted in Clemency Canning P198.

[346] Ibid P199.

[347] WYL250/9/Vol. 26/51.

[348] Outram M.F. P305/6.

[349] Norton J.B. P120.

[350] Private Letters P415/6.

[351] Outram M.F. P307.

[352] Moore R.J. P25.

[353] Hutchins F.G. P87.

[354] Moore R.J. P164.

[355] Ibid P164/5.

[356] Mason Philip P317.

[357] Ibid P318.

[358] Goldsmid Vol. II P363.

[359] Outram M.F. P343/4.

[360] Quoted in Stephen Wood: Movement for Temperance in the British Army P24 (OUL 1984).

[361] Goldsmid Vol. II P402.

[362] Trotter P223.

[363] Woodruff, Philip: The Men Who Ruled India Vol. II P15.

INDEX.

A

Abdul-Rahman Khan 76
Abdul Rashid 71
Abu Khan 76
Addiscombe Military Training
    College 36
Aden 160, 161, 162, 164, 185
Afzul Khan 72
Agra 208, 245
Ahwaz 191, 192
Alambagh 219, 220, 225, 226,
    227, 228, 231, 232,
    233, 234, 235, 236,
    237, 245, 277
Alexandria 148, 149, 150, 160
Ali Akbar 117
Ali Hasan, Sheikh 118, 151
Ali Murad 109, 115, 116, 117,
    118, 119, 120, 121,
    122, 123, 124, 126,
    150, 151
Ali Pasha 104
Allahabad 180, 204, 207, 210,
    211, 236, 241, 245,
    247, 250
Allyghur 208
Anderson, James 4, 7, 32
Anderson, Lieutenant J.C. 147
Anderson, Margaret 4, 49
Anna Sahib 142
Anstey, Chisolm 157
Arthur, Sir George 129, 131,
    137, 143, 145
Ashley, Lord 134

Auckland, Lord 60, 70, 85, 86,
    90, 94, 100

B

Babaji Ahirakar 140
Baba Farki 147, 155
Baroda 19, 53, 146, 147, 148,
    149, 150, 151, 153,
    155, 156, 157, 158,
    159, 160, 161, 243
Barrackpore 174, 249
Bashiratganj 218
Belgam 139
Bell, Ross 90
Benares 180, 204, 207, 209,
    210
Bentham, Jeremy 15, 172
Bentinck, Lord William 45
Bhao Traimbak 155
Bhils 27, 28, 29, 30, 31, 32,
    33, 34, 35, 36, 37, 41,
    42, 54, 58, 178
Bibarak 109
Bisset, Doctor 7
Bombay xiii, 14, 15, 16, 19,
    21, 22, 27, 28, 29, 38,
    39, 43, 44, 46, 47, 48,
    50, 51, 52, 53, 55, 62,
    66, 67, 68, 79, 85, 86,
    87, 90, 96, 105, 112,
    113, 114, 127, 129,
    130, 131, 136, 137,
    138, 139, 141, 142,
    143, 144, 145, 146,

147, 148, 150, 151,
153, 154, 155, 156,
157, 158, 159, 160,
161, 164, 185, 191,
193, 199, 202, 242,
243, 247, 249, 250,
252, 254, 263
Briggs, Colonel 28
Brigham, Major 227
Brighton 136, 156, 180, 253
Brown, Captain 117
Bruce, Captain 227
Budargarh 139, 140
Bunni Bridge 219, 233
Burasjun 186
Burnes, Sir Alexander 68
Bushire 182, 183, 185, 186,
187, 188, 189, 193
Butler, Harcourt 240, 265

C

Calcutta 1, 2, 14, 29, 60, 95,
96, 98, 100, 101, 136,
138, 139, 141, 143,
145, 147, 148, 149,
157, 166, 169, 177,
179, 180, 189, 200,
202, 204, 207, 210,
211, 227, 236, 245,
246, 247, 250, 252,
253, 266, 276
Campbell, Brigadier William
238
Campbell, Sir Colin 217, 227,
231, 232, 236, 246
Canning, Lady 202
Canning, Lord Charles John
177, 179, 184, 202,

210, 217, 239, 241,
242, 245, 250
Charbagh Bridge 220, 221,
228
Chatarwala Kothi[-- chakar-
wala] 237
Chattar Munzil 222, 229
Clarendon, Lord 193
Clerk, George 98, 146, 147,
150, 254
Coghlan, Colonel William 164
Colville, Sir Charles 21
Conway, Captain 127
Cotton, Sir Willoughby 62

D

Daji Pandit 140
Dalhousie, Marquis of; Lord;
James Andrew Ramsay
147
Delhi 1, 12, 13, 109, 164, 201,
204, 206, 208, 213,
226, 227, 267, 275
Dilkusha 168, 220, 228, 230,
231, 237
Dinapur 202, 209
Dost Muhammad 60, 61, 69,
70, 71, 72, 73, 74, 75,
76, 79, 86, 118, 184
Dr Ogilvy 16

E

Eastwick, Lieutenant Herbert
64
Ellenborough, Lord 79, 94,
101, 105, 106, 107,
113, 138, 146, 151,
241, 244, 250

Elphinstone, Mountstuart 29, 35
England, General 96, 103, 106, 108
Esnia Nayak 34
Esson, Reverend 9
Ethersley, Commander 189
Euphrates River 115
Eyre, Major Vincent 212

F

Faizabad 207, 209, 224
Falkland, Lord 29, 147
Farquharson, Colonel 39, 51
Fateghar 227
Fatehpur 204, 211
Fath Singh 47
Fayrer, Doctor Joseph 169
Fitzgerald, Lord Edward 134
Franks, Brigadier-General T.H. 236
French, Captain 152

G

Ganges River 2, 168, 204, 206, 207, 209, 211, 214, 217, 218
Goa 12, 139, 142
Gordon, Captain 10
Gough, Sir Hugh 138
Govinda Novak 32
Graham, Douglas 37
Grant, Sir Hope 227
Grant, Sir Robert 44, 55, 147
Gujarat 42, 46, 51, 61, 62, 123
Gumti 220, 237, 238
Gwalior 138, 207, 227

H

Hadji Khan Kakar 73
Haileybury College 35, 36
Haliburton, Major 225
Hammersley, Lieutenant 95, 96
Hardinge, Sir Henry 139
Harteh 190
Hatnia Nayak 34
Havelock, Henry 2, 185, 204, 222, 229, 231
Henderson, Colonel 10
Hobhouse, Sir John Carn 97
Hyderabad 13, 58, 59, 62, 63, 64, 65, 66, 80, 86, 87, 90, 106, 108, 109, 110, 112, 113, 115, 121, 122, 123, 124, 125, 126, 127, 128, 129, 131, 135, 136, 166, 173
Hyder Khan 70, 72

I

Indore 42, 43, 138
Indus River 58, 59, 62, 65, 66, 68, 69, 80, 88, 106, 110, 115, 126, 128
Inglis, Colonel James 214, 220

J

Jackson, Coverley 203
Jacob, Colonel John 125
Jalalabad 94, 233, 235
Jessop, William 3
Jocelyn, Lord 145, 150
Jubbar Khan 76
Jubbul Khan Nawab 73

Jung Bahadoor, Maharajah 236

K

Kabul 60, 61, 69, 71, 72, 73,
    75, 76, 79, 92, 93, 95,
    96, 97, 111
Kagal 140, 141
Kaisarbagh 220, 221, 225,
    231, 237
Kalogan 212
Kalpi 227
Kandahar 62, 68, 69, 70, 71,
    76, 92, 94, 95, 96, 98,
    102
Kanpur 1, 2, 168, 177, 180,
    202, 204, 205, 206,
    207, 209, 210, 211,
    212, 214, 220, 225,
    226, 227, 228, 231,
    233, 235, 236
Karachi 63, 85, 86, 88, 90,
    106, 108, 110, 126, 188
Karun River 188, 189
Keane, Sir John 44, 62, 66, 85
Khairpur 106, 110, 112, 116,
    117, 120, 121, 122,
    123, 125
Kharag Island 182
Khyber Pass 58, 93, 97
Kolhapur, Rajah of 140
Konkaji 20

L

Lawrence, Henry 98, 148, 180,
    203, 220, 226
Lawrence, John 201, 241, 243,
    250, 254
Lothian, Lord 178

Low, Colonel John 103, 125
Lower Sind 58, 59, 86, 90,
    105, 106, 120, 121,
    122, 123, 124
Lucknow ix, xiii, 1, 2, 148,
    163, 164, 165, 166,
    167, 168, 172, 173,
    174, 175, 179, 200,
    202, 203, 204, 206,
    207, 209, 210, 212,
    213, 214, 215, 217,
    218, 219, 220, 221,
    222, 225, 227, 228,
    229, 231, 232, 233,
    234, 236, 237, 238,
    239, 241, 243, 254,
    257, 265

M

Macaulay, Zachary 44
Macnaghten, William 61, 66,
    67, 70, 93
Mahableshwar 143
Mahdeo Singh 32
Malcolm, Major 161
Malcolm, Sir John 39
Mangalwar 218
Manohar, Fort 142
Mansantosh, Fort 142
Martiniere 228, 237
Marx, Karl 241
Matari 127
Meerut 201
Metcalfe, Sir Charles 35
Miani 125, 127, 128, 138
Mihrab Khan 79, 80, 82, 91
Mihtar Musa Khan 76
Mill, James 176

Mill, John Stuart 176
Mir Mir Mohamed 59, 109, 125
Mir Murad Ali 59
Mir Rustam 109, 112, 115, 116, 117, 118, 119, 120, 125, 133
Mir Sher Mohammed of Mir-pur 88
Mir Sobdar Khan 59, 65
Mohammed Akbar Khan 93
Mohammed Hussain 116
Mohammed Khan 85, 116, 119
Mohomed Sadik 94, 101
Mohomed Sharif 94, 95
Moira, Lord 104
Montgomery, Robert 240
Moti Mahal 228, 229
Moti Munzil 221
Muhammad Ali Shah 165, 166
Muhamra 186, 188, 189, 190, 191, 192, 193
Murad Mirza, Prince 184
Musa Bagh 238

N

Nagpur 149
Nana Sahib 205, 206, 227
Napier, Colonel Robert 207, 250
Napier, Sir Charles xvii, 14, 104, 107, 114, 116, 119, 134, 149, 245, 266, 273
Napier, William 144
Narsu Pant 147, 151, 153, 155, 160

Nasir-ud-din Hyder 165
Nasir Khan 59, 88, 91, 92, 101, 106, 109, 110, 112, 116, 118, 125, 126
Nawaz, Shah 91
Nimar 138, 139, 141
Nott, General William 71
Nur Mohamed 59

O

Omeira 192
Ord, Richard 20
Oudh 1, 13, 14, 129, 163, 164, 165, 166, 167, 168, 169, 170, 172, 173, 174, 175, 176, 177, 180, 201, 203, 212, 213, 214, 218, 225, 227, 231, 232, 233, 234, 239, 240, 241, 243, 244, 245, 251, 252, 253, 265, 267, 278
Outram, Benjamin 4, 267, 269
Outram, Francis (Frank) 6, 7, 22, 38, 39
Outram, Frank 18, 52, 179, 208, 209, 245, 247, 266
Outram, Joseph 3, 39
Ovans, Captain 28
Ovans, Colonel 140

P

Palmer, Colonel 96
Palmerston, Lord 150, 253
Panhala 140
Partab Singh 53
Peel, Sir Robert 79, 134, 139,

159
Persia, Shah of 64, 89, 183, 192
Peshwar Bajirao II 205
Phund Sawant 142
Pitt the Younger, William 15
Pollock, General George 97
Pottinger, Henry 63, 80, 138
Preedy, Captain 126
Punjab 61, 91, 109, 137, 145, 149, 243, 251

Q

Quetta 68, 77, 79, 90, 91, 93, 96, 99, 100, 103

R

Ramay, James Andrew, Earl of Dalhousie 147
Ranjit Singh 61, 62, 137
Renaud, Major 204
Reshire 185
Rigby, Captain 28
Ripon, Lord 134, 137, 144
Russell, William Howard 163

S

Sakarand 125
Samangarh, Fort 139
Satara 140, 143, 146, 171
Satlaj River 145
Sawant-Wari 142, 143
Shah of Persia 64, 89, 183, 192
Shat-u-l-Arab 189
Sher Singh 109, 137
Shuja, Shah 29, 60, 61, 62, 64, 66, 67, 71, 73, 75, 76, 77, 78, 86, 92, 94, 95,

97, 101
Shujah'u-l'Maluk 186
Sikandrabagh 230
Sleeman, Major-General William 167
Sonmiani 83, 85
Stacey, Colonel 91, 93, 96
Stalker, General 185, 188, 189
Stratford, Lord 160, 184
Suraj Mall 47
Syed Mohamed Khan 183

T

Thackeray 21, 22

W

Wajid Ali Shah 166
Wallace, Colonel 140
Wellesley, Arthur; Marquis xix
Wellington, Duke of 29, 97, 134, 135, 137, 159
Wheeler, Major-General Sir Hugh Massey 205
Wiilshire, General 80, 81, 83
Wilberforce, William 44
Wood, Sir Charles 70, 169, 171, 266, 271
Wright, John 3

Y

Yemeni 161

ABOUT THE AUTHOR

This is Roy Digby Thomas' third book. The first two, "Digby: The Gunpowder Plotter's Legacy" and "George Digby: Hero and Villain," recounted the lives of two significant figures in England in the 17th Century.

His latest book, "Outram in India: The Morality of Empire" deals with the life of James Outram in the 19th Century. It is based on three years of research into British rule in India, and Outram's role there. But it is more than just a straightforward biography. Like the two previous books, it portrays an outsider's struggle against the Establishment, and what happens when an individual's conscience and morality clashes with the accepted way of doing things.

In the last fifty years new information has come to light which enables a reappraisal both of the morality of the English East India Company's rule in India, and Outram's role as a servant of the Company. This has led to a fresh approach on a subject which, since the independence of India after the Second World War, has not receieved enough attention.

Printed in the United Kingdom
by Lightning Source UK Ltd.
121664UK00001B/4-45/A